Herman Melville's
world of whaling

Herman Melville's world of whaling

by

Maria Ujházy

Second edition

Akadémiai Kiadó, Budapest 1986

First edition 1982
Second edition 1986

ISBN 963 05 4230 7

© Akadémiai Kiadó, Budapest 1982

Printed in Hungary

To my Parents, Gyula and Lily Salusinszky,
who taught me to love "man, in the ideal".

"For small erections may be finished by their first architects; grand ones, true ones, ever leave the copestone to posterity. God keep me from ever completing anything. This whole work is but a draught — nay, but the draught of a draught."

Moby-Dick, p. 142.

Contents

Acknowledgements   9

Part I From obscurity to fame: Herman Melville valued and revalued

Part II Biographical prelude

Chapter 1

The road to the forecastle   55

Chapter 2

Unfolding within himself: the making of an author and the undoing of his
reputation   62

Part III Cooking up the blubber

Chapter 1

Identification   71
   1. "I mean to give the truth of the thing"   71
   2. The Extracts   75
   3. Ishmael   78
   4. The dense webbed bed of welded sinews   82
   5. The dark Hindoo half of nature   84
   6. From storm to storm   88
   7. The vast practical joke   91
   8. Hyena chuckle   96
   9. Sunshine   100
  10. Fishy fundamentals of jurisprudence   101

Chapter 2

Striking at pasteboard masks: Ahab's sound and fury   107
   1. Ahab's "Everlasting No"   107
   2. Gamming   110
   3. The wondrous old man   115
   4. Blasphemous Ahab   116

5. Ahab's madness   122
6. Ahab's transcendentalism   126
7. Providence   131
8. Indifferent as his God   136
9. The Voice of God   141
10. Undecipherable hieroglyphics   142
11. If   143
12. Artistic reflections   147
13. Mythology   148

Chapter 3

Counterpoint   159
1. What makes a good voyager   159
2. Self-reliance   161
3. The monkey-rope   164
4. Merger   168
5. A wicked book   170

Notes   172

Selected bibliography   187

Acknowledgements

To write this book "I have swum through" two libraries: one at the Hungarian Academy of Sciences, the other at the British Museum. My thanks are due to the staff in both places. Their ready assistance, understanding and initiative assured the continuous flow of source material.

From its inception, my work had been encouraged and aided by Professor Miklós Szenczi of Budapest University. His wisdom and advice kept me on the track. No words would adequately express my gratitude to him.

I received invaluable help from the incisive criticism of Eric Mottram of London University.

Throughout my work benefited immensely from the inspiring suggestions and the unsparing scrutiny of Lenke Bizám of the Hungarian Institute of Philosophy.

Most of my thanks, however, go to my husband. He was partner in this "launching upon the deep", and no chapter of this book emerged but propelled by the stream of his comments and advice.

Budapest, 1981

Maria Ujházy

PART I

From obscurity to fame:
Herman Melville valued and revalued

Eight days after his death, Herman Melville was commemorated in *The New York Times* of October 6, 1891, under the heading: "The Late Hiram Melville".[1] The column contained a letter entitled "A Tribute by One Who Knew Him" and was signed "O.G.H.", supposedly the initials of O. G. Hillard. Hillard may not have been responsible for the rechristening, nor did it happen in any of the other thirty odd obituaries, notices, tributes and articles marking Melville's passing published during the last four months of 1891. Nevertheless, it pinpointed what the other notices suggested: that at the time of his death Herman Melville was little known and by few. The thirty items—five of which were reprints—were printed in some seventeen newspapers and four magazines. They were brief and pathetically succinct.

On September 29, 1891, in its Obituary Notes column, this is all *The New York Times* wrote about Melville's death:

"Herman Melville died yesterday at his residence, 104 East Twenty-sixth Street, this city, of heart failure, aged seventy-two. He was the author of 'Typee', 'Omoo', 'Mobie (sic) Dick', and other seafaring tales, written in earlier years. He leaves a wife and two daughters, Mrs. M. B. Thomas and Miss Melville."[2]

The same day, *The New York Daily Tribune,* more appreciatively, carried a 234 word obituary notice, incidentally the shortest in that column: Captain Gustavus A. Hull was commemorated in 550 words, Rudolph Garrigue, president of the Germania Fire Insurance Company and John H. Hodges, a partner in a firm dealing in pictures, each in 370 words. The notice gives a brief account of Melville's life and only mentions *Typee* from among his works, remarking that "This was his best work, although he has since written a number of other stories, which were published more for private than public circulation".

The New York *The Press* entitled its brief obituary notice: "Death of a Once Popular Author" and frankly admitted:

"Probably, if the truth were known, even his own generation has long thought him dead, so quiet have been the latter years of his life."[3]

There were obituaries that did not mention any of his works, or only some, and even those with erroneous titles. On September 30, the Boston *Transcript* remembered him as the grandson of Thomas Melville and the husband of Elizabeth Shaw, but did not refer to him as an author. The Boston *Morning Journal* called him "the well-known author of popular seafaring stories" and went on: "So little has been heard of him personally in the late years that many people imagined he was dead and yet his literary honours were well won and deserved." Nevertheless, the *Morning Journal* could not recall a single work by name. Neither did the Boston *Herald* of October 4, 1891, mention any works in its brief, 150 word obituary. Instead, it recalled the "eloquent" and "florid" oratory of Herman's brother Gansevoort. Nor did the "Hiram" letter in *The New York Times* on October 6 mention by name a single one of Melville's works.

The Boston *Evening Transcript* of September 29, on the other hand, gave a list of works including the following items.

"... a philosophical romance 'Redburn'; 'Plute (sic) Jacket;—or the World on (sic) a Man-of-War'; 'Moby Dick'; 'Pierre'; 'Israel Potter'; 'The Prazza (sic) Tales'; ... "

An obituary in the New York *The World* on September 29 listed among his works "'Ouvoo' (sic); 'Piute (sic) Jacket; or the World on (sic) a Man-of-War'."[4]

Paradoxically, we find that in some sense, Melville's fame was retrieved from oblivion through his death. By the beginning of October 1891, the obituaries tended to grow in number and length. Already on the 2nd, *The New York Times* carried a 960 word memorial article deploring "the total eclipse" of this "literary luminary", and calling Melville "a born romancer", who wrote "alluring" and "fantastic tales" about "the Polynesian Islands and their surrounding seas".[5] The same day the writer of an article in the Boston *Post* wished "Melville had explained before his death the reasons of the fierce and long-established hatred between the White Whale and Captain Ahab".[6]

Six days later, on the 8th of October, Richard Henry Stoddard[7] in the New York *Mail and Express* declared *Typee* and *Omoo* to be "landmarks in American literature, in which the name of Herman Melville must ever hold an honorable place". In the same breath however, Stoddard denigrated these "landmarks", condescendingly attributing their fame to the fact that Melville's countrymen, being then "less literary in their tastes and demands than at present, were easily captivated by stories of maritime life like 'Omoo' and 'Typee', and 'Moby Dick'".[8]

Death certainly gave Melville new value and made him topical. On the other hand, maybe Horace Elisha Scudder, editor of the Boston *Atlantic Monthly*, did not voice an altogether solitary view in a personal letter written one year before Melville's death: "So much more frankness of speech can be used when a fellow is apparently out of hearing ... I believe we had better wait for our shot at Melville, when his personality can be more freely handled."[9]

14

Ironically, Melville was being remembered for the very reason he hoped he would not be. In June 1851, when *Moby-Dick* was nearing completion he wrote to Hawthorne:

"What 'reputation' H. M. has is horrible. Think of it! To go down to posterity is bad enough, any way; but to go down as a 'man who lived among the cannibals'! When I speak of posterity, in reference to myself, I only mean the babies who will probably be born in the moment immediately ensuing upon my giving up the ghost. I shall go down to some of them, in all likelihood. 'Typee' will be given to them, perhaps, with their gingerbread."[10]

In fact, hardly three years after its publication, Melville wanted to dissociate himself from the reputation *Typee* had gained for him. In a letter of January 28, 1849, accompanying the MS of *Mardi,* he wrote to his English publisher, John Murray:

"Unless you should deem it *very* desirable do not put me down on the title page as 'the author of Typee & Omoo'. I wish to separate 'Mardi' as much as possible from those books."[11]

Ten months later, on November 4, 1849, in the Journal he kept of his voyage to London and the Continent, Melville wrote self-deprecatingly:

"This time tomorrow I shall be on land and press English earth after the lapse of ten years—*then* a sailor, now H. M. author of 'Peedee', 'Hullabaloo' & 'Pod-dog'."[12]

When in 1860 his brother Allan was arranging the publication of his poems, Melville expressed the same worry, beseeching him: "For God's sake don't have *By the author of 'Typee' 'Piddledee' & c.* on the title-page".[13]

Yet when he died, in all the United States there was but one single paper, the Springfield (Mass.) *Republican* of October 4, 1891, that extolled "the marvellous romance of 'Moby Dick, the White Whale'" as "the crown of Melville's sea experience", asserting that: "Certainly it is hard to find a more wonderful book than this."[14] But all the other press notices that chronicled Melville's death or commemorated him in the three months following, implicitly or explicitly placed the spotlight on *Typee*. Several made absolutely no mention of *Moby-Dick*.[15] The October 1 issue of *The New York Daily Tribune,* in its account of Melville's literary career, referred to his friendship with Hawthorne and his years at Pittsfield, Mass., and wrote: "It was at this place that most of Melville's writing was done". Yet in the whole 580 word article *Typee* and *Pierre* are the only novels mentioned, and there is not the slightest hint at *Moby-Dick*.

All this was a far cry from the evaluation Melville himself seems to have formed. Evert Augustus Duyckinck, editor at Wiley and Putnam's (the publishing house that brought out the first editions of *Typee*) and a friend and literary promoter of Melville, in the *Cyclopaedia of American Literature* (1855) written with his brother George Long Duyckinck drew a clear line between the inherent values of Melville's works and their reception by the public. Of *Typee* he wrote:

"The spirit and vigorous fancy of the style, and the freshness and novelty of the incidents, were at once appreciated. There was, too, at the time that undefined sentiment of the approaching practical importance of the Pacific in the public mind which was admirably calculated for the reception of this glowing, picturesque narrative. It was received everywhere with enthusiasm, and made a reputation for its author in a day."

Duyckinck regarded *Moby-Dick* "... the most dramatic and imaginative of Melville's books. In the character of Captain Ahab and his contest with the whale, he has opposed the metaphysical energy of despair to the physical sublime of the ocean. In this encounter the whale becomes a representative of moral evil in the world. In the purely descriptive passages, the details of the fishery, and the natural history of the animal, are narrated with constant brilliancy of illustration from the fertile mind of the author."[16]

Melville seems to have accepted this assessment, for when, 18 years later, in 1873, M. Laird Simons, about to bring out a new edition of the Duyckincks' *Cyclopaedia*, asked Melville if he wished any change in the article on him, Melville responded:

"As to the Article in question I don't remember anything in it which would be worth your while to be at the trouble of adding to or omitting or amending."[17]

That in his social contacts Melville left no doubt as to the direction his thoughts were taking can be seen in many of his letters and also in the recollections of some who had personally met him. In 1859, two divinity students visited Melville on his Pittsfield farm. Both were sons of Hawaiian missionaries, and both were eager to see and hear "the renowned author of Typee, Omoo, &c." One, John Thomas Gulick, recorded his impressions in his journal, the other, Titus Munson Coan, wrote about the visit in a letter to his mother, and once more in December 1891, in the Boston *Literary World*. Both men were disappointed in their expectations.

"His conversation and manner," John Thomas Gulick wrote, "as well as the engravings on his walls, betray little of the sailor... Though it was apparent that he possessed a mind of an aspiring, ambitious order, full of elastic energy and illumined with the rich colours of a poetic fancy, he was evidently a disappointed man, soured by criticism, and disgusted with the civilized world and with our Christendom in general and in particular. The ancient dignity of Homeric times afforded the only state of humanity, individual or social, to

16

which he could turn with any complacency. What little there was of meaning in the religions of the present day had come down from Plato. All our philosophy and all our art and poetry was either derived or imitated from the ancient Greeks."

In his 1891 article for the Boston *Literary World,* T. M. Coan quoted from the letter written to his mother in 1859:

"In vain I sought to hear of Typee and those Paradise islands, but he preferred to pour forth his philosophy and his theories of life. The shade of Aristotle arose like a cold mist between myself and Fayaway."

The article then relates how T. M. Coan's first impressions were confirmed when he visited Melville some twenty-five years later:

"I visited him repeatedly in New York, and had the most interesting talks with him. What stores of reading, what reaches of philosophy, were his!
    He took the attitude of absolute independence toward the world. He said, 'My books will speak for themselves, and all the better if I avoid the rattling egotism by which so many win a certain vogue for a certain time.' "[18]

Richard Henry Stoddard, author and critic, another acquaintance of Melville's old age, wrote in his *Recollections, Personal and Literary* (1903):

"Whether any of Melville's readers understood the real drift of his mind, or whether he understood it himself, has often puzzled me." (p. 143.)

The discrepancy between what Melville meant, what his critics and reviewers suggested he meant, and what his readers expected he meant had been a problem since the publication of his first two books, and Melville was fully aware of it. "What I feel most moved to write, that is banned,—it will not pay. Yet, altogether, write the *other* way I cannot. So the product is a final hash, and all my books are botches"—he wrote to Hawthorne in June 1851. He recalled Biblical Solomon, "the truest man who ever spoke"[19] and added his suspicion "that he a little *managed* the truth with a view to popular conservatism; or else there have been many corruptions and interpolations of the text".[20] (A remarkable anticipation of the later authenticated fact that interpolations *had* been made in the text of *Ecclesiastes,* originally attributed to King Solomon for the sake of canonization.)
    Melville seems to have been intrigued by this "managing" of the truth. Already two years earlier in a letter to Evert A. Duyckinck he expressed his belief "that the muzzle which all men wore on their souls in the Elizebethan day" had "intercepted Shakspers full articulations ... even Shakspeare, was not a frank man to the uttermost. And, indeed, who in this intolerant Universe is, or can be?"[21] In "Hawthorne and His Mosses", published in the New York *Literary World* in

August 1850, Melville had written: "... In this world of lies, Truth is forced to fly like a scared white doe in the woodlands; and only by cunning glimpses will she reveal herself, as in Shakespeare and other masters of the great Art of Telling the Truth,—even though it be covertly, and by snatches."[22] In *Moby-Dick,* Father Mapple in the New Bedford Whaleman's Chapel pronounced "delight" upon "him ... who against the proud gods and commodores of this earth, ever stands forth his own inexorable self. ... who gives no quarter in the truth, and kills, burns, and destroys all sin though he plucks it out from under the robes of Senators and Judges". And he invoked "woe to him who seeks to please rather than to appal!... whose good name is more to him than goodness!... who would not be true, even though to be false were salvation!"

In December 1885, Melville hailed with enthusiasm the *Essays and Phantasies* of James Thomson,[23] the atheist poet and essayist, sent to him from Leicester, England, by James Billson,[24] a classical scholar with similar secularist views. In one of his essays, Thomson presents the Dickensian character of Bumble the beadle as the symbol of the oppressive domination of bourgeois morality and conventions: "We can write freely of the acts of our government", Thomson writes, "we can freely discuss our political questions (or, more precisely, questions in the sphere of political expediency) ... but, ... if the English paper or book ventures beyond the bounds of Bumbledom's restrictions in religion or morals, it is effectually suppressed by Bumble,—he won't buy it, however brilliant and thoughtful and honest it may be. Imperialism imposes fines, imprisonment, banishment; Bumble simply imposes death by starvation."[25] In his letter to Billson, Melville wrote:

> "It is long since I have been so interested in a volume as in that of the 'Essays & Phantasies'.—'Bumble'—'Indolence'—'The Poet'—&c., each is so admirably honest and original and informed throughout with the spirit of the noblest natures, that it would have been wonderful indeed had they hit the popular taste. They would have to be painstakingly diluted for that—diluted with that prudential wordly element, wherewithall Mr. Arnold has conciliated the Conventionalists while at the same time showing the absurdity of Bumble. But for your admirable friend this would have been too much like trimming—if trimming in fact it be. The motions of his mind in the best of his Essays are utterly untrameled and independent, ... It is good for me to think of such a mind—to know that such a brave intelligence has been—and may yet be, ... As to his not achieving 'fame'—what of that? He is not the less, but so much the more. And it must have occurred to you as it has to me, that the further our civilization advances upon its present lines so much the cheaper sort of thing does 'fame' become, especially of the literary sort."[26]

A conclusion Melville had also voiced in *Pierre:* "Though the world worship Mediocrity and Common Place, yet hath it fire and sword for all contemporary Grandeur."[27]

18

In fact, it had already occurred to Melville thirty-four years earlier that his age and civilization would not reward Truth with Fame: "Try to get a living by the Truth—and go to the Soup Societies", he wrote to Hawthorne in June 1851. "Let any clergyman try to preach the Truth from its very stronghold, the pulpit, and they would ride him out of his church on his own pulpit bannister. It can be hardly doubted that all Reformers are bottomed upon the truth, more or less; and to the world at large are not reformers almost universally laughing-stocks? Why so? Truth is ridiculous to men."[28]

To get a living by writing, Melville knew that he had to do what E. A. Poe regarded as "the hardest task in the world": "coin" his "brain into silver at the nod of a master".[29] In his letter of October 29 1847 to his English publisher, John Murray, he wrote: "... Circumstances paramount to every other consideration, force me to regard my literary affairs in a strong pecuniary light." For, as he wrote to Hawthorne four years later in June 1851: "Dollars damn me; and the malicious Devil is forever grinning in upon me, holding the door ajar."[30]

And so Melville, too, tried to "manage the truth" as best he could, and seemed to follow the advice King Media gave to Babbalanja, the philosopher of *Mardi:*

> "Meditate as much as you will, Babbalanja, but say little aloud unless in a merry and mythical way. Lay down the great maxims of things, but let inferences take care of themselves. Never be special; never, a partisan. In safety, afar off, you may batter down a fortress; but at your peril you essay to carry a single turret by escalade."[31]

What happened, however, was that the inferences were first ignored, then forgotten, and then twisted out of recognition. Ninety years after his death, is Melville safe and "afar off" enough to "batter down" the "fortress" he was sparring at? Or is the "fortress" even better guarded in our own time than when *Mardi* was written?

Melville won instant fame with his first two books: *Typee* (1846) and *Omoo* (1847). Frank Luther Mott in *Golden Multitudes* lists them as "Better Sellers" for 1846 and 1847, when "Over-All Best Sellers" were Joel T. Headley's *Napoleon and His Marshals* and Grace Aguilar's *Home Influence*. ("Over-All Best Sellers" in 1841, 1842, 1844, 1848, and 1850 were pirated editions of the works of Dickens, Thackeray and the Brontës.)[32]

Typee was published on March 17, 1846, by Wiley and Putnam in New York; John Murray of London published Part One on February 27, and Part Two on April 1. Thus, the American first edition was sandwiched between the two parts of the English first edition. This was an ingenious arrangement because the first favourable notices from the English press were already arriving by steamer[33] before the book was issued in the United States. Moreover in England, *The Athenaeum* published its first review of the book on February 21, six days ahead of its publication there. With the authority that British literary opinion exercised over the American press at the time, this gave a green light to Melville in America. With the exception of *Pierre* all of Melville's later novels were also published practically concurrently in both New York and London.

The first American edition of *Typee* came out in two thousand copies. It met, on the whole, a favourable press reception, and was selling at a rate that induced the publisher to bring out two re-issues during the summer. Meanwhile, John Murray in England anticipated a bigger market. He brought out five thousand copies in the first instance, and by December 3, 1847, had sold 4,104.[34]

Encouraged by this initial success and in order to widen its reading public, John Wiley, the senior member and American manager of Wiley and Putnam's, persuaded Melville to expurgate the book and omit passages disparaging the Christian missionaries, and those with a sexual tinge. The Revised Edition was published in August 1846.[35]

In a letter to his English publisher of July 1846, Melville advised him to follow Wiley and Putnam's example:

"... there is a present demand for the book which the publishers can not supply—a new edition is in preparation. ... This ... will be a Revised one, ... all passages which are calculated to offend the tastes, or offer violence to the feelings of any large class of readers are certainly objectionable ... I have rejected every thing, in revising the book, which refers to the missionaries ...

... I earnestly trust that you will issue a Revised Edition. Depend upon it Sir, that it will be policy so to do. Nor have I decided upon this revision without much reflection and seeking the advice of persons every way qualifyed to give it."[36]

But, for whatever reason, John Murray never revised the English edition[37] and reprinted it seven more times during Melville's lifetime (in 1847, 1848, 1850, 1855, 1861, 1866, and 1877).

Meanwhile, in America, Melville was completing his second novel, *Omoo,* which he sold to the more liberal-minded Harper and Brothers, who remained Melville's American publisher for several years to come. (In 1849, they reissued *Typee,* using the Revised Edition. This text was then reprinted by Harper's six times—in 1850, 1855, 1857, 1865, 1871, and 1876.) *Omoo,* a sequel to *Typee,* shared *Typee*'s fame. First published by John Murray in London on March 30, 1847 and by Harper's in New York on May 1, it was reprinted six times by Murray's during Melville's lifetime (1848, 1849, 1850, 1861, 1865, 1877) and reprinted four times by Harper's in the year of its first publication, and then in 1855, 1863, and 1868.[38]

Published in the same year as *Typee* was reissued on both sides of the Atlantic, the two travelogues were often reviewed concurrently. Apart from attacks by evangelical journals on account of Melville's strictures on missionary practice, both books were hailed as "captivating", "charming", "delightful", "entertaining", "singularly attractive", "original", "bewitching", "spirited", "brilliantly coloured", etc., etc.[39]

The "inferences" took good "care of themselves". The religious scepticism implied in these "delightful romances" went unnoticed.

From then on, for the next decade, nearly all of Melville's works were identified as by the "author of 'Typee' and 'Omoo'".[40]

When, in the winters of 1857–60, in need of money and weary of writing, Melville embarked on his Midwestern lecture tours, newspaper reports still associated his name with *Typee* and *Omoo* (with the single exception of the Cincinnati *Enquirer* of February 2, 1858, which referred to *Typee, Omoo,* and *Moby-Dick* as the best of his works) and no doubt his audiences must have been disappointed, as some of the reports in fact indicate, when the "author of 'Typee' and 'Omoo'", instead of telling them glamorous stories of his South Sea adventures, talked in a serious and philosophical vein streaked with unobtrusive but pungent satire about "Statuary in Rome", "The South Seas" and "Travelling".

It is questionable whether Melville could have assured his later novels a success similar to that of *Typee* and *Omoo* even if he had continued writing in the same vein. When *Typee* and *Omoo* were being issued, the naval victories of the Revolution and of the War of 1812 were still a living memory in American minds and sea fiction appealed to national self-assurance. Moreover, it was the period of the golden age of American shipping which had started in 1815 but had come to an end by 1850. In the course of those 35 years, as Thomas Philbrick states, "American seamen came to challenge and even displace the British hegemony of many of the most important areas of maritime activity". By 1850 "the tonnage of the American fishing fleet was over five times greater than it had been in 1815, ... by the 1840s the American whaling fleet comprised more than three quarters of the world's total".[41] The sea was inherent in the life and imagination of Americans and the book market was inundated with a flood of nautical novels.

After 1850, however, there was a sharp decline in the market for sea fiction. The war with Mexico (1846–1848), resulting in an enormous expansion of United States territory, together with the discovery of gold in California in 1848, greatly accelerated the population shift westward, away from the sea. In the northeastern states, industrialization and the intensifying conflict with the southern states diverted interest from the sea to the mainland. American nautical fiction withered away and the vogue of sentimental and domestic tales came rapidly to predominate.

Thomas Philbrick believes that "the relative unpopularity of Melville's later fiction may also be a result of the fact that he was firmly established in the mind of the reading public as a nautical writer, a producer of the kind of fiction that was no longer in demand. Thus, even if Melville had attempted to return to the methods and concerns of *Typee* or *White-Jacket* in the late 1850s, it seems unlikely that he would have regained his earlier popularity. Certainly no other American writer enjoyed popular acclaim for treatment of nautical materials from the middle 1850s until the revival of interest in maritime affairs about the time of the Spanish–American War" (1898).[42]

21

In the event, Melville, not only continued to go to sea in most of his novels, but wrote more and more the way he felt "most moved to write". And it did "not pay".[43] The "two jobs" (*Redburn* in 1849 and *White-Jacket* in 1850) which he had "done for money"[44] were relative successes, although less so than *Typee* and *Omoo:* during Melville's lifetime *Redburn* was reprinted by Harper's three times (1850, 1855 and 1863) and once by Bentley's in England (1853); *White-Jacket* was reprinted once by Harper's (1855) and once in London (1855).[45] *Mardi* (1849), with its multifarious satirical allusions and implications, gave the first warning to critics.

At first they handled *Mardi* as the work of a popular young author, and on both sides of the Atlantic wrote highly of the "richness of imagination", the "fanciful descriptions of nature", "his skill in sketching", "his pictorial power", "the wild grandeur of his imagination", the book's "unique style", "beautiful language", "genial humour", "graphic descriptions", "oriental delights", "spirited and graceful sketches of land and ocean", etc.

In the United States, where the immediate reception of *Mardi* was much more favourable than in Britain, some critics also commended the philosophical and political references, in general terms alluding to the "philosophy and originality of thought", "an infinite fund of wit, humour, pathos, and philosophy", "a lively, pungent, instructive and exceedingly clever bundle of ... thoughts and imaginings", and "high philosophical speculation". Anticipating many twentieth-century critics, Evert Duyckinck was the first to interpret Melville's social satire in terms of "human nature": "'Mardi' probes yet deeper. ... The individual world of man, the microcosm, is to be explored and navigated. ... 'Mardi' is ... a satirical voyage in which we discover human nature." (*Literary World,* April 21, 1849.)

But as time passed, critics in the United States too, more and more came to share their English counterparts' bewilderment at this "frantic romance", this "prose run mad", this "rubbishing rhapsody" and "trash" "little better than insane ravings", this "hodge-podge", this "rambling philosophical romance", regretting, as the British *John Bull* (April 21, 1849) did,

> "that a pen so talented ... should have been made use of for the dissemination of sceptical notions ... and to talk down the verities of the Christian faith by sophistry ... ... we could heartily wish Mr. Melville had confined himself to the lively and picturesque scenery of which his pencil is a master, and if he pleased, to such subjects as offer a fair scope for the indulgence of his satirical vein, without introducing crude metaphysics and unsound notions of divinity".

In Britain, *Mardi* was not reprinted until 1923; in America, Harper's reprinted it in 1855 and 1864, after which it was not reprinted again until 1923.[46]

Moby-Dick (1851; the first English edition was entitled *The Whale*) met a mixed reception at first, both in Britain and the United States. In several instances the book was treated as another sea romance of Melville's "by far the most powerful

22

and original contribution that Herman Melville has yet made to the Romance of Travel", as the London *Weekly News and Chronicle* put it in November 1851[47] and was lauded for its "strange fascination", the author's "radiant imagination", his "fine vein of comic humour", "descriptive powers", "poetical imagination", "freshness of style and exquisite tact", the adventures ... deliciously exciting", "descriptions ... graphic and pictorial", "delineation of character ... Shakespearean", the "graphic and instructive sketches of the fishery, of sea-life in a whaling vessel", "acuteness of observation"[48] etc. It was variously called "a prose Epic on Whaling", "a pregnant allegory", a work "which, in point of richness and variety of incident, originality of conception, and splendor of description, surpasses any of the former productions of this highly successful author"[49] and "a work of great power and beauty", "one of the cleverest, wittiest and most amusing of modern books".[50]

But critics and reviewers were at a loss for pinpointing its genre: the book would not fit any literary convention known to them. On November 8, 1851, the London *Britannia* was musing: "There is so much eccentricity in its style and in its construction, ... and in the gradual development of its strange and improbable story, that we are at a loss to determine in what category of works of amusement to place it. It is certainly neither a novel nor a romance, ... for who ever heard of novel or romance without a heroine or a single love scene?" The London *Examiner* of the same day remarked: "But all the regular rules of narrative or story are spurned and set at defiance."

Other critics had graver misgivings.

The London *Spectator* of October 25, 1851, called it "rhapsody run mad", the *Atlas* of November 1 believed that "extravagance" was its "bane", and that the author had allowed "his fancy not only to run riot, but absolutely to run amuck", the *Athenaeum* of October 25 maintained that "this absurd book" contained "much trash belonging to the worst school of Bedlam literature". The London *Morning Chronicle* of December 20 found in the book little else than "sheer moonstruck lunacy" and the Charleston, South Carolina *Southern Quarterly Review* of January 1852 declared that the "Mad Captain"'s "ravings" and "the ravings of Mr. Melville himself, ... are such as would justify a writ *de lunatico* against all parties".

Nor did the purport of *Moby-Dick* evade the vigilant eyes of several reviewers. The London *John Bull* of October 25, 1851, was well aware that it was "far beyond the level of an ordinary work of fiction ... not a mere tale of adventures, but a whole philosophy of life that it unfolds". The critic strongly resented the occurrence of "worse than heathenish talk ... calculated to give ... serious offence", openly declaring that "This feature of Herman Melville's new work we cannot but deeply regret" and deploring that "he should have defaced his pages by occasional thrusts against revealed religion which ... cannot but shock readers accustomed to a reverent treatment of whatever is associated with sacred subjects". On the same day the *Athenaeum* clearly sensed that this was "a most provoking book" and the *Spectator* that it contained "satiric reflection upon the conventionalisms of civilized life".

"An air of irreverence pervading many parts" of the book also worried the New York *Argus* of November 14, 1851,[51] and Melville's close friend, Evert A. Duyckinck, part-owner and editor of the New York *Literary World*, wrote in a similar vein on November 22, 1851. Calling *Moby-Dick* an "intellectual chowder of romance, philosophy, natural history, fine writing, good feeling, bad sayings", and appreciating the "thorough exhaustive account admirably given of the great Sperm Whale", he protested against "this piratical running down of creeds and opinions", which was "out of place and uncomfortable", for: "We do not like to see what, under any view, must be to the world the most sacred associations of life violated and defaced . . . Nor is it fair to inveigh against the terrors of priestcraft, . . . petrifying us with imaginary horrors, and all sorts of gloomy suggestions, all the world through."[52]

The Boston *Post*, quoting the disparaging views of the London *Athenaeum*, reckoned the price of a dollar fifty which Harper's had set on the volume "far too costly", as it did not believe the book "worth the money asked for it, either as a literary work or as a mass of printed paper", and declared: "Published at twenty five cents, it might do to buy, but at any higher price, we think it a poor speculation." (At an auction on January 27, 1977 in New York, an American dealer did not think it a poor speculation to pay fifty-three thousand dollars for a three-volume set of the 1851 London edition of *The Whale*, as the London *Times* reported the following day.)

The New York *Commercial Advertiser* of November 28, 1851, expected "the greatest diversity of opinion" as to the merits of the novel. "There are few readers who will not be at first repulsed by its eccentricity", it prophesied, then expressed its own objections: "We regret to see that Mr. Melville is guilty of sneering at the truths of revealed religion. On page 58, he makes his hero, 'a good Christian—born and bred in the bosom of the infallible Presbyterian church', unite with a Polynesian in worshipping and offering incense to an idol, and in this connexion virtually questions the authenticity of the first commandment."

From the beginning of 1852 *Moby-Dick* was decried with gathering momentum. In January, the New York *United States Magazine and Democratic Review* asserted that Melville had "survived his reputation", for his books published after *Typee* and *Omoo* showed "a decided retrogression"; with *Moby-Dick*, he "destroyed all his chances of immortality". This book, with "all his rhetorical contortions, all his declamatory abuse of society, all his inflated sentiment, and all his insinuating licentiousness" seemed to have reached "the very ultimatum of weakness to which its author could attain".

The same month the Philadelphia *Peterson's Magazine* praised the book as "a skilfully told narrative of sea-adventures", but thought that it was also "a philosophical romance" and wished "the story (had) been compressed one-half, and all the transcendental chapters omitted", for then "it would have been decidedly the best sea-novel in the English language. No man", the paper added, "can serve two masters, even in fiction; and Mr. Melville, by attempting it, has spoilt his book." Another disappointed review was published in *Today: A Boston Literary Journal,* which especially objected to "the humor of those parts where sacred things are made light of—as for instance, the scene in which the hero joins his pagan friend in worshipping an idol and defends his course by half a page of wretched sophistry", as it was "revolting to good taste, and may still ... be dangerous to many of those persons who will be likely to read the book".

In July 1853, *Moby-Dick* was dismissed by the London *New Monthly Magazine* as a "furibund story", of which "the style is maniacal—mad as a March Hare—mowing, gibbering, screaming, like an incurable Bedlamite, reckless of keeper or strait-waistcoat".[53]

Moby-Dick was reprinted by Harper's in 1863, and was not published again until 1892.[54]

H. W. Hetherington tells us that "the total number of copies of *Moby-Dick* printed and sold in America up to and including 1887 was 3,797. On the other hand during less than three years, ... up to January, 1849, 6,392 copies of *Typee*" were sold. "During the single year 1887 were sold 200,000 copies of *Ben-Hur* (1880) ... The sales of *Moby-Dick* were ... as nothing to those of Susan Warner's *The Wide Wide World* (1850) or Mrs. E. D. E. N. Southworth's *The Curse of Clifton* (1852)."[55]

Whilst *Moby-Dick* had received at least some commendation, no such fortune was to accrue to Melville's next novel: *Pierre* (1852). *Pierre* is a satire upon the sentimental novels that dominated the American literary scene in the mid-nineteenth century. Like *Billy Budd,* published posthumously in 1924, it argues the inapplicability of the Christian moral doctrines, for, if consistently followed, they turn good into evil, if pragmatically applied, they serve hypocrisy. Yet *Pierre* is a flawed book. The travesty in it is too close an imitation of the sentimental novel for its satirical effect to be pungent. It is not consistent enough, and explicit didacticism often intrudes. The novel in fact *was* "a final hash".

Pierre was unequivocally rejected on both sides of the Atlantic. Critics deplored that Melville should "abuse his really fine talents as he does", that he should have "produced more and sadder trash than any other man of undoubted ability among us". *Pierre* contained "incoherent ravings", which "might be supposed to emanate from a lunatic hospital"; it was "perhaps the craziest fiction extant",[56] and one critic "feared" that "Herman Melville has gone 'clean daft'".[57]

Nor were the critics altogether insensitive to the intent of this "raving lunatic", and explicitly warned the public. "The most immoral *moral* of the story", Evert or George Duyckinck wrote in *The Literary World* of August 21, 1852, "if it has any moral at all, seems to be the impracticability of virtue ... Mr. Melville's chapter on 'Chronometricals and Horologicals', if it has any meaning at all, simply means that virtue and religion are only for gods and not to be attempted by man. But ordinary novel readers will never unkennel this loathsome suggestion." So did John R. Thompson, too, protest against the sacrilegious implications of *Pierre* in the September, 1852 issue of the Richmond, Virginia *Southern Literary Messenger,* of which he was editor and proprietor: "But badly as we think of the book as a work of art, we think infinitely worse of it as to its moral tendency. . . . if one does not desire to look at virtue and religion with the eye of Mephistopheles, or, at least, through a haze of *ambiguous* meaning, in which they may readily be taken for their opposites, he had better leave *Pierre or the Ambiguities* unbought on the shelves of the bookseller." But the strongest outcry came from George Washington Peck in the *American Whig Review* of November 1852: "Mr. Melville has done a very serious thing, a thing which not even unsoundness of intellect could excuse. He might have been mad to the very pinnacle of insanity; he might have torn our poor language into tatters, . . . he might have done all this and a great deal more, and we should not have complained. But when he dares to outrage every principle of virtue; when he strikes with an impious, though, happily, weak hand, at the very foundations of society, we feel it our duty to tear off the veil with which he has thought to soften the hideous features of the idea, and warn the public against the reception of such atrocious doctrines."[58]

During Melville's lifetime, *Pierre* was reprinted by Harper's (in 1855), but was not accepted by any English publisher[59] and was not published again on either side of the Atlantic until 1922.[60]

Pierre was followed by a virtual eclipse of Melville's fame. The press reaction to *Israel Potter* (1855) and to *The Piazza Tales* (1856) was on the whole favourable, but short-lived. The few notices on *The Confidence-Man* (1857) and his volume of poetry, *Battle-Pieces and Aspects of the War* (1866), contained more stricture than applause. Of his other three volumes of poetry *Clarel* (1876) was published at the expense of Melville's uncle, *John Marr* (1888) and *Timoleon* (1891) were both privately issued in 25 copies each.[61] His last novel, *Billy Budd* was only published posthumously, in 1924.

In 1866, Melville managed to obtain the post of customs inspector in New York harbour, which he held for twenty years, resigning at the end of 1885 after receiving substantial family bequests and attaining financial independence for the first time in his life.

In the chapter entitled "My Life in the Custom-House" of his *Recollections, Personal and Literary*,[62] Richard Henry Stoddard relates how, when 28, at the personal intervention of President Pierce, he "was created" "an Inspector of Customs of the Port of New York" and remarks:

"My fortune *was* made after all." He then adds: "As all roads led to Rome, so all New York humanity gravitated toward the Custom-House—merchants, bankers, politicians, besides everyone who was fit for nothing elsewhere, and so thought he deserved a job in the Custom-House."

He also describes his introduction some time later to a new appointee:

"I bowed to the gentleman . . . in whom I recognized a famous writer whom I had met some twenty-five years before: no American writer was more widely known in the late forties and early fifties in his own country and in England than Melville, who, in his earlier books, 'Typee', 'Omoo', 'Mardi', and 'White-Jacket', had made himself the prose poet of the strange islands and peoples of the South Seas."

Five years after Melville had retired from the custom-house, the New York *Literary World* wrote on December 6, 1890:

"There are more people today, writes Edward Bok, who believe Herman Melville dead, than there are those who know he is living . . . famous writer of sea stories—stories which have never been equalled perhaps in their special line. Mr. Melville is now an old man, but still vigorous . . . 44 years ago, when his most famous tale, *Typee,* appeared, there was not a better known author than he, and he commanded his own prices. Publishers sought him and editors considered themselves fortunate to secure his name as a literary star.[63] And today? Busy New York has no idea he is even alive, and one of the best informed literary men in this country laughed recently at my statement that Herman Melville was his neighbour by only two city blocks. 'Nonsense' said he. 'Why, Melville is dead these many years'. Talk about literary fame? There's a sample of it!"

Ten months later, on October 10, 1891, the same journal devoted the 25th and last but one item of its obituary column to the following notice:

"Mr. E. W. Bok not long since called the attention of the public to the fact that Mr. Herman Melville, the author of *Typee,* was still living in New York. Mr. Melville died in that city September 28, at the age of 72 . . . "[64]

The oblivion into which Melville had fallen among his compatriots was also confirmed by an English observer, William Clark Russell (1844–1911), a sailor in the merchant marine in his teens, and subsequently a writer of sea fiction. Melville had entered a cordial correspondence with him in 1886, dedicating *John Marr* to him in 1888; Russell dedicated his *An Ocean Tragedy* to Melville in 1889. In 1892, in an article for the February issue of *The North American Review* entitled "A Claim for American Literature", Russell extolled the literary merits of Melville and Richard Henry Dana, Jr., as those of "men of genius, but sailors first of all" and wrote about Melville:

"His books are now but little read. When he died the other day—to my sorrow! for our correspondence had bred in me a deeper feeling than kindness, and esteem,—men who could give you the names of fifty living American poets and perhaps a hundred living American novelists, owned that they had never heard of Herman Melville; which simply means that to all intents and purposes, the American sailor is a dead man and the American merchant service ... a dead industry. Yet a famous man he was in those far days ... now he is neglected; yet his name and works will not die."

In 1849, Melville wrote to Evert A. Duyckinck:

"All ambitious authors should have ghosts capable of revisiting the world, to snuff up the steam of adulation, which begins to rise straightway as the Sexton throws his last shovelfull on him.—Down goes his body & up flies his name."[65]

But no "steam of adulation" was to rise from his grave. The American Literary Histories, Anthologies, Cyclopaedias of the turn of the century and right up to the Melville Centenary in 1919 gave him a very low rating; it was something of a surprise when there appeared a revival of interest in Melville.

The verdict of the 1902 edition of the *Encyclopaedia Britannica* was summary: "Melville was the product of a period in American literature when the fiction written by writers below Irving, Poe, and Hawthorne was measured by humble artistic standards."[66] In 1909, Melville was not included in W. C. Brownell's *American Prose Masters,* nor was he listed among the authors in John Erskine's *Leading American Novelists,* published in 1910.[67]

In *A Literary History of America* (London: T. Fischer Unwin, 1901) Barrett Wendell, Professor of English at Harvard College, while devoting entire chapters to Irving, Cooper, Poe, Whittier, Longfellow and Hawthorne, mentioned Melville only in the chapter entitled "The Knickerbocker School":

"There are certain names which we might have mentioned: Mrs. Kirkland, for example ... wrote some sketches of life in the Middle West ... Herman Melville, with his books about the South Seas, which Robert Louis Stevenson is said to have declared the best ever written, and with his novels of maritime adventure, began a career of literary promise, which never came to fruition. Certain writers too, who reached maturity later, had already made themselves known, Bayard Taylor, for example, and George William Curtis; ... " (p. 229.)

George E. Woodberry, Professor of Comparative Literature at Columbia University, in his *America in Literature* (London and New York: Harper and Brothers, 1903) did not even mention Melville; the revised edition of 1921 *(Appreciation of Literature and America in Literature,* only includes Melville in a long list of also-rans in a chapter entitled "An Encyclopaedic View":

"The sea-novel was developed by Herman Melville (1819–1891) in 'Typee' (1846) and its successors, but these tales, in spite of their being highly commended by lovers of adventure, have taken no more hold than the work of Simms."

Another Columbia professor, William P. Trent devoted considerably more space to Melville in his *A History of American Literature, 1607–1865* (London: William Heinemann, 1903). In the chapter "The Romancers" he writes rather reluctantly:

"Fortune ... has at last smiled again upon (Melville) ... since a generation fond of narratives full of not too improbable adventure and of tropical glow has accepted, with at least fair complacency, the republication of books that won the warm commendation of Robert Louis Stevenson. The author of *Typee* was born ... "

Here a short biography follows, in the course of which Professor Trent writes:

"But as early as 1849 the quasi-speculative, chaotic romance entitled Mardi gave premonition of aberration and of the eventual frustration of a promising career. Melville's greatest achievement still awaited him ... he published in 1851 his masterpiece, Moby-Dick, or the White Whale. If it were not for its inordinate length, its frequently inartistic heaping up of details, and the obvious imitation of Carlylean tricks of style and construction, this narrative of tremendous power and wide knowledge might be perhaps pronounced the greatest sea story in literature." (pp. 389–91.)

On a previous page (p. 383) Melville's place in literary history is clearly indicated:

"There were at least a dozen new writers who belonged more or less to the school of romancers ... They were in no case great, and only one of them, Herman Melville, has attained the honour of being seriously considered by the present generation. Only four of these half-alive romancers will require special discussion ... "

The half-alive romancers were John Pendleton Kennedy (1795–1870), Dr. Robert Montgomery Bird (1803–1854), William Gilmore Simms (1806–1870) and Herman Melville.

In 1905, William P. Trent had another edition published, revised for the use of schools: *Brief History of American Literature* (New York: D. Appleton and Co., 1905). Here he writes:

"Besides Hawthorne and Poe and the older writers contemporary with Cooper there were at least a dozen romancers well known between 1830 and 1850, whose works are now completely forgotten, although not devoid of merit. One romancer, who began to publish toward the end of the period, Herman Melville, has had of late some revival of fame, but his case is practically unique. As we have already seen, only Kennedy, Bird and Simms need be grouped with Melville as representing minor writers of fiction, whose work deserves brief mention." (p. 138.)

Later he refers to Melville as "the sailor-author". (p. 140.) As for *Moby-Dick,* he states that here

> "his powers culminated. It is in parts probably not exceeded in strength and general interest by any other romance of the sea." Yet "The numerous books he wrote gave painful proofs of mental aberration" and "in spite of the genuine merits of Kennedy, Bird, Simms and Melville, it remains true that the really significant fiction of the period ... is to be found in the works of Hawthorne and Poe". (p. 140.)

W. P. Trent was the editor of *A History of American Literature,* published in 1918 by G. P. Putnam's Sons, New York and the Cambridge University Press, supplementary to the *Cambridge History of English Literature.* Carl van Doren's Chapter VII ("Fiction"), in dealing with Melville under "Contemporaries of Cooper" (pp. 320–23), indicates that a dramatic change in the assessment of Melville was under way. Carl van Doren calls Melville "the most original and perennial of Cooper's contemporaries", and *Moby-Dick* "the best of his and one of the best of American romances" and adds:

> "The immense originality of *Moby-Dick* must warrant the claim of its admirers that it belongs with the greatest sea romances in the whole literature of the world."

This, however, was not to redeem Melville from the conventional verdict he had earned himself since writing *Mardi:*

> "His death ... removed from American literature one of its most promising and most disappointing figures,"

though Carl van Doren casually adds:

> "Of late his fame has shown a tendency to revive."

(In the 1924 edition, this sentence was changed to: "Of late his fame is undergoing an energetic revival in both America and England.")

If it was so, then an important part was played in this revival by those "admirers" of Melville whom Carl van Doren hinted at. For it was the small nuclei of admirers, both in America and in England, which kept Melville's memory alive throughout the thirty years that elapsed between his death, and his apotheosis after 1921 as a great American classic.

Who were they, and what made them admire Melville?

The slow revival of interest in Melville towards the end of the century started chiefly in England and mainly sprang from two sources: a renewed interest in sea fiction, and the English secularists' discovery of Melville's humanism and realism.

Interest in sea fiction, which had declined in the fifties, was revived by the colonizing expeditions of the 1880s and, more directly, by the novels of R. L. Stevenson. Stevenson was an admirer of Melville and wrote to a friend in 1888:

> "I shall have a fine book of travels, I feel sure; and will tell you more of the South Seas after my few months than any other writer has done—except Herman Melville perhaps, who is a howling cheese."[68]

Stevenson had brought, as J. St. Loe Strachey put it in *The Spectator* of June 24, 1893, "the South Seas into fashion again". And Strachey added: "With this renaissance of the South Seas, it was inevitable that there should come a demand for the republication of *Typee, Omoo, Moby-Dick* and *White-Jacket*."[69]

In fact, Melville himself had helped Arthur Stedman, subsequently his literary executor, in preparing the new editions of these novels. In December 1889, Henry S. Salt[70] had written to Melville[71] on behalf of Walter Scott, the publisher, proposing a new edition of *Typee* and *Omoo* in the Camelot Series. However, John Murray, owner of the copyright of these two novels, refused his consent, as Melville duly informed Salt on February 25, 1890:

> "Concerning 'Typee'.—As I engaged to do, I wrote to Mr. Murray. The information contained in the reply is such, and the manner of conveying it is such, that I consider myself bound, by considerations both of right and courtesy, not to sanction any English issue of the book—(during my lifetime) other than that of the original purchaser and publisher.—Were matters otherwise, I should be glad to accede to your proposition."[72]

When after Melville's death *Typee, Omoo, White-Jacket* and *Moby-Dick* were reissued in 1892 and 1893 they were published as romances of the sea and hailed as such. In his introduction to the 1892 edition of *Typee* (G. P. Putnam's Sons, London and New York), Arthur Stedman, the editor, wrote: "With *Moby-Dick or The Whale* (1851) Melville reached the topmost notch of his fame." While "the book represents to a certain extent the conflict between the author's earlier and later methods of composition", it still belongs to "the highest domain of romance". "How many young men have been drawn to sea by this book is a question of interest." Stedman deplores that Melville "did not . . . take warning from *Mardi*, but allowed himself to plunge more deeply into the sea of philosophy and fantasy", which led to a deterioration in his works. Coming to *Israel Potter*, Stedman declares it "hardly worthy of the author of *Typee*".

A year later, in 1893, Murray's English editions of *Typee* and *Omoo* were introduced by Henry S. Salt, who declared *Typee* "the undoubted masterpiece" of Melville's "earlier period", whilst *The Whale* was "the crown and glory of the later phase, less shapely and artistic than *Typee*" surpassing it "in immensity of scope and triumphant energy of execution".

31

In both Introductions, one senses a certain ambivalence in the assessment of the relative merits of the two "masterpieces", *Typee* and *Moby-Dick*. Stedman saw *Moby-Dick* as marking "the topmost notch" of Melville's fame, but still spoke of Melville in conventional terms as "the author of *Typee*". Salt seeks to strike a balance with a compromise: both are masterpieces in their own right, the one of Melville's "earlier period", the other of his "later phase".

Published and republished as one of Melville's several romances, *Moby-Dick* intrigued readers and critics more and more as it gradually dawned upon them that there was more here than merely a story of fantastic adventures at sea.

However, two writers (one the Englishman, William Clark Russell,[73] the other the Canadian Archibald MacMechan,[74] Munro Professor of English at Dalhousie University, Halifax, Nova Scotia) had unequivocally declared in favour of *Moby-Dick* years before it was reissued in 1892. Moreover, contending with assessments of Melville as "a born romancer" and writer of "fantastic tales"[75], and of *Moby-Dick* as belonging to "the highest domain of romance",[76] they both emphasized that Melville's greatest merit in *Moby-Dick* was that the poetry and the story were based on "rough realities" and the book was "a record . . . of fact idealized". They pronounced their judgement in the 1880s, the very nadir of Melville's popularity; for in the fourteen years between 1877 and 1892, no work of Melville's had been published except the twice 25 copies of *John Marr* (1888) and *Timoleon* (1891), and even those issued privately by Melville himself.[77]

William Clark Russell wrote an article for the September issue of the London *Contemporary Review* in 1884 (Vol. 46, pp. 343–63) in which he rated *Moby-Dick* Melville's "finest work". He also pointed out that

> "*Moby-Dick* is not a sea-story—it is a medley of noble impassioned thoughts born of the deep, pervaded by a grotesque human interest, owing to the contrast it suggests between the rough realities of the cabin and the forecastle, and the phantasms of men conversing in rich poetry, and strangely moving, and acting in that dim weather-worn Nantucket whaler."

Archibald MacMechen addressed a letter to Melville in 1889:

> "For a number of years I have read and re-read *Moby-Dick* with increasing pleasure with every perusal: and with this study, the conviction has grown up that the unique merits of that book have never received due recognition . . . I am anxious to set the merits of your books before the public and to that end, I beg the honour of correspondence with you. It would be of great assistance to me, if I could gather some particulars of your life and *literary methods* from you, other than given in such books as Duyckinck's dictionary."[78]

Melville would not satisfy this request: however MacMechan's letter gave him "pleasure, as how should it not, written in such a spirit". "But", he wrote, "you do not know, perhaps, that I have entered my eighth decade. After twenty years nearly, as an outdoor Custom House Officer, I have latterly come into possession of unobstructed leisure, but only just as, in the course of nature, my vigor sensibly declines. What little of it is left I husband for certain matters as yet incomplete, and which indeed may never be completed."[79]

Not discouraged, Professor MacMechan wrote a lengthy article on *Moby-Dick,* published in October, 1899, in the *Queen's Quarterly,* under the title: "The Best Sea Story Ever Written". Here he asserted:

"In my poor opinion much less than justice has been done to an American writer, whose achievement is so considerable that it is hard to account for the neglect into which he has fallen.
     This writer is Herman Melville, who died in New York in the autumn of 1891, aged eighty-three. . . . To find how complete neglect is, one has only to put question to the most cultivated and patriotic Americans North or South, East or West, even professed specialists in the nativist literature, and it will be long before the Melville enthusiast meets with sympathy or understanding. The present writer made his first acquaintance with *Moby-Dick* . . . nearly twenty years ago; and since that time he has seen only one copy of the book exposed for sale, and met only one person (and that not an American) who had read it. . . . the only place where real appreciation of him (Melville) is to be found of recent years is in one of Mr. Clark Russell's dedications. There occurs the phrase which gives this paper its title."

The article then points out that Melville "cuts himself off" from all the "advantages" of the conventions of sea romance:

"Whalers are commonly regarded as a sort of sea-scavangers. He convinces you that their business is poetic; and that they are finest fellows afloat. . . . The book is not a record of fact; but of fact idealized . . . "

". . . Whaling is the most peculiar business done by man upon the deep waters. A war-ship is but a mobile fort or battery; a merchant-man is but a floating shop or warehouse: fishing is devoid of any but the ordinary perils of navigation; but sperm-whaling, according to Melville, is the most exciting and dangerous kind of big game hunting . . . "

". . . Whaling is peculiarly an American industry; and of all whale-men, the Nantucketers were the keenest, the most daring, and the most successful. Now . . . the industry is almost extinct. The discovery of petroleum did for it. Perhaps Melville went to sea for no other purpose than to construct the monument of whaling in this unique book . . . "

"... This book is at once the epic and the encyclopaedia of whaling. It is a monument to the honour of an extinct race of daring seamen; but it is a monument overgrown with the lichen of neglect. Those who will care to scrape away the moss may be few, but they will have their reward."

And reward they had. Some even a quite surprising one, like the English secularists[80] of the end of the century, who discovered marked congeniality between their philosophy and Melville's. Henry Stephen Salt,[81] an atheist, member of the Fabian Society and a close friend of G. B. Shaw, was one of them. Other names are recorded in Melville's correspondence. But the first among them to "scrape away the moss" was James Thomson, the atheist poet and essay writer.[82]

In 1874, the year he completed *The City of Dreadful Night,* James Thomson wrote an article in *The National Reformer* on Walt Whitman. Here he mentioned Melville, who at that time was serving his eighth year in the New-York custom-house:

"I know but one other living American writer who approaches him (Whitman) in his sympathy with all ordinary life and vulgar occupations, in his feeling of brotherhood for all rough workers, and at the same time in his sense of beauty and grandeur, and his power of thought. I mean, Herman Melville, the author of 'Typee', 'Omoo', 'Mardi', 'The Whale', etc., but Melville is sometimes strangely unequal to his better self, and has lavished much strength in desultory doings."

Bertram Dobell, bookseller and publisher, poet, critic and editor, rationalist in outlook[83] and Thomson's friend and literary executor,[84] wrote in his monograph on Thomson:

"Early in 1881, Thomson, who had already visited Leicester, and made there a number of good and generous friends, was invited to write an 'Address' in verse to be recited at the opening of the New Hall of the Leicester Secular Society, and also to be present on the occasion of its delivery. These requests he willingly acceded to; and on March 5, he travelled, in company with Mr. and Mrs. Wright, to Leicester, where he stayed, enjoying the hospitality of several friends, for the next four days. On this occasion he first made the acquaintance of Mr. John W. Barrs, who was henceforth to prove one of his most devoted admirers and most generous friends. On June 4 in the same year, Thomson again went to Leicester, having been invited thither by a number of the friends whose hospitality he had enjoyed on his previous visit. The following extract from his diary sums up the story of his stay there on this occasion:

'To Leicester on June 4th with the Wrights and Adeline (Holyoake). Myself kept out of town seven weeks—one week at Quorndon with Phil Wright and brothers; three days in Leicester with Mr. Michael Wright;

one day with Mr. Gimson; all the other five-and-a-half weeks with the Barrs at Forest Edge, Kirby Muxloe, four miles out of Leicester. Unbounded hospitality; splendid holiday.'"[85]

H. W. Hetherington[86] believes that it was on this occasion that Thomson "introduced to Jack[87] and his sister and their friend James Billson, who often came over from his nearby country place ... some books by ... Herman Melville". James Billson, a lawyer and classical scholar, was to become in 1893–94 President of the secularist Leicester Literary and Philosophical Society.

Three years later—and two years after the death of James Thomson—in 1884, a correspondence began between James Billson and Melville which went on for four years. In his first letter Billson complained about Melville's books being hard to procure. They were "in great request":

"As soon as one is discovered (for that is what it really is with us) it is eagerly read & passed round a rapidly increasing knot of Melville readers."

In his reply, Melville sent his "best wishes to yourself and your circle".[88]

Sensing that Herman Melville would find the ideas of their late friend, James Thomson, congenial, Billson and his secularist friend John W. Barrs sent several volumes of Thomson's works from Leicester to New York. In his replies, Melville expressed high appreciation of Thomson's prose and poetry. In December 1888, he wrote to James Billson:

"... 'The City of Dreadful Night', one can hardly overestimate it, massive and mighty as it is, — its gloom is its sublimity ... "[89]

In 1890, Henry Stephen Salt (1851–1939), a mutual friend of John W. Barrs, James Thomson and Bertram Dobell, entered into a similar correspondence with Melville. Salt was a classical scholar, a monographer of Shelley, biographer of Thoreau, author, critic; he was an atheist and a vegetarian, a founder and Honorary Secretary of the Humanitarian League, a member of the Fabian Society and a close friend of G. B. Shaw. In his autobiographical *Company I Have Kept* (London: Allen and Unwin, 1930, p. 109.) he recalls:

"It was from that widely-read student of good books, Bertram Dobell, that I had first heard of Melville's works; and so grateful was I for the information that I sedulously passed it on to others. I remember, in particular, bringing *Moby-Dick* to the notice of William Morris, and how a week or two afterwards I heard him quoting it with huge gusto and delight. Among other well-known men who realized Melville's genius have been Robert Buchanan, R. L. Stevenson, Edward Carpenter, Clark Russell, and John Masefield. Stevenson is said to have considered Melville's books about the South Seas to be the best ever written on the subject. ... I was brought into touch with

. Herman Melville through my biography of the pessimist poet James Thomson.[90] He was a great admirer of Melville, and Melville in his turn highly valued *The City of Dreadful Night*. Knowing this, I had sent him a copy of my book, and in consequence received from him two or three letters, in one of which he very characteristically wrote that Thomson's poem is 'the modern Book of Job, under an original form, duskily looming with the same aboriginal verities'."[91]

It was in *The City of Dreadful Night* (1874)[92] that the sceptic James Thomson wrote:

"..
I find no hint throughout the Universe
Of good or ill, of blessing or of curse;
I find alone Necessity supreme.

....
That all the oracles are dumb or cheat
   Because they have no secret to express;
That none can pierce the vast black veil uncertain
Because there is no light beyond the curtain;
   That all is vanity and nothingness.

....
The world rolls round for ever like a mill;
It grinds out death and life and good and ill;
It has no purpose, heart or mind or will."

Salt was a great admirer of Melville's and wrote an article about him in *The Scottish Art Review* in November 1889. (Vol. II. No. 18.) Like William Clark Russell and Archibald MacMechan, he, too, emphasized the authenticity and realism of Melville's art, a view common to most of Melville's admirers at the turn of the century right up to the early 1920s:

"The chief characteristic of Herman Melville's writings is this attempted union of the practical with the ideal. Commencing with a basis of solid fact, he loves to build up a fantastic structure, which is finally lost in the cloudland of metaphysical speculation. He is at his best, as in *Typee*, when the mystic element is kept in check, and made subservient to the clear development of the story; or when, as in certain passages of *Mardi* and *Moby-Dick*, the two qualities are for the time harmoniously blended. ... As a portrayer of character Melville is almost always successful. His sea-captains, from the effeminate 'Miss Guy' to the indomitable Ahab, and his seamen ... are lifelike pictures."

Deploring that Melville's fame had fallen into obscurity, Henry S. Salt wrote:

"In an age, which has witnessed a marked revival of books of travel and adventure, and which, in its greed for narrative or fiction of this kind is often fain to content itself with works of a very inferior quality, it is a cause for regret that the author of *Typee* and *Mardi* should have fallen to a great extent out of notice, and should be familiar only to a small circle of admirers, instead of enjoying the wide reputation to which undoubted genius entitles him". Melville was "now so far forgotten by a later and ungrateful generation as to be too often confused with Herman Merivale on the one side, or Whyte Melville on the other."[93]

It was these admirers of the realism and secularism of his books who kept Melville's memory alive throughout the thirty years from his death to the revival of his fame in the wake of 1919, the centenary of his birth.

In the course of the preceding eight years, no work of Melville's was published. In 1920, 1921, and 1922 *Typee, Omoo, White-Jacket* and *Moby-Dick* were reissued on both sides of the Atlantic. The Standard Edition of *The Works of Herman Melville* was published in sixteen volumes by Constable and Co., London, in 1922–24, and Melville's first full-length biography: Raymond M. Weaver's *Herman Melville: Mariner and Mystic* (New York: George H. Doran Co.) in 1921. Newspapers and magazines published memorial articles about Melville, invariably calling him a "romancer" and a sea fiction writer, but also emphasizing the authenticity and realism of his writings. *The New York Times* of July 20, 1919, praised their "verisimilitude", *The New York Tribune* of August 4 declared: "In his own odd fashion he put down for all time the essence of the off-shore ocean . . . an achievement which, we guess, promises Melville the security of fame for long to come." In the London *Athenaeum* of January 28, 1921, Augustine Birrell wrote a long eulogy of *Moby-Dick,* pointing out as one of its most striking features the "mingling of an ever-present romanticism of style with an almost savage reality of narrative . . . It is romantic from end to end, and eloquent throughout, but is also grim and real."

Even F. L. Lucas' review of Raymond Weaver's psychoanalytical biography of Melville in *The New Statesman* of April 1, 1922, held Melville to be "the creator of an epic of the sea and of human life" and pronounced *Moby-Dick* to be "not an allegory spun into a story, but a story strong enough to shoulder a dozen allegories or none at all".

In the centennial year of Melville's birth, the most decisive commemorative article, written by Frank Jewett Mather, professor of art and archeology at Princeton University, appeared in a short-lived American weekly, *The Review*. Published in two parts, on the 9th and the 16th of August 1919, it came to altogether thirteen columns. This was the first major article on Melville that gave an all-around account of his life and work. Mather had high praise for Melville's art, unequivocally held *Moby-Dick* to be his "greatest book", and clearly recognized its symbolic implications.

We learn that Mather was first introduced to Melville by Edwin Lucas White, the poet, who gave him *Moby-Dick* to read.

"That reading made a Melvilleite out of me. I bought everything Melville published—it took me ten years to do it, and my collection was only completed with the two privately printed pamphlets of poems, through the gracious gift of Melville's daughter. I read my collection up and down with increasing delight. Gradually I learned that to love Melville was to join a very small circle. It was like eating hasheesh ... I owe to my enthusiasm for Melville acquaintance with extraordinary persons on both sides of the seas; for no ordinary person loves Melville. So on the centenary of his birth it is a double debt of gratitude which I repay most inadequately in giving some account of one of the greatest and most strangely neglected of American writers."

Mather then proceeds to give a full account of Melville's life and work, and in face of conventional assessments declares unequivocally:

"*Moby Dick* ... is Melville's most characteristic and, I think, his greatest book. Still, for the average reader Melville is merely the author of *Typee* and *Omoo*."

Mather argues in a vein similar to that of Henry S. Salt when discussing the symbolism of *Moby-Dick:*

"*Moby Dick* has the tremendous advantage of its concreteness. Captain Ahab's mad quest of the white whale imposes itself as real, and progressively enlists and appalls the imagination ...

... The tragic and almost incredible motive of the quest of the demon whale gains credibility from the solid basis of fact, as mad Captain Ahab himself is based, so to speak, on his ivory leg ...

But *Moby Dick* is more than what it undisputedly is, the greatest whaling novel. It is an extraordinary work in morals and general comment ... Melville finds a suggestion or a symbol in each event and fearlessly pursues the line of association ... It is the interplay of fact and application that makes the unique character of the book ...

... The effect of the book rests on the blend of fact, fancy and profound reflection, upon a brilliant intermingling of sheer artistry and moralizing at large."

Regarding Melville's artistic decline after *Moby-Dick,* Mather hints at his isolation:

"... he had greatly isolated himself. By telling the truth about the Polynesian missionaries he had sorely ruffled the devout, and had increased the offense by skeptical asides in his novels. From the New England writers, most of whom too clearly revealed 'the stripedness of their German and Neo-Platonical origins' he stood off. He came to a New York in the literary doldrums. Solitude easily became a habit which stuck.

... What he lacked was possibly only health and nerve, but perhaps even more, companionship of a friendly, critical and understanding sort."[94]

From August 1919, for some 18 months, *Moby-Dick* was more widely acclaimed in England than in the United States. As Jay B. Hubbell notes in *Who Are the Major American Writers?* (1972), in the centenary year of Melville's birth, Professor Percy H. Boynton of Chicago University published a *History of American Literature* in which Melville's name does not even appear.

In London, in the *Bookman* of August 1919, F. C. Owlett called *Moby-Dick* "the finest sea book ever written in English."[95] In March 1920, the authoress Viola Meynell exclaimed in *The Dublin Review:*

"Readers of the book will see that this is the greatest of seawriters whom even Conrad must own as master.* Barrie confessedly owes him his Captain Hook. Great isolated fame Herman Melville must have in many an individual mind which having once known him, is then partly made of him for ever. But how little *Moby-Dick* is generally known is exemplified by a writer in *The Times Literary Supplement* recently who, in a clever article on Herman Melville, did not even mention this book, as if his fame really rested on those better-known and comparatively insignificant stories, *Typee* and *Omoo*. Though *Moby-Dick* has been published in England and has been included in the 'Everyman' series, it is at present out of print."

The same year, in her Introduction to the Oxford University Press edition of *Moby-Dick,* she wrote:

"*Moby-Dick* is the high-water mark of Herman Melville's achievement. ... And if one concludes at the end of it that Herman Melville is one of the greatest of all imaginative writers, it is as much for each page of scientifically accurate description as for any other part of it. There has never been such imaginative description of fact. The infinite detail of the whale, its measurements, its blubber, its oil, its lashless eyes, its riddled brow—these are the reality with which the wild spirit of thought is interlocked. It is the

---

* He did not. In 1907 he refused to write a preface to an edition of *Moby-Dick* which the Oxford Press intended to publish. "It struck me as a rather strained rhapsody with whaling for a subject and not a single sincere line in the three vols of it"—he explained in a letter. (*Moby-Dick As Doubloon*, p. 123.)

opposite school from that which prefers to dispense with reality as a start for imagination, and can find it more easily in fairies and fantasies and imps and gnomes than in these ropes and buckets. That taste would rather not stop to measure and examine a whale when it can have a fairy whom fancy can make any size, and whose robe may be of rainbow colours."

Meanwhile critics in the United States were still hesitant.

For Van Wyck Brooks the centenary of Melville's birth "passed two summers ago, unnoticed". In a lengthy article published in the New York *Freeman* on October 26, 1921, he ironically reports on the sudden interest in Melville under English influence:

"(Melville) did not even die in the historical manuals: the rising generation was assured, ... that his talent was quite as great as that of a dozen seventh-rate poets and romancers who had been his contemporaries. That his talent was a sovereign talent, or had at least its sovereign moments (let us insist only on moments), his fellow-countrymen had not observed: it was only in England that he had been justly appreciated. ... Well, it was only a question of time: sooner or later the darkness that surrounds this extraordinary man was certain to yield before our indefatigable national appetite for investigation and research. Next year Melville will have been forgotten again. ... But for the next six months there is to be a Melville boom. Ishmael is to emerge at last: he is to have his little hour. ... A complete edition of Melville's works is said to be in preparation, to follow the appearance of Professor Weaver's biography."

Unable to comprehend the purport of the book and the relationship between fact, fiction and philosophy, Van Wyck Brooks holds up to ridicule the structure and style of *Moby-Dick:* "To those, indeed, for whom literature is a question of the theme, of the intention, no book could be more exasperating than 'Moby Dick'," he warns the reader. "Melville constantly loses the thread of his tale, ... he loses himself in the details of cetology, he tells us about ambergris and about the erroneous and 'less erroneous' pictures of whales ... he has a chapter on the tails of whales, another on the spouting of whales, another on 'Jonah Historically Regarded'; he speculates, he mythologizes, ... Melville is an American Borrow, a Borrow of the sea."

A year later, Van Wyck Brooks was seconded by another notable American critic, Arthur Hobson Quinn. Reviewing Raymond Weaver's biography of Melville in the October 1922 issue of *Yale Review*, he declared "Melville's besetting weakness" to be "his lack of humor, and his inability to distinguish fact from fiction" (a view A. H. Quinn consistently reiterated in his *The Literature of the American People*. New York: Appleton-Century-Crofts, 1951, pp. 245–6.).

The evaluation given by Van Wyck Brooks was, however, repudiated by the American critic Carl Van Vechten, who, in January 1922 stated in the New

Orleans *Double Dealer* that he had "scant patience with those who consider 'Moby-Dick' only a sea story", and asserted: "It is surely Melville's greatest book, surely the greatest book that has yet been written in America, surely one of the great books of the world."

The six months Van Wyck Brooks had allowed for "a Melville boom" had elapsed when in September 1922 the London *The Nation & The Athenaeum* reported that the "vogue of Herman Melville" was still gathering momentum. The article related how "a recent cheap edition of 'Moby Dick' has resulted in a common confession that the book is a masterpiece, and in a general curiosity about its author". The article then continued:

"That book, indeed, appears to have been a wonder treasured as a sort of secret for years by some select readers who had chanced upon it. They said little about it. We gather that they had been in the habit of hinting the book to friends they could trust, so that 'Moby Dick' became a sort of cunning test by which genuineness of another man's response to literature could be proved. . . .

To-day, Herman Melville is admitted to be one of the best things America has done. So whole-hearted, indeed, has been the admiration of English critics for 'Moby Dick' that the more intellectual of the American critics have, quite naturally, retorted that the White Whale is not such a fine whale after all. It might have been bigger, or different. It is not the kind of whale to which a modern American man of letters would have given birth. Which, we will admit, is probable; yet, nevertheless, the significance of 'Moby Dick' is so portentous that a deep curiosity concerning its author and his other works is natural."

Thrice six months after his forecast, Van Wyck Brooks felt the need to read *Moby-Dick* again and state in a lengthy article in the New York *Freeman* of May 16, 1923:

"It seems to me now less chaotic, better shaped, than it seemed at first: nothing has surprised me more than to discover how conscious Melville was of what he was doing. . . . It seemed to me intolerable that he had not removed the chapters on whales in general, on whaling, whales' heads, pitchpoling, ambergris, the try-works, etc., and published them separately: they were glorious, but I could not believe that they had been deliberately introduced to retard the action. It struck me that the action should have been retarded as it were within the story. I do not feel this now. The book is an epic, and an epic requires ballast. Think of the catalogue of ships in Homer, the mass of purely historical information in the 'Aeneid', the long descriptions in 'Paradise Lost': how immensely these elements add to the density and the volume of the total impression, and how they serve to throw into relief the gestures and activities of the characters! The freight of

41

inanimate or partially inanimate material gives 'Moby-Dick' its bottom, its body, in the vintner's phrase; and I am convinced that Melville knew what he was about.

It is only when we have grasped the nature of the book that we begin to perceive how cunning is its craftsmanship throughout. ... 'Moby-Dick' is our sole American epic, no less an epic for being written in prose."

Soon Melville became a fashionable writer among men of letters on both sides of the Atlantic. Two factors contributed to his new fame. One was, that in the 1920s there was a general revaluation of American literature. Until then it was treated as a branch of English literature. Now American writers and critics were becoming conscious of a separate national identity in letters. This literary nationalism was searching for national classics. Melville, whose works so pregnantly and inherently reflect the North-eastern United States of his time, was promptly declared a great American classic.

Another coinciding factor was the new vogue of the Freudian analysis of works of art as projections of the inner mysteries of the author's soul. An early example of this radically new treatment of *Moby-Dick* was published in *The Times Literary Supplement* of July 26, 1923, by J. W. N. Sullivan, who stated: "'Moby Dick' is not, as it has been so often called, the greatest of sea stories, it is not a vast, elaborate account of the hunting of a mighty and mysterious whale. It is an account of the mighty, mysterious, and troubled soul of Herman Melville."[96]

Subsequently, the psychoanalytical trend was followed by the new critical, the structuralist, the archetypal, the existentialist and the neopositivist approach. Melville, with his "inferences" carefully constructed "in a merry and mythical way"[97], and with his ambiguities was easy prey for all exegetes.

If Melville had indeed had a ghost "capable of revisiting the world",[98] it is doubtful whether he would have recognized himself in the image that emerged in this fanciful Melville revival, nor even understood what was meant by the following:

"Essentially was he a mystic, a treasure-seeker, a mystery-monger, a delver after hidden things spiritual and material. The world to him was a darkly figured hieroglyph; and if he ever deciphered the cabalistic sign, the meaning he found was too terrible, or else too wonderful, to tell."[99]

When *Moby-Dick* was first published by Bentley's in England in 1851 as *The Whale,* some 80 phrases and passages that either made satirical references to religious doctrine, or contained social criticism, were deleted.[100]

Since the 1920s several unexpurgated editions have appeared; and neither the religious scepticism nor the social criticism, so strongly resented by the contemporaneous press, have roused much animosity. On the contrary: revalued and reinterpreted, the book has been appropriated by the literary establishment and tamed to serve the status quo. What Bentley's bowdlerized, and the mid-nineteenth century press condemned, has now been explained away.

42

In the course of the past sixty years, "the Melville boom" has grown into "the Melville industry", producing over 3,000 items of literary criticism on Melville.[101] An interesting shift has taken place in the treatment of *Moby-Dick*. Whereas previous to the Melville revival of the 1920s *Moby-Dick* was mostly considered as a more or less outstanding piece of sea fiction with superfluous and objectionable philosophical digressions, from the 1920s on, the book has been chiefly praised for the symbolical implications of its philosophical speculations, whilst the factual, nautical and cetological elements have frequently been frowned upon as digressive and unintegrated.

Opinions may differ as to how far the Melville criticism of the past sixty years has cleared or obfuscated the way to the understanding and enjoyment of *Moby-Dick*. Focusing on the same book, but widely disparate in their reflections, it often seems that the different approaches to *Moby-Dick* cast more light on their authors than on their common subject. Thus, the study of the many modern interpretations of *Moby-Dick* might well serve to elucidate the dominant trends of 20th century literary criticism, and to cast light on the numerous allegorizing efforts, which, true to St. Paul's admonition (II. Corinthians, III. 6) trust "the spirit" that "giveth life" more than "the letter" that "killeth", and infuse the spirit of their own choice into the letters of Melville's.

The dehistorization of *Moby-Dick* has come into full swing. Hints of religious scepticism and critical references to contemporary social conditions on land and sea, the enormous exploitation of whalemen and even of their captain exposed with such glowing satire by Melville (in chapters 6, 16, 48, 49, 54, 60, 62, 64, 66, 89, 132), have been, if not translated into existentialist or mythopoeic language, ignored or snubbed. Some critics have even wished these passages out of existence, and after assiduous dissections of the novel, declared it to be two novels in one, alleging either that Melville started to write a nautical romance, but when through the first third, changed his mind and wrote a philosophical allegory,[102] or, that he wrote a "dramatic" and an "ideational" novel "in a single creative act".[103]

Once critics no longer felt themselves bound to consider the social and historical context of the novel or view it in its totality, they allowed themselves to disintegrate the book and rationalize this into theory, as e.g. Raymond W. Short did: "The symbolical potentials develop dynamically with the story, and it is questionable if they are retroactive; if, for instance, the connotations of the rope which binds Fedallah to his fate and hangs Captain Ahab in Chapter 135 should carry back to the rope as described in Chapter 60."[104] *Moby-Dick* has become a *"Loose-Fish"* to all "the ostentatious smuggling verbalists".[105]

In the course of this century, *Moby-Dick* has been more written about than read, and the method of critic-exegetes, whether of the psychoanalytical, new critical, mythopoeic, structuralist, existentialist, or neopositivist persuasion, seems to echo its "The Doubloon" chapter. A few notable examples might serve as illustration.

D. H. Lawrence, in his *Studies in Classic American Literature* (1923), calls *Moby-Dick* "the greatest book of the sea ever written", but regards the White

Whale as "the deepest blood-being of the white race", the "sacral-sexual consciousness of man", and his chase as a suicidal and maniac hunt carried on by "white mental consciousness".

Psychoanalyzing *Moby-Dick*, E. L. Grant Watson in "Moby-Dick" published in *The London Mercury* in 1920, declares the book to be "the story of the author's own fiercely vivid life-consciousness". The White Whale is the "symbol of madness", of nature's beauty, terror and mystery, and his "whiteness is the whiteness of insanity". Ahab is "the atheistical captain of the tormented soul".

A rather myopic close reading produced this algebra of William S. Gleim's "A Theory of *Moby-Dick*" (*The New England Quarterly*, 1929): water represents truth, the whale symbolizes Fate, the ship is the symbol of the world and of time. The ocean is the symbol of space. "All of which signifies that the world is encompassed ... and controlled by Fate, and also that Fate is inimical to the world." Queequeg personifies Religion, and Starbuck personifies Reason. Ahab is Melville and he personifies the Ego, the will and the soul. His death, like that of his Biblical namesake, shows that there is no way of avoiding the power of Fate.

Ahab comes to an "identification with Evil" according to Charles Olson in "Lear and Moby Dick" (*Twice a Year*, 1938). Harry Slochover in *"Moby-Dick:* The Myth of Democratic Expectancy" (*American Quarterly*, 1950) points out that Ahab's "dictatorship" foreshadows the ruthless ethic that free individual enterprise was to formulate and that his "sin" and his fate contain "a warning of what is in store for a man who would be God". Ahab is stringently censured by Charles H. Cook, Jr. in "Ahab's Intolerable Allegory" (*Boston University Studies in English*, 1955) for trying to identify the source of his suffering and strike at it. Cook rebukes Ahab for externalizing "his own portion of evil" in regarding the Whale as an "incarnation of the world's evil". That was "the tragic flaw" in his character, his effort to give a single meaning to "the baffling multiplicity and incomprehensibility of the universe".

All the variants of allegorical interpretation are justified by the structuralist semiology of William Hull in *"Moby-Dick:* An Interpretation" (*ETC: A Review of General Semantics*, 1947/48); he calls the book a "system-function" in which "invariant relations" join "variables". The basic diagram of *Moby-Dick* is the following: "Man's relation to whale, conditioned by sea, is disastrous in the degree to which he identifies levels of abstraction". All three variants can be given variable values (man: Ahab, Ishmael-Ahab, Western culture, the crew, mankind, etc.; sea: the physical ocean, the human unconscious, the unknown, unattainable universe, etc.; whale: the sperm whale, whaling, industry, science, legend and history, the unknowable, etc.). Content is given to the system-function "by the reactions in the individual reader. Thus an indefinite number of meanings is possible."

The skilful combination of the psychoanalytical, the archetypal and the existentialist approach together with an appeal to American national consciousness has made Richard Chase's interpretations of *Moby-Dick* protean enough to be widely acceptable. In his monograph, *Herman Melville: A Critical Study* (1949), Richard

Chase asserts that Melville's writings, just as his psyche, can be reduced (or aggrandized) to a myth which has "two central themes: the Fall and the Search, the Search for what was lost in the Fall or for the earthly and possible substitutes for what was lost".

Inspired by both Freud and Jung, Chase suggests that the idea of the Fall was based on Melville's own instinctive sense of "disaster and loss" as "the one real truth about life" and was corroborated by the early experience of his family's bankruptcy and by his later studies of comparative mythology. But the Fall, of course, had also played a prominent role in the myth of the pastoral origins of the North-American states, of their lofty ideals and of the loss of all these through the corrosive influences of industrial civilization. Chase duly remarks: "The myth of the Fall seemed to be also an American myth, a so-far undefined legend of the Promethean nation which had revolted and fled from the high tyranny of British rule, an Ishmaelite nation betrayed by the Old World as a father might betray a son, forcing him to revolt and seek his own fortune . . . America became for Melville the Prometheus of the West—the Titan whose momentous creative act had been his revolt against Zeus. The Promethean American is the hope of the world's people. In him is the divine creative *élan,* with its promise of endurance, growth, and fructifying civilization. But the revolt of Prometheus is in the past, and as Melville pictures him, he is now the suffering hero, persecuted by a heavenly father . . . who seeks to re-establish the stagnant reactionism which the revolutionary *élan* of Prometheus had once smashed. The question Melville asks is: Will America turn out to be the true Prometheus who successfully opposes the will of Zeus, . . . or will America turn out to be a false Prometheus who in his suffering becomes, like Zeus himself, a blind and self-destructive tyrant?"

When Ahab tries to combat the divine tyrant of Greek and Old Testament mythology, incarnated in the White Whale, he tragically fails, for instead of being a true, redeeming Prometheus, he degenerates into a tyrant himself, and thus becomes a false one.

Chase also finds another myth implicit in *Moby-Dick:* capitalism. In this sense *Moby-Dick* is "a hymn to the technical skill of the heroes and the marvelous perfection of their machine, . . . a saga of the exploitation of nature and man for profit or for righteousness". In this "capitalist myth" every fatal casualty is "at once the murder of an industrial worker and the ritual sacrifice of a hero".

Eight years later, in *The American Novel and Its Traditions* (1957), Chase offers an existentialist reading of *Moby-Dick:* the novel is a "moral fable". The action takes place "in a universe of extreme contradictions" and "there is no transcendent ground where the painful contradictions of the human dilemma are reconciled." Melville is moved by "the absurdity of such a creature as man, . . . prisoner of the cruel contradictions with which, in his very being, he is inexorably involved." What Ahab does is "in the nature of man" and that is "to seek but not to find." Ishmael realizes that "the only promise to happiness" is "the blissful, idyllic, erotic attachment to life and to one's ideal comrades".

45

Newton Arvin in his highly informative critical biography, *Herman Melville* (1950), attests to the realism of *Moby-Dick* in dealing with "the life of American whalers" and then proceeds to suggest four "planes of significance" on which the book may be read: "the literal, the oneiric or psychological, the moral, and the mythic." In this context, Moby Dick becomes "the archetypal Parent" who inflicts "a kind of castration" on Ahab. Ahab reacts with "Oedipal bitterness" and is overcome by a neurotical desire for destruction and suicide. He commits the archetypal sins of pride, arrogance and disobedience, for which he has to suffer. Ishmael is saved by acquiescence in a "balanced vision" of both good and evil and finds his peace in a kind of "naturalistic theism" and "cosmic submissiveness".

Henry A. Murray in "In Nomine Diaboli" (*The New England Quarterly*, 1951) hails the "rapprochement of psychology and literary criticism" and contrives the following interpretation of *Moby-Dick:* Ahab is "an embodiment of that fallen angel or semi-god who in Christendom was variously named Lucifer, Devil, Adversary, Satan". The White Whale embodies "the Old Testament Calvinistic conception of an affrighting Deity and his strict commandments, the derivative puritan ethic of nineteenth-century America and the society that defended this ethic". "Captain Ahab-Lucifer ... has summoned the various religions of the East to combat the one dominant religion of the West." Stated in psychological terms, Ahab, representing the "primitive drives, values, beliefs, and practices which the Hebraic Christian religionists rejected and ... forced into the unconscious mind of western man" is really "captain of the culturally repressed dispositions of human nature, that part of the personality which psychoanalysts have termed the 'Id'". In which case the White Whale "can be none other than the internal institution which is responsible for these repressions, namely the Freudian Superego." But this role is imposed on Moby Dick through "the projection of Captain Ahab's Presbyterian conscience". Thus "the simplest psychological formula for Melville's dramatic epic is this: an insurgent 'Id' in mortal conflict with an oppressive cultural Superego". But Ahab, "possessed of all Satan's pride and energy", is doomed to failure, because he is "motivated by his private need to avenge a private insult", is a nihilist and proceeds with "egoistic self-inflation and unleashed wrath". The whale escapes, signalizing the survival of "the dominant ideology" of Melville's day: "that peculiar compound of puritanism and materialism, of rationalism and commercialism, of shallow, blatant optimism and technology, which proved so crushing to creative evolutions in religion, art, and life."

This ending seems to indicate "Melville's capitulation in the face of overwhelming odds". But since his subsequent novels testify to his "embattled soul" refusing to surrender, *Moby-Dick* may rather be "taken as a comment on the strategic crisis of Melville's allegorical life".

In "The Reconciliation of Ishmael: *Moby-Dick* and the Book of Job" (*The South Atlantic Quarterly*, 1958), C. Hugh Holman explicitly brings *Moby-Dick* into line with Biblical exegesis. His reading makes the voyage of the *Pequod* "an adventure of the human soul". Ishmael is "the principal agent" and in the course of the novel he matures from "a spiritual outcast" and "a worthy bearer of his Biblical name" into an acquiescent Job, who, impressed by the terrors and the wonders of Leviathan Moby Dick, "has learned ... the lesson of acceptance" and "to know woe without becoming mad", there being "no sane alternative". With no more answer to "the riddle of evil and suffering" than was imparted to Job, he submits to the "incomprehensible reality" of "the mixed good and evil in all things, the prevalence of suffering in the world, the horror in which at times the universe seems formed" with Job-like humility.

In 1963, John Halverson in "The Shadow in *Moby-Dick*" (*American Quarterly*) applies Jungian psychology to the novel and describes its plot as "the journeys of the soul" of Ishmael and Ahab "on the sea of the unconscious". Queequeg and Pip are their "helpful shadows", and the salvation of Ishmael and the damnation of Ahab are the consequences of the one's accepting, and the other's rejecting their helpful shadow.

In the same year, applying myth criticism, H. Bruce Franklin in *The Wake of the Gods* gives a Jungian explanation for Ahab's overpowering influence upon the crew: Ahab has succeeded in fashioning Moby-Dick into a myth that appeals to their unconscious understanding of the mythology of the demon hunt. On etymological and historical evidence Bruce Franklin suggests that the cosmic struggle of Ahab and the whale is based on the Egyptian Osiris–Typhon myth. The ancient Egyptians identified everything in nature malignant to man as Typhon, usually represented by some aquatic monster, and believed him to be hunted by Osiris, a priest-king-god. "Just as Moby Dick embodies Typhon, Ahab embodies Osiris." Subsequently Bruce Franklin remarks: "The battles of faith have long since left the fields of the literalness, the exclusiveness, and the originality of the Judaic–Christian revelation; the psychological facts of religion no longer engage directly with the historical facts; Osiris is neither an opponent nor an avatar of Christ." The "psychological facts of religion" extensively elaborated by Carl Jung are among the buttresses of the modern apologetics of religion. Franklin duly points out: "Melville saw Egyptian mythology as the direct source of the Hebrew mythology and therefore of the myth of the Christ. ... He drew from this source his own version of the savior myth—*Moby-Dick*, which he submits to us as a kind of truth not found in Christian, Hebrew, or Egyptian mythology." Yet Bruce Franklin's mythopoeic interpretation cannot but provide an inconsistent and controversial explanation to Osiris–Saviour–Ahab's tragic end, unfollowed as it is by resurrection. As Bruce Franklin points out, what makes Moby Dick "in mythic fact that great demon" is that "Ahab succeeds in defining him psychologically, metaphysically, and morally as the Dragon, the Leviathan, the Typhon". "Psychological, metaphysical and moral definitions, however, do not seem to have the same mythic effect reflexively. In this respect Bruce Franklin calls it "Ahab's monomania" that "makes him re-enact the role of the dragon-slayer, makes him play Osiris to Moby Dick as Typhon, perhaps therefore Christ to Moby Dick as Leviathan." Thus, when it comes to defining himself, Ahab no longer affects a "mythic act", but is monomaniac and play-acting. Based on this re-definition, the argument concludes in declaring that this "playing the role of a god is the most complete ungodliness" that forfeits "the resurrection and the life".

According to Maurice Friedman's existentialist interpretation in *Problematic Rebel. The Image of Modern Man (Melville, Dostoievsky, Kafka, Camus)* also published in 1963, Ahab is "not only the best example in literature of Kierkegaard's 'demonic shut-inness', he is also the best example of Martin Buber's 'second stage of evil', in which man reaches the threshold of self-deification and absolute self-affirmation." He is "the essential breakthrough to the Modern Promethean" who "arrogates to himself all the authority of truth which resided before either in God, . . . or in the Platonic or idealistic absolute. . . . For modern man neither of these truths is any longer possible, since 'God is dead'. The 'death of God' means the death of both the Biblical image . . . and the Greek Platonic image of an absolute order and an absolute good in harmony with which man can live. In the face of a basically inscrutable reality, the only way left to man to find any meaning in his existence is to identify truth with himself." Ishmael, on the other hand, is "the Modern Exile". He is baffled "in his attempt to understand the Leviathan". The White Whale himself is "an unrevealed and unrevealing god who stands ready in an era of the 'death of God' to fill the now absent place of divinity." Ishmael's god is faceless and imageless, because he is "the 'dead god' who cannot speak at all—the god who is no god." Friedman asserts that *Moby-Dick* is both "a celebration of the American whaling industry and of expanding American civilization" and "a deep recognition of the tragedy of such expansion—the inevitable, tragic limitations that are encountered by the American frontiersman, the giant industrialist, or, for that matter, modern man in all his forms since the Renaissance. These are the limits of existence."

The structuralist method of John Seelye in *Melville: The Ironic Diagram* (1970) reduces *Moby-Dick* to a pattern of "static and kinetic elements" that "may be figured as a line and circle." The kinetic and linear element provided by Ahab's quest and his onrush towards the Whale is ironically countered by the static and circular elements provided by "the static, discursive cetology chapters, . . . the various 'rounds' of opinion" and Ishmael's "essays in skepticism" insisting on the relativity of perception. All are "summed up by the relativistic roundness of the world itself, which turns the line of inquiry into a circle". Ishmael survives, for, with "ironic equanimity" he comes to the "circular view" of the "disparate elements of the world" being bound together in a harmonious circular whole that contradicts "the straightforward, singlepurposed intention of the quester". The "concentric circles" of the vortex in which the *Pequod* and its crew are caught and drawn to death and destruction, "provide a final configuration of the paradoxical force with which Ishmael has been dealing throughout—the circle which is the antithesis of the line, and its synthesis as well, here on this round globe".

Robert Zoellner in *The Salt-Sea Mastodon* (1973) by means of reductive structuralism and exegetic jugglery achieves semantic identifications, inversions and modifications which suggest that Ahab is Claggart, is "technological man in the latter half of the twentieth century", is "all of us"—affronted and provoked by

48

the serenity, tranquillity and benignity exhibited by the White Whale alias Billy Budd, nature, the world, the cosmos. What Melville terms the "horrible vultureism of earth" and "the universal cannibalism of the sea" is translated by Zoellner as "constructive and life-generating rather than destructive and life-obliterating ... masculine dynamism". Even the countless victims of the whaling industry Melville compassionately commemorates are revivified: they do not die a "terminal", but a "vitalistic" death, for in terms of "cyclic cosmology" "the Great South Sea becomes a kind of vitalistic broth, a mystic medium in which all those things which have died will never die, but only sleep ... no slightest movement of the cosmic medium, no least vibration of the cyclic continuum, no life, no thought, no dream, no impulse is ever lost; all things remain in being, in restless slumber until, in some far turn of the ever-rolling waves, they may come back again." Zoellner asserts that Ishmael comes to perceive that the ocean is "lovely", just as "the tropical weather through which the *Pequod* sails", that Moby Dick is mild and serene and that "Moby-Dick and the lovely world through which he swims are not two things, but one thing", all of which "affirms the fundamental goodness of existence and the preponderant salubrity of cosmic activity". Zoellner points out what Melville failed to indicate: Ishmael, in the course of the novel, attains "a final harmony" between himself "and his world" by understanding that "the world, though terrible, is good. The cosmos, though frightful, is benign", a statement rather hard to reconcile with what Melville wrote: "The sun hides not the ocean, which is the dark side of this earth, and which is two thirds of this earth. So, therefore, that mortal man who hath more of joy than sorrow in him, that mortal man cannot be true—not true, or undeveloped. With books the same. The truest of all men was the Man of Sorrows, and the truest of all books is Solomon's and Ecclesiastes is the fine hammered steel of woe." Nor is there any attempt made at such reconciliation in *The Salt-Sea Mastodon*. Melville's woeful reference to Ecclesiastes is never mentioned there.

Robert Zoellner claims that Ishmael finds solution to his theological dilemma in rejecting the "overkill", "megaton" Jehova of New England and embracing what Zoellner terms a "truncated transcendentalism or metanaturalism". For all its pantheism and repudiation of Calvinistic Christianity, this faith, in Zoellner's argument remains theistic enough to revert to a Biblical answer for "the final puzzle of the novel": "Why does Ahab disturb the benign, violate the peaceable, strike out at the good?" In line with the Judaeo–Christian doctrine of Original Sin and of a perfectly created universe corrupted by human depravity, Zoellner answers: "To be human is to be aware, and to be aware is to lack serenity. The serenity of nature thus becomes an affront to our condition, the quietude of the world a mockery of our estate. In this situation, the overwhelming impulse is to reach out and mark nature with our pain." But, if "to be human is to be aware, and to be aware is to lack serenity", then, for all its efforts to reconstruct *Moby-Dick,* Zoellner's interpretation still leaves open the question of how could Ishmael, as alleged, achieve his "metanaturalistic", "insular Tahiti" serenity, having become aware of the need to do so?

Michael T. Gilmore in his Introduction to the collection of *Twentieth Century Interpretations of Moby-Dick* (1977) strikes the note of neopositivistic agnosticism. In his reading *Moby-Dick* "addresses the problem of knowing in a context that is metaphysical rather than social or moral". Ahab is "Melville's consummate 'knower', and his hunt for the white whale may be regarded as an epistemological quest". Throughout the novel, "Melville dwells on the connection between whaling and the pursuit of knowledge", the implication being that "Truth such as that sought by Ahab in his hunt for the white whale, is neither desirable nor attainable by man". Ishmael can never gratify his desire for "full comprehension" of the whale and "the outcome of *Moby-Dick,* in which the white whale escapes, demonstrates the futility of Ahab's quest and reaffirms the inscrutability of existence".

Following the same track, Brian Way in *Herman Melville: Moby-Dick* (1977) asserts Melville's "use of the language of religion, in particular of the word reverence, implies a notion of transcendence, a sense that the phenomena he describes cannot be fully understood in purely material terms, and that the universe will always remain ultimately beyond man's understanding and control". He then proceeds to claim that in *Moby-Dick* Melville was concerned with the problem of how "to salvage religious experience from the wreck of formal belief . . . whether it was possible to create a religion without God". His conclusion, that "Melville found a part of what he was looking for in his feeling of reverence for the natural world" is properly tuned to the latest note in contemporary religious apology.

With Melville's religious scepticism tidily tucked out of sight, Brian Way completes the emasculation of *Moby-Dick* by diluting its social criticism: "Indeed *Moby-Dick* is often discussed, from a Marxist or romantic anarchist point of view, as if it were a purely anti-capitalist book. This seems to me to be entirely false: as in the case of democracy, Melville weighs capitalism in the balance, finds that it involves certain dangers and possesses certain inherent shortcomings, but does not ultimately reject it. . . . in his description of the fine houses and gardens of New Bedford harpooned from the depths of the sea, and the beautiful women clothed and perfumed from the profits of the fishery, he is responding to that same American opulence which Scott Fitzgerald was to celebrate in the 1920s. Some of Melville's satire of capitalism, too, is of that genial light-hearted sort which stops well short of the severest censure."

Many more items could be cited to denote the variety of the exegesis of *Moby-Dick*. Yet for all their diversity, the examples also indicate uniformity. Invariably the desired interpretations are achieved by taking certain aspects or particulars out of the context of the novel, generalizing them into abstractions, equating these with other abstractions, and then applying the equations to the general purport of the novel. With logic thus violated, the resulting exegetical variants readily lend themselves to substantiating the intent of the critic, though hardly that of the book.

Exegesis, however, is not the sole representative of the Melville scholarship of our age. *Moby-Dick* might still be a Loose Fish, but its identification has been significantly aided by scholarly investigations which have, in the course of the past fifty years, resulted in such invaluable source-materials as Jay Levda's *Melville Log; The Letters of Herman Melville,* collected and edited by Merrell R. Davis and William H. Gilman; Melville's lectures and the list of Melville's readings, both compiled and edited by Merton M. Scalts, Jr.; contemporaneous and subsequent Melville criticism variously compiled, selected and edited by Hugh W. Hetherington, Watson G. Branch, Hershel Parker and Harrison Hayford respectively; Melville's *Biography* by Leon Howard; the *Herman Melville Reference Bibliography (1900–1972)* compiled by Beatrice Ricks and Joseph D. Adams; the annotated editions of *Moby-Dick, The Confidence-Man, Clarel, Billy Budd* and *Selected Poems* by Luther S. Mansfield, Howard P. Vincent, Elizabeth S. Foster, Walter E. Bezanson, Harrison Hayford, Merton M. Sealts, Jr., and Hennig Cohen, respectively; and the Northwestern-Newberry Edition of *The Writings of Herman Melville.* Circumspect elucidations of Melville's writings based on a wide range of historical and philological informations have been provided in a number of monographs and articles, among which, in regard to *Moby-Dick, The Fine Hammered Steel of Herman Melville* by Milton R. Stern, *Melville's Quarrel with God* by Lawrence Thompson, *The Trying-Out of Moby-Dick* by Howard P. Vincent, *The Example of Melville* by Warner Berthoff, *The Design of the Argument in Moby-Dick* by Howard C. Horsford, *Melville and Geology* by Elizabeth S. Foster and *Pierre Bayle and Moby-Dick* by Millicent Bell are especially enlightening.

Anyone today who wishes to analyze *Moby-Dick* with due consideration of its historical and social background, its organic integrity will find himself indebted to the eminent scholars mentioned above. The present book could not have been written without the results of their researches.

PART II

Biographical prelude

CHAPTER 1

The road to the forecastle

"I am like one of those seeds taken out of the Egyptian Pyramids, which, after being three thousand years a seed and nothing but a seed, being planted in English soil, it developed itself, grew to greenness, and then fell to mould.[1] So I. Until I was twenty-five, I had no development at all. From my twenty-fifth year I date my life. Three weeks have scarcely passed, at any time between then and now, that I have not unfolded within myself. But I feel that I am now come to the inmost leaf of the bulb, and that shortly the flower must fall to the mould. It seems to me now that Solomon was the truest man who ever spoke."[2]

Melville wrote these lines to Nathaniel Hawthorne in June 1851. In the same letter he intimated:

> "In a week or so, I go to New York, to bury myself in a third-story room, and work and slave on my 'Whale' while it is driving through the press. *That* is the only way I can finish it now."

What happened to Melville in the first twenty-four years of his life? What gave rise to his sudden development in his twenty-fifth? How did he "unfold" within himself? How is Biblical Solomon related to the "inmost leaf of the bulb"? And what is the essence of the "inmost leaf" and of the offshoot that grew concurrently: *Moby-Dick?*

These are the questions the present and subsequent chapters seek to answer.

Herman Melville was born in the year the United States of America was going through its first economic crisis. "... the Babe is ... doing well & is a very promising Child", Allan Melvill wrote to grandfather Thomas Melvill on the 13th August, 1819 and promptly added: "Business is absolutely stagnant, ... we still have numerous failures & more anticipated ...".[3]

But by the following June, Allan Melvill's "little Barque" had "weathered the storm which has wrecked the fortunes of thousands, & scattered ruin around her in all directions".[4]

He had a flourishing wholesale business in New York, importing from France and selling to the world of fashion such luxury goods as women's silk gloves, linen braids, leghorn hats, and fabrics like crepe, velvet and tulle. The epitome of the Protestant businessman, he was devout, self-righteous and patriotic; very ambitious, and obsessed with a relentless zeal to vindicate divine grace through business success. He had friends and acquaintances among important politicians and statesmen, and set up house in the neighbourhood of, and had social intercourse with, respectable attorneys, merchants, bankers, businessmen and landowners—the most influential members of a society which, as all along the Northeastern Seaboard right up to the post-Civil War period, was dominated by commercial, landowning and banking interests.[5] Herman Melville was born into the Northeastern Establishment.

Allan Melvill moved to New York State in 1814, after his marriage into the wealthy Gansevoort family. Previously, he had had an import business in Boston, where he was born. A brother was a well-to-do banker there. His father, Thomas Melvill, was Naval Officer of the Port of Boston, a post to which he had been appointed by George Washington in 1789 for his service as a major in the Revolution. In town he was renowned as the "last of the Mohawks" for his participation in the Boston Tea Party in 1773. He was descended from a Scottish Presbyterian family. His son Allan took great pride in tracing the family lineage back to medieval Scottish nobility and to a Hungarian ancestor.

"I cannot describe my sensations while walking on the ground where once stood the dwelling and Birth (place) of my venerated progenitor", he wrote to his father on May 31, 1818,[6] after visiting the parish of Scoonie, where his great-grandfather, the Reverend Thomas Melvill, had been Presbyterian minister for several decades. Allan had gone to Scotland to investigate a potential claim to a share in the £ 100,000 estate of the deceased General Robert Melvill of Edinburgh, of whom his father had been the closest surviving kin. Finding the estate entailed on others beyond legal recovery and disappointed in his expectations of a heritage, Allan nonetheless turned the trip to good use for some moral aggrandizement:

"Your greatgrandfather"—his letter goes on—"was a grandson of Sir John Melvill of Carnbee, who was knighted by James the 6th & made baron of Granton 28th July 1580, on which you may depend as a well-authenticated historical fact, *confirmed by living testimony*—I have also traced you back in direct lineal descent to Sir Richard de Melville, Knight in the reign of Alexander the 3rd in the year 1268, & have discovered that *the branch at Boston,* & my great Uncle John then at Grenada, are expressly recognized in Douglas Baronage of Scotland[7] of which I shall purchase if possible a cheap edition, as belonging to the Melvilles of Carnbee & termed an ancient and illustrous House of the founders of which Crawford & Douglas Peerage of Scotland both say, were *related* to Queen Margaret consort of Malcolm Canmere & came with her from Hungary[8]—you may also tell my good Mother,* that Mrs. Meason inform'd me that the Scollays of the Orkneys, from whom her husband is descended, sprang originally from the Kings of Norway, & so it appears we are of a royal line in both sides of the House— after all it is not only an amusing but a just cause of pride, to resort back

* Née Priscilla Scollay

56

through the ages to such ancestry, & should produce a correspondent spirit of emulation in their descendents to the remotest posterity."

Allan Melvill seems to have preferred the Hungarian origin to the Norman alternative. But in Douglas's *Peerage of Scotland* there is no mention of the Hungarian ancestor being "related" to Queen Margaret,[9] this must have been an amplification on Allan Melvill's part to bear out "a royal line on both sides of the House".[10]

Originally, Thomas Melvill was to follow in his grandfather's footsteps and was educated for a Presbyterian ministry at the College of New Jersey (now Princeton University). But, like many other New England intellectuals of his time, he rebelled against the restrictive authoritarianism of the Presbyterian Church and turned to the rising Unitarian movement for religious faith in a benevolent, rational and dependable God. In the first half of the 19th century, Unitarianism was a spreading creed among of the New England upper class, in opposition, on the one hand, to the authoritarianism of the Calvinistic churches and, on the other, to the waves of highly emotionally charged religious revivalism sweeping over the States.

On the maternal side, there was no aristocratic lineage, but there was solid wealth. Maria Gansevoort was the daughter of General Peter Gansevoort, famous for his defence of Fort Stanvix during the Revolution. He was one of the wealthiest men in Albany, the capital city of New York State. He possessed a large tract of wooded land in Northumberland County, probably granted to him for his military service,[11] used for lumbering. Descended from early Dutch settlers, the family was a devout member of the Reformed Dutch Church, the most rigid follower of Calvin's tenets in the United States. It was this church that joined Allan and Maria in marriage and baptized their children.

Herman received his early formal education in a non-denominational New York private school, where he shared the company of children of well-to-do, middle-class parents. But the wealth of his parents rested on very shaky foundations.

In an economy where production was largely directed by commission merchants, as was the case in the Northeastern States right up to the Civil War, trade in general, and importing and exporting in particular, rested upon a credit basis. Allan Melvill, urged by his ambition and belief in "justification by faith", drained every available source of loans and credit, both inside the family (his father and his brother-in-law) and outside it. By overextending his credit severalfold, he became extremely vulnerable to the vicissitudes of the fierce competition that was raging around him and in which, according to Robert Greenhalf Albion "ninety-three in the hundred of untold thousands" went bankrupt.[12]

So did Allan Melvill in 1830. He subsequently accepted the management of the Albany branch of a New York fur company, hoping eventually to secure capital with which to re-establish himself on his own.

The family moved to Albany, the capital of New York State.

With a population of some 30,000, less than one-tenth of that of New York, Albany was a thriving trading town. Shipments of grain, lumber and fur, arriving from the west and north through the Erie Canal opened in 1825, passed through Albany on their way down the Hudson to the port of New York, keeping all those involved in the traffic steeped in prosperity and in the firm Calvinistic belief that wealth and virtue had been paired off by the same Divine Inscrutability as poverty and sin. Albany was also the abode of the Gansevoorts.

Melville never knew his maternal grandfather, General Peter Gansevoort, who died in 1812. His grandmother died in 1830, and from then on, uncle Peter Gansevoort was the virtual head of the family. This uncle played an important and beneficent role in Melville's life. It was he who often helped the family over an exigency, and who, in the last year of his long life (1876), financed the publication of *Clarel*. He had an affluent law practice and a great deal of property. He was also a state Assemblyman, a state Senator and a Judge of the Court of Common Pleas. The Gansevoort family were patricians, and through their alliance with them the Melvills too, when they moved to Albany, came to belong to the same caste.

For two years, Herman Melville was sent to a Calvinist private school catering for the sons of wealthy families. His classmates were to become merchants, bankers, lawyers, clergymen, or to go into some trade as butchers, shoemakers, carpenters, etc. In fact, the Albany Academy meant to qualify its students for business pursuits, and its curriculum included, besides the classics, practical and technological and other practical studies.

Meanwhile, Allan Melvill was making strenuous efforts to re-establish himself in business. In December 1831, he returned from a trip to New York with a severe cold, but as his brother-in-law, Peter Gansevoort, reported in a letter in January 1832, "persisting in giving attention to his business—He devoted himself so closely and assiduously, as to produce a state of excitement, which in a great measure robbed him of his sleep". Occasional "alienation of mind" ensued and then "the melancholy spectacle of a deranged man."[13] He died about a fortnight later. W. H. Gilman remarks that there is no real evidence of Allan Melvill's insanity. He most likely died of pneumonia.[14]

Backed by his uncle Peter, Melville's elder brother Gansevoort undertook to operate the business which their father had established before his death. It consisted of a fur and cap retail store and a manufacturing plant. It was at this time that the spelling of the family's name was changed. Gansevoort added the final "e", probably with the desire to obscure his relationship, so that the bad business reputation of his father, who had died owing thousands of dollars to creditors in Albany and New York, should not impinge upon his own.[15]

Gansevoort did well in the fur trade. Uncle Peter was one of the directors of the New York State Bank, and through his help Gansevoort got substantial bank loans. His enterprise flourished and in two years the family were back in wealthy and elegant surroundings.

Herman left school in 1832 and became a clerk in the New York State Bank. Not yet thirteen, in his time he was not the only boy of his age and background to give up school for business. Youngsters of many well-to-do families left school at thirteen or fourteen to become apprentices or clerks and work their way up the scale in business or some trade. But the prospect of becoming a banker one day does not seem to have appealed to Herman too much, for he left the Bank in 1834 and went to Pittsfield to work for his uncle Thomas Melvill on his farm. (In 1850, he was to buy an adjoining farm and live there for thirteen years.)

Uncle Thomas belonged to the Episcopal Church, and thus during the year Herman spent with his family, one more creed was added to his religious education.

Farming, however, did not satisfy him at the age of fifteen. Next year he returned to Albany and went to work for Gansevoort until he was seventeen. In the meantime, he also attended courses in classics, English and practical sciences at the Albany Classical School, ruled by its principal in the spirit of Presbyterianism.

Inheriting Dutch Calvinism from his mother, Unitarianism from his father, witnessing allegiance to the Episcopal Church in his uncle's house, and receiving education in establishments alternately under non-denominational, Dutch Reformed, Presbyterian and Congregational leadership, the spectrum of Herman Melville's religious education came to include the hues of all the creeds dominant at the time along the Northeastern Seaboard. The girl he was to marry some ten years later was being brought up in a Unitarian family.

In 1837, Gansevoort went bankrupt. He was one of the many who fell victim to the worst economic crisis the USA had had to face till that time. Preceded by an orgy of speculation in western lands and overinvestment in internal improvements, it started in 1835 with crop failures and farmers unable to meet their obligations to land speculators and merchants, who, in their turn could not repay their loans to the banks. Bank notes lost their value and foreign credits were withdrawn. What is more, important mercantile houses failed in England towards the end of 1836, with resultant cuts in the demand for American cotton. The depression continued for over five years, a period long enough to reduce an offspring of a patrician family to the ranks of the most wretched and despised lot in mid-nineteenth century New England society: the whalers. For by 1841 Herman Melville was a-whaling on board the Acushnet. But he had turned to this only as a last resort.

First he tried school-teaching in Pittsfield. One badly paid and exhausting term sufficed to send him back to Albany. The following year (1838) the Melvilles moved to Lansingburgh, a neighbouring village of some three thousand inhabitants, wealthy and philistine; here they could live more economically. Even so, the family fortunes were running out and Gansevoort fell ill in 1838. Uncle Peter's rescue loans only helped to tide them over from one month to another, and Peter Gansevoort, himself in debt largely on his sister Maria's and on nephew Gansevoort's account, found it more and more difficult to help. Herman tried another spell on his uncle's farm, but returned after three months and enrolled in the Lansingburgh Academy for a course of surveying and engineering.

59

In an era when there seemed to be almost no limit to the prospects for the building of canals and for other internal improvements, this looked like an excellent idea. But never in American history was there a worse time to apply for a civil engineer's job than in 1839.

The big boom in canal building had been closely correlated with the land speculation going on throughout the century. The various states had had their canals built mostly with borrowed money, much of which had come from England. The 1837 crash, due in no small part to the speculative overinvestment in canals, lost the states their foreign credits; pressed by the English creditors, many of them declared bankruptcy. Nearly all sold out to private concerns, and ceased to finance public improvements. Nor was there a change when the depression gave way to a new cycle. After the 1840s, canals were neglected as capital moved into railway construction, where huge profits were to be expected. New York State was exceptional in that it continued to invest funds to expand the Erie Canal—opened in 1825—and to improve its facilities. Nevertheless, Herman Melville's application for a position in the Engineering Department of the Canal was not accepted.

Whilst applying for the job in April of 1839, Melville also submitted his first MS for publication in the *Democratic Press and Lansingburgh Advertiser* under the title of "Fragments from a Writing Desk". *The Democratic Press* published two of these "Fragments"; no more was heard of their author for the next seven years.

On May 23, 1839, his mother wrote to Uncle Peter: "Herman has gone out for a few days on foot to see what he can find to do." The following day Gansevoort informed their younger brother, Allan: "Herman has returned from his expedition, without success". A few days later Allan Melville noted in his journal: "My brother Herman sailed for Liverpool before the mast."[16]

So it had come to this after all. "Sad disappointments in several plans which I had sketched for my future life; the necessity of doing something for myself, united to a naturally roving disposition, had now conspired within me, to send me to sea as a sailor",—he narrated in the first chapter of *Redburn*, a novel he wrote in 1849 as a potboiler, capitalizing on the shock he experienced at the age of 20, when, face to face with the grimness of forecastle life, he suddenly realized, after having been seated for quite a long while inside the coach, what it felt like to be one of the wheels.*

Herman Melville left New York harbour on the 5th of June 1839. He sailed before the mast, that is, as an ordinary sailor, on board a merchant vessel which carried bales of cotton to Liverpool and brought back iron bars, copper, earthenware, tin plates, wire, blankets and hemp. Yet whatever hardships, sufferings and exertion this experience entailed, it did not imply any loss of social

---

* "There are classes of men in the world, who bear the same relation to society at large, that the wheels do to a coach; and are, just as indispensable ... Now, sailors form one of these wheels" and "Indeed, the bad things of their condition come under the head of those chronic evils which can only be ameliorated, it would seem, by ameliorating the moral organization of all civilization." *Redburn*, pp. 176—177.

status. With New York—as R. G. Albion states—standing "second only to London among all the seaports of the world in the tonnage of its shipping by the middle of the nineteenth century" the son of many a wealthy northeastern merchant went to sea without losing caste, and with the prospect of rising in the merchant service, possibly to captaincy; and "a few years in command of a brig or ship had figured in the background of many leading merchants".[17] But evidently Melville had no such aspirations, for after his Liverpool trip, he returned in early October 1839, to his mother's home in Lansingburgh. By this time, his mother had become "entirely impoverished".[18]

Once more Melville tried teaching, this time in a nearby village school, but the school closed down the following year. Then, in June 1840, he set out to do what thousands of his fellow Americans did at the time: he went West. Uncle Thomas Melvill, encumbered with debts, had leased his Pittsfield farm to his son and, in 1838, settled in Galena, Illinois. There he became Public Notary and also Secretary of the Chamber of Commerce. With his help, Herman Melville hoped to find some job in teaching or business. Historically, his expectations were justified: but the timing of his venture was unfortunate. Illinois was still suffering from the economic crisis that had hit all the states in 1837. Emerson visited Illinois ten years later and noted in his Journal: "The hard times of Illinois were from 1837 to 1845 and onwards, when pork was worth twelve shillings a hundred and men journeyed with loads of wheat and pork a hundred miles or more to Chicago, and sold their wheat for twenty-six cents a bushel, and were obliged to sell their team to get home again."[19]

By November 1840, Herman Melville was back in the East, job-hunting in New York, where his brother Gansevoort was studying law. "Herman is still here"—Gansevoort wrote to their younger brother, Allan—"He has been and is a source of great anxiety to me—He has not obt^d a situation— . . . has had his hair sheared & whiskers shaved & looks more like a Christian than usual—".[20]

On December 31, 1840, Herman Melville was on the crew list of the *Acushnet,* a whaler, jointly owned by eighteen citizens of Massachusetts State.[21] On January 3, 1841, the *Acushnet* weighed anchor. Once more Melville was "sailing before the mast", this time not to return before October 1844, the year from which he would "date"[22] his life.

Unfolding within himself: the making of an author and the undoing of his reputation

Herman Melville was not the only of his family to be a sailor. He had five cousins serving at sea and an uncle by marriage on his father's side who was a captain, merchant and ship owner. Four of his cousins were naval officers and one was a whaler; subsequently, one of the officers had to resign his commission, took to drinking and became a whaler, too. They had all set out to sea under family circumstances similar to those of Herman Melville. Later, his younger brother, Tom, was also to follow suit as a whaleman.

The three years Melville spent as a sailor provided him with experience that served him for a lifetime: "If I shall ever deserve any real repute in that small but high hushed world which I might not be unreasonably ambitious of;—he wrote in *Moby-Dick*—if hereafter I shall do anything that, upon the whole, a man might rather have done than to have left undone; if, at my death, my executors, or more properly my creditors, find any precious MSS. in my desk, then here I prospectively ascribe all the honour and the glory to whaling; for a whale-ship was my Yale College and my Harvard."[1] The company of men subjected to yet defying the forces of nature and the oppression of their masters kept haunting him and inspiring most of his fiction. He was nearing seventy when he recalled them in one of his last poems.

> "*Life is storm—let storm!* you rung.
> Taking things as fated merely,
> Child-like though the world ye spanned;
> Nor holding unto life too dearly,
> Ye who held your lives in hand—
>
> . . . .
>
> Nor less, as now, in eve's decline,
> Your shadowy fellowship is mine.
> Ye float around me, form and feature:—
> Tattooings, ear-rings, love-locks curled;
> Barbarians of man's simpler nature,
> Unworldly servers of the world.
> Yea, present all, and dear to me,
> Though shades, or scouring China's sea."[2]

Between January 1841, and October 1844, Herman Melville served on three whalers cruising the Pacific Ocean, jumped ship, got involved in a threat of mutiny, spent four weeks on one of the Marquesas Islands among the allegedly cannibalistic Typees, six weeks in Tahiti freshly brought under French rule, three and a half months in Hawaii and returned to Boston by serving 15 months on board a US warship. Discharged from naval service, Melville terminated his sailor's career, and would not again board a ship except as a cabin passenger.

When he returned to his mother in Lansingburgh, he found that conditions had improved. The country had recovered from financial depression, there was more money around. Gansevoort, his elder, and Allan, his younger brother, were both lawyers, sharing an office in Wall Street. Gansevoort, moreover, was a prominent orator in the presidential campaign which was just culminating, haranguing on behalf of James K. Polk, the Democratic candidate, and was expecting a Government appointment as a reward after a Democratic victory.

The family gave Herman a warm welcome. Tradition has it, that excited by the account of his adventures, family and friends urged him to put them into book form. Nautical travel chronicles and fiction sold well and many an old salt had tried his hand at it.

To meet contemporary requirements, Melville amplified his personal recollections by drawing on other books of Pacific voyages for geographical and ethnographical information, and added some of his own fancy and philosophy. The result was a blend of travel chronicle, fiction and social and religious criticism, entitled in England: *Narrative of a Four Months' Residence among the Natives of a Valley of the Marquesas Islands,* and in America, *Typee: A Peep at Polynesian Life.*

In July 1845, Gansevoort obtained his long awaited reward and was appointed Secretary of the American Legation in London. This enabled him to accomplish the deed which has assured him a solid place in literary history: he took his brother's MS with him and arranged for its publication by John Murray. The book came out in London in February 1846 and was published three weeks later by Wiley & Putnam in New York, and brought Melville fame overnight.

Encouraged by his success, Melville set to work on a sequel, which was published in 1847 under arrangements similar to those of *Typee*. *Omoo* ("rover" in the dialect of the Marquesas Islands) deals with the horrors of a whaling cruise, Melville's adventures in Tahiti and Hawaii, and is an indictment of missionary activity in these lands.

It was at this juncture, whilst *Omoo* was being printed, that Melville applied for a Government job as a clerk in the Treasury Department at Washington. Fortunately for posterity, he was refused, and by October 1847, had begun his third novel, *Mardi*. This one, however, was to be of a different kind.

Picaresque in genre and ornate with romantic devices, it was loaded with criticism of contemporary social, political and religious practice. Moreover, it reflected voracious reading. Melville had been introduced to the intellectual and cultural world of New York.

He got married in August 1847. His wife, Elizabeth, was the daughter of Lemuel Shaw, Chief Justice of Massachusetts, a friend of his deceased father. With the help of a loan from this generous father-in-law, the Melvilles set up house in New York, together with Herman's newly wed younger brother, Allan, his mother and sisters. Here Melville would live until 1850.

It was at this time that the "strange combination of vowels & consonants"[3] of Evert A. Duyckinck's name (Melville almost invariably misspelt it) attached itself to the Melville Saga.

Evert A. Duyckinck was an editor of Wiley and Putnam's in New York, and was in charge of the publication of *Typee*. That is how his friendship with Melville started. He was also editor of *The Literary World*, to which Melville contributed sketches and reviews.

Duyckinck introduced Melville to the literary circles of New York. More important, he gave him access to his seventeen-thousand volume library.[4] Melville's recorded borrowings from Duyckinck's library, from the New York Society Library and from the Library of the Boston Athenaeum, his book acquisitions in New York, Boston and London[5] show that he read very extensively. He read literature—American, English, European, classical Greek and Roman—philosophy, history, theology, natural history, geology, mineralogy, books on the fine arts, and, of course, books on whaling, sailing and travelling. Numerous references and adopted phrases in *Mardi* and *Moby-Dick* suggest that in the four years between September 1847—when he settled in New York—and July 1851—when he finished *Moby-Dick*—he read works by Beaumont and Fletcher, Boswell, Sir Thomas Browne, Robert Burton, Samuel Butler, Carlyle, Coleridge, Darwin, Defoe, Dickens, William Godwin, Ben Jonson, Charles Lamb, Marlowe, Shakespeare, Smollett, Thackeray, Pierre Bayle, Cyrano de Bergerac, Chateaubriand, Cuvier, Dante, Goethe, Montaigne, Rabelais, Rousseau, Schiller, Mme de Staël; in 1849, he bought himself the 37 volume set of Harper's Classical Library. It was "a varied scope of reading little suspected by his friends, and randomly acquired by a random but lynx-eyed mind, in the course of the multifarious, incidental, bibliographic encounterings of almost any civilized young inquirer after Truth".[6]

How his reading—which naturally was likely to be more extensive than the documentary evidence indicates[7]—affected Melville's unfolding within himself is reflected in the discrepancy between what, at its inception, he promised to his English publisher *Mardi* would be: "another book of South Sea Adventure (continued from, tho' wholly independent of, 'Omoo')" which "clothes the whole subject in new attractions & combines in one cluster all that is romantic, whimsical & poetic in Polynusia",[8]—and the multifarious, philosophical and satirical novel that was completed in January 1849.

The change of Melville's "mood",[9] as he himself referred to it, can also be traced in his letters.

On the 25th of March 1848, he wrote to John Murray, his English publisher: "My romance I assure you is no dish water nor its model borrowed from the

Circulating Library. It is something new I assure you, & original if nothing more . . . It opens like a true narrative—like Omoo for example, on ship board—& the romance & poetry of the thing thence grow continually, till it becomes a story wild enough I assure you & with a meaning too".[10] John Murray seems to have sensed the message, for he answered in an "Antarctic tenor". Undeterred, Melville proceeded, and on the 28th January 1849, begged Murray: "Unless you should deem it *very* desirable do not put me down on the title page as 'the author of Typee & Omoo'. I wish to separate 'Mardi' as much as possible from those books."[11]

Two months later the change was complete. Even *Mardi* became objectionable. In the same letter in which he announced to Duyckinck that he had bought a set of Bayle's *Dictionary* he referred to *Mardi* as "that affair of mine", and that "it seems so long now since I wrote it, & my mood has so changed, that I dread to look into it, & have purposely abstained from so doing since I thanked God it was off my hands".[12]

Mardi was eventually refused by John Murray on the ground that it was fiction and did not contain any useful information. Or were there any other considerations? Emily Morse Symonds, writing under the pseudonym of George Paston, recollects in *At John Murray's:*

"Murray was never to publish another book for Melville not even his masterpiece—*Moby-Dick*.[13] His change of front may be explained by a letter from the virtuous Sir Walter Farquhar to the 'good' Lord Ashley[14], which was forwarded to Albemarle Street.[15]

My dear Ashley, wrote Sir Walter, I am anxious that you should speak to Mr. Murray on the subject of two volumes in the Home and Colonial Library[16], entitled *Typee* and *Omoo,* by Herman Melville. In the original prospectus of this series it is stated to be the publisher's intention to publish a number of useful and entertaining volumes—the utmost care being at all times exercised in the selection of the works, *so that they shall contain nothing offensive to morals or good taste.*

Now I do not hesitate in saying that while, in the great majority of the volumes, Mr. Murray has redeemed his pledge, he has entirely departed from it by allowing the publication of *Typee* and *Omoo.* By a rather unsparing editorial pruning both these volumes might have been less objectionable—under any circumstances their tone is, I think, reprehensible throughout. They are not works that any mother would like to see in the hands of her daughters, and as such are not suited to lie on the drawing-room table . . . I think it important to elicit from him (Murray) some assurance that there shall not appear in his series another volume similar in character, for without such assurance I shall be reluctantly compelled to cease subscribing to the series."[17]

It was Richard Bentley who published *Mardi* in London in March 1849, and Harper and Bros. one month later in New York.

Far from being "useful and entertaining", the book remained enigmatic even to the person closest to the author: his wife and copyist. "I suppose by this time you are deep in the 'fogs' of 'Mardi'—if the mist ever does clear away, I should like to know what it reveals to *you*"—she wrote to her step-mother on April 30, 1849[18], using the same metaphor the London *Athenaeum* applied a week earlier in its review of *Mardi:* "Matters become crazier and crazier—more and more foggy—page by page—until the end ... is felt to be a happy release."[19] A similar metaphor was used by Evert A. Duyckinck, too, who, although writing of *Mardi* in terms of praise, remarked in *The Literary World* of April 21, 1849: "The discourse of these parties is generally very poetical, at times quite edifying, except when they get into the clouds, attempting to handle the problems of the universe."

However Melville thanked God that *Mardi* was off his hands, it still remained close enough to his heart—and his pocket—for him to resent the "broadside" fired into it in England[20] and subsequently in the United States. With the wisdom of hindsight the reason for the unfavourable reception of the book was quite clear to Richard Bentley, the English publisher, for he explained to Melville:

"As you observe the English critics generally have fired quite a broadside into 'Mardi'. This I cannot help thinking, has arisen in a great measure from the nature of the work: the first volume was eagerly devoured, the second was read—but the third was not perhaps altogether adapted to the class of readers whom 'Omoo' and 'Typee', and the First Volume of 'Mardi' gratified. The effect somehow or other has been decidedly to check, nay I almost say, to stop the sale of the book."[21]

Bentley used firmer terms when, after his experiences with *The Whale,* a new Melville novel* was offered for print:

"I cannot consent to ignore all my experiences of your previous works—in England they have all with the exception of 'Omoo' and 'Typee' proved failures. Will you allow in all frankness, and certainly not intended by me to be said in any other than the most friendly spirit, to say, that I conceive if you had revised your work 'Mardi', to the latest, the 'Whale', and restrained your imagination somewhat, and had written in a style to be understood by the great mass of readers—nay if you had not sometimes offended the feelings of many sensitive readers you would have succeeded in England. Everybody must admit the genius displayed in your writings; but it would have been impossible for any publisher with any prudent regard to his own interests to have put out your books here without revisal, and occasional omission."[22]

Melville, though confident that *Mardi* "will reach those for whom it is intended; and ... that ... in its higher purposes, has not been written in vain" understood

* *Pierre*

66

Bentley's message and was contrite: "I need not assure you how deeply I regret, that for any period, you should find this venture of 'Mardi' an unprofitable thing for you; & I should feel still more grieved, did I suppose it was going to eventuate in a positive loss to you."

Nor was he being hypocritical in so writing: *Redburn* was on its way "thro' the press". Melville's new baby son had to be provided for, and that "certain something unmanageable in us, that bids us do this or that, and be done it must—hit or miss"[23] had to be subdued. *Redburn* was to be "a thing of a widely different cast from 'Mardi': a plain, straightforward, amusing narrative of personal experience—the son of a gentleman on his first voyage to sea as a sailor—no metaphysics, no conic sections[24], nothing but cakes & ale".[25]

Redburn was published by Bentley in England late in September 1849, and in the middle of November by Harper's in New York. Another potboiler, *White-Jacket,* based on Melville's experiences of service on board an American man-of-war and exposing the hardships and the degradation sailors in the US navy were being subjected to was published by Harper's in New York and Bentley's in London at the beginning of 1850.

From both of these successful offsprings Melville wholeheartedly dissociated himself: "No reputation that is gratifying to me, can possibly be achieved by either of these books" he wrote to his father-in-law. "They are two *jobs,* which I have done for money—being forced to it, as other men are to sawing wood. And while I have felt obliged to refrain from writing the kind of book I would wish to; yet, in writing these two books, I have not repressed myself much—so far as *they* are concerned; but have spoken pretty much as I feel.—Being books, then written in this way, my only desire for their 'success' (as it is called) springs from my pocket, & not from my heart. So far as I am individually concerned, & independent of my pocket, it is my earnest desire to write those sort of books which are said to 'fail'."[26]

Nevertheless, the success of *Redburn* was welcome. "Redburn ... to my surprise ... seems to have been favorably received", he wrote to Duyckinck. "I am glad of it—for it puts money into an empty purse.[27] But I hope I shall never write such a book again—Tho' when a poor devil writes with duns all round him, & looking over the back of his chair—& perching on his pen & diving in his inkstand—like the devils about St: Anthony—what can you expect of that poor devil?—What but a beggarly 'Redburn'! And when he attempts anything higher—God help him & save him! for it is not with a hollow purse as with a hollow balloon—for a hollow purse makes the poet *sink*—witness 'Mardi' ... What a madness and anguish it is, that an author can never—under no conceivable circumstances—be at all frank with his readers.—Could I, for one, be frank with them—how would they cease their railing—those at least who have railed."[28]

This Melville wrote to Duyckinck from London, whither he went in October 1849, to conclude negotiations for the publication of *White-Jacket.*

On the lst of February 1850, Melville returned to New York after a visit to England, France and Germany, enriched with books and new literary acquaintances.

In September of that year, with money borrowed from his father-in-law, he bought a farm in Pittsfield, Berkshire, Massachusetts and lived there with his family until 1863, when he sold the farm to his brother, and moved back to New York with his family.

Did he buy the farm in the hope that it would make him "independent" of his "pocket"? If so, the farm never met his expectations. A year later, however, he seems to have fulfilled his "earnest desire to write those sort of books which are said to fail". He completed a book which was regarded as a failure by his own and, with few exceptions, by the next two generations. The third proclaimed it a masterpiece.

PART III

Cooking up the blubber

CHAPTER 1

Identification

1. "I mean to give the truth of the thing"

Having swum "through libraries and sailed through oceans",[1] by May 1850, Melville was working on *Moby-Dick*. On the first day of that month, he wrote to Richard Henry Dana, Jr.:[2]

> "About the 'whaling voyage'—I am half way in the work ... It will be a strange sort of book, tho', I fear; blubber is blubber you know; tho' you may get oil out of it, the poetry runs as hard as sap from a frozen maple tree;—& to cook the thing up, one must need throw in a little fancy, which from the nature of the thing, must be ungainly as the gambols of the whales themselves. Yet I mean to give the truth of the thing, spite of this."[3]

With "cooking-up" also meaning "concocting", the metaphor pertinently indicates what it is that distinguishes *Moby-Dick* from all the numerous other contemporary whaling narratives.

With all the hazards and hardships, there was not much room for romance on board a whaler, and illusions would swiftly vanish. "Yes, yes! give me this glorious ocean life, this salt-seal life ... Let me roll around the globe, ... with ... an endless sea before!" Redburn enthused at the outset of his voyage. But "soon these raptures abated": "Miserable dog's life is this of the sea! commanded like a slave, and set to work like an ass! vulgar and brutal men lording it over me, as if I were an African in Alabama. Yes, yes, blow on, ye breezes, and make a speedy end to this abominable voyage!" he commented after a while. "What are sailors?" Melville asked in *Redburn*, and then answered:

> "What in your heart do you think of that fellow staggering along the dock? Do you not give him a wide berth, shun him, and account him but little above the brutes that perish? Will you throw open your parlors to him; invite him to dinner? or give him a season ticket to your pew in church?—No. You will do no such thing; but at a distance, you will perhaps subscribe a dollar or two for the building of a hospital, to accomodate sailors already broken down; or for the distribution of excellent books among tars who can not read. And the very mode and manner in which such charities are made, bespeak, more than words, the low estimation in which sailors are held. It is useless to gainsay it;

71

they are deemed almost the refuse and offscourings of the earth; and the romantic view of them is principally had through romances."

The condition of the sailors was, in fact, indicative of the whole social system:

"By their very vocation they are shunned by the better classes of people, and cut off from all access to respectable and improving society; consider all this, and the reflecting mind must very soon perceive that the case of sailors, as a class, is not a very promising one.

Indeed, the bad things of their condition come under the head of those chronic evils which can only be ameliorated, it would seem, by ameliorating the moral organization of all civilization."[4]

Whalers had the distinction of being despised even by their fellow sailors in the merchant marine and the navy.

"Why is it", Melville asks in *Moby-Dick* "that all Merchant-seamen, and also all Pirates and Man-of-War's men, and Slave ship sailors, cherish such a scornful feeling towards Whale-ships; this is a question it would be hard to answer". Whalemen were at the very bottom of society in the Northeastern states:

"This business of whaling has somehow come to be regarded among landsmen as a rather unpoetical and disreputable pursuit ... the world declines honoring ... whalemen."

All this at a time, when

"whalemen of America ... outnumber all the rest of the banded whalemen in the world; sail a navy of upwards of seven hundred vessels; manned by eighteen thousand men; ... and every year importing ... $ 7,000,000."[5]

J. Ross Browne wrote in his *Etchings of a Whaling Cruise:*

"There are now in active employment more than seven hundred whaling vessels belonging to the New England States, manned by nearly twenty thousand hardy and intrepid men. It is a reproach to the American people that, in this age of moral reform, the protecting arm of the law has not reached these daring adventurers. We are indebted to them for the extension of our commerce in foreign countries; for valuable additions to our stock of knowledge; for all the benefits resulting from their discoveries and researches in remote parts of the world and yet they are the most oppressed class of men in existence. History scarcely furnishes a parallel for the deeds of cruelty committed upon them during their long and perilous voyages.

The startling increase of crime in the whale fishery demands a remedy. Scarcely a vessel arrives in port that does not bring intelligence of a mutiny.

Are the murderous wrongs which compel men to rise up and throw off the burden of oppression unworthy of notice? Will none make the attempt to arrest their fearful progress? Such a state of things surely calls for investigation."[6]

Melville was adamant in denouncing any attempts to glamorize the sailors or their conditions. He warmly appreciated Richard Henry Dana, Jr.'s *Two Years Before the Mast* (1840) and J. Ross Browne's *Etchings of a Whaling Cruise* (1846) for their true accounts of the sailors' life. Reviewing J. Ross Browne's *Etchings* for *The Literary World* of 6, March 1847, he wrote:

"From time immemorial many fine things have been said and sung of the sea. The days have been, when sailors were considered veritable mermen; and the ocean itself, as the peculiar theatre of the romantic and wonderful. But of late years there have been revealed so many plain, matter-of-fact details connected with nautical life that at the present day the poetry of salt water is very much on the wane. The perusal of Dana's 'Two Years before the Mast', for instance, somewhat impairs the relish with which we read Byron's spiritual 'Address to the Ocean'.[7]

Mr. J. Ross Browne's narrative tends still further to impair the charm with which poesy and fiction have invested the sea. It is a book of unvarnished facts ... Indeed, what Mr. Dana has so admirably done in describing the vicissitudes of the merchant sailor's life, Mr. Browne has creditably achieved with respect to that of the hardy whaleman's ...

Considering the disenchanting nature of the revelations of sea life with which we are presented in Mr. Browne's book, we are inclined to believe that the shipping agents employed in our various cities by the merchants of New Bedford will have to present additional inducements to 'enterprising and industrious young Americans of good moral character,' in order to persuade them to embark in the fishery ...

Give ear, now, all ye shore-disdaining, ocean-enamoured youth, who labor under the lamentable delusion, that the sea—the 'glorious sea' is always and in reality 'the blue, the fresh, the ever free!' Give ear to Mr. J. Ross Browne ... We shudder at all realities of the career they will be entering upon ... "[8]

Both in England and the United States one of the most popular authors of the "many fine things" that "have been said and sung of the sea" and of the sailors, was the English dramatist, composer and sea-song writer, Charles Dibdin (1745–1814). Melville referred to him and quoted him in several instances.[9] He was annoyed with the virtuous, patriotic, acquiescent, merry and carefree sailor image of Dibdin's verses, such as:

"Tight lads have I sail'd with, but none e'er so sightly
    As honest Bill Bobstay, so kind and so true,
He'd sing like a mermaid, and foot it so lightly,
    The forecastle's pride, and delight of the crew!"[10]

Or:

"Jack dances and sings, and is always content,
    In his vows to his lass he'll ne'er fail her,
His anchor's a-trip when his money's all spent—
    And this is the life of a sailor.*

Alert in his duty he readily flies,
    Where the winds the tired vessel are flinging,
Though sunk to the sea-gods, or toss'd to the skies,
    Still Jack is found working and singing.

'Longside of an enemy, boldy and brave,
    He'll with broadside on broadside regale her,
Yet he'll sigh to the soul o'er that enemy's grave,
    So noble's the mind of a sailor.
. . . .
In a fostering Power while Jack puts his trust,
    As Fortune comes, smiling he'll hail her,
Resign'd, still, and manly, since what must be must,
    And this is the mind of a sailor."[11]

In *Billy Budd*, in connection with the Nore mutiny of 1797, Melville remarked with no little glee:

"The event converted into irony for a time those spirited strains of Dibdin—as a song-writer no mean auxiliary to the English Government at the European conjuncture—strains celebrating, among other things, the patriotic devotion of the British tar."[12]

In *White-Jacket* he is even more explicit in exposing the way Dibdin misrepresented sailors and their lives in the navy:

"Dibdin's ditties . . . most of them breathe the very poetry of the ocean. But it is remarkable that those songs—which would lead one to think that man-of-war's men are the most care-free, contented, virtuous, and patriotic of mankind—were composed at a time when the English Navy was principally

* This verse is ironically quoted in *White-Jacket*.

74

manned by felons and paupers, ... Still more, these songs are pervaded by a true Mohammedan sensualism; a reckless acquiescence in fate, and an implicit, unquestioning, dog-like devotion to whoever may be lord and master. Dibdin was a man of genius; but no wonder Dibdin was a government pensioner at £ 200 per annum."[13]

When Melville wrote *Moby-Dick*, he was resolved "to give the truth of the thing". He sharply and explicitly projected upon his canvas the hazards and hardships of the whaling industry and the misery of those who worked in it. Yet what was contrived, had the magic of art, with dimensions extended to their logical extremities. Thus in *Moby-Dick* the hazards of the industry become a doom hovering over the scene until the final catastrophe; the hardships reduce the crew to helpless victims of the superior forces of nature and of society; the ship's company and all those associated with it come to represent the world's population on the one hand and a cross-section of New England society on the other; the whale-chase assumes epic dimensions; the captain develops into a tragic Don Quixote of fatal, idealistic single-mindedness; and the Whale appears huge, colourless and ferocious, challenged by men who believe it to have been divinely created.

2. The Extracts

The novel begins with a flourish. Under the title of "Etymology" the Whale is announced in twelve different languages. This is followed by a chapter called "Extracts", in which eighty quotations testify to the age-old relationship between man and whale; they hint at the whale's power and hugeness; the difficulty and toughness of the hunt and the importance of the quarry. The sources tapped are paraded in chronological order and range from *Genesis* to a contemporaneous whale song. There is poetry, drama, there are chronicles, narratives, psalms, speeches, correspondence, and natural and political history. Melville probably took the pattern from Robert Southey's seven volume *The Doctor* (1834–47), where each volume opens with a "Prelude of Mottoes", also quotations from various sources, but which carry no message except that of commending the book in general terms. Part of the message of Melville's eighty extracts is denoted by the contrast between the first and the last:

"'And God created great whales.'

Genesis"

"'Oh, the rare old Whale, mid storm and gale
   In his ocean home will be
A giant in might, where might is right,
   And King of the boundless sea.'

Whale Song"

75

Five of the eighty are extracts from the Bible and should be considered in the light of their special implication for the novel. They are quotations from *Genesis* I, 21; *Job* XLI, 32; *Jonah* I, 17; *Psalms* CIV, 26; and *Isaiah* XXVII, 1. In the Old Testament there are, of course, several more references to a huge aquatic animal, as in *Job* VII, 12; XLI, 1; *Psalms* LXXIV, 13,14; *Isaiah* LI, 9 and *Ezekiel* XXIX, 3, XXXII, 2. The terms used in the ancient Hebrew text are vague and vary.

"A great fish" ("prepared" by the Lord) is mentioned in *Jonah* I, 17. We find לִוְיָתָן (Leviathan) in *Job* XLI, 1, *Psalms* LXXIV, 14, CIV, 26 and *Isaiah* XXVII, 1. In all the other places the word is תַּנִּין (Tannin) or its variants, which might be regarded as plural cases, or dialectical variations, or as meaning either "jackals" (plural) or "serpent" (singular). No specific names seem to have been used in ancient Hebrew to distinguish between the various huge and dangerous animals people might come across in sea or river, and all the relevant terms in the ancient Hebrew Old Testament refer to a long, serpent-like animal. In the King James Version of the Bible, used by Melville, these terms were variously translated as: whale, Leviathan, dragon and serpent. (The New English Bible tends to prefer the vague "sea-monster", and only uses "whale" in *Job* XLI, 1, with "Leviathan" in the footnote as an alternative.) In *Moby-Dick*, Melville first identifies all the variants of the English translation as whales. Then, with a sly twist, he identifies the whale with the dragon:

> "Akin to the adventure of Perseus and Andromeda—indeed, by some supposed to be indirectly derived from it—is that famous story of St. George and the Dragon; which dragon I maintain to have been a whale; for in many old chronicles whales and dragons are strangely jumbled together, and often stand for each other. 'Thou art, as a lion of the waters, and as a dragon of the sea', saith Ezekiel; hereby, plainly meaning a whale; in truth, some versions of the Bible use that word itself."[14]

In truth, *Ezekiel* XXXII, 2 in the King James version says:

> "... Thou art like a young lion of the nations, and thou art as a whale in the seas"

with a footnote to "whale", that reads: "Or, dragon." "Thou" refers to Pharaoh.

Incidentally we find the same identification in Book IV, Chapter 33, of Rabelais's *Gargantua and Pantagruel:*

> "Pantagruel sighted in the distance a huge and monstrous spouting whale... began to wail and cry ... 'Let's run away. Why I'll be blowed if it isn't the Leviathan described by the great prophet Moses in his life of that holy man Job.* ... I think it's the same sea-monster that was sent in the old days to

---

* This sentence is quoted in the eleventh Extract.

gobble up Andromeda . . . Oh, if only there were some valiant Perseus here to slay him at a blow!"[15]

In the Extracts, then, Melville presents the whale as the common denomination of several stories of both the Bible and of non-Judaeo–Christian mythology; he also shows as identical the "whales" that "God created" (*Genesis* I, 21, quoted in the first Extract) and "saw that it was good" (same verse), and "Leviathan the piercing serpent, even Leviathan that crooked serpent", whom "the Lord with his sore and great and strong sword shall punish" (*Isaiah* XXVII, 1, quoted in the fifth Extract).

Biblical self-contradiction and the parallelisms between Biblical and non-Biblical mythology have long been considered strong arguments against the divine inspiration of the Bible. Thus, already in the overture, Melville strikes one of the basic notes of his novel: religious scepticism, nurtured in the mid-nineteenth century by the theory of evolution and the findings of geology, ancient history and comparative religion. But a literal reading of the Old Testament had often tended to induce religious scepticism. St. Paul was wise enough to warn the Corinthians that "the letter killeth, but the spirit giveth life" (II. *Corinthians* III, 6); and St. Augustine, in his *Confessions,* gives an exultant account of his rescue from Manicheanism on hearing "one passage after another in the Old Testament figuratively explained". He then relates:

> "These passages had been death to me when I took them literally, but once I had heard them explained in their spiritual meaning I began to blame myself for my despair."[16]

The answer to Biblical criticism is Biblical exegesis.

Yet, Melville, in a bantering style, warns the reader not to take the Extracts too seriously, "for veritable gospel cetology". They are a "higgledy-piggledy" collection of "what has been promiscuously said, thought, fancied, and sung of Leviathan, by many nations and generations".[17]

As a result, however, the whale, or Leviathan, is introduced as a focal object of human activity, inquisition and imagination.

It therefore follows from the Extracts that this story of a particular whale will be the story of human struggle as gigantic as the object pursued.

"To produce a mighty book, you must choose a mighty theme"—Melville writes in a subsequent chapter.[18]

And who is the fictitious compiler of the Extracts that establish the mightiness of the theme?

A "poor devil of a Sub-Sub". It is for him and his likes that the author wishes he could clear out "Hampton Court and the Tuileries" and "the seven-storied heavens".[19]

3. Ishmael

The action begins with Ishmael, the narrator, going to sea. Although Biblical names were common in New England, no Ishmael (or Ahab, for that matter) is mentioned in contemporary records. But in contemporary literature Melville's narrator had several namesakes. The romantic, roaming outcast Ishmael character was, of course, popularized by Byron. But Melville's aversion to the Byronesque hero is evident from his ironical reference to "Byron's Address to the Ocean" which Wellingborough Redburn "had often spouted on the stage at the High School at home"[20], or his scornful hint in *Moby-Dick* at the "moody" verse that "Childe Harold ... ejaculates".[21]

It is more likely, then, that in calling his narrator Ishmael, Melville was aware of what Pierre Bayle wrote about the Biblical Ishmael in his *Dictionary Historical and Critical*.[22] Melville acquired the solid volumes in the spring of 1849, as we know from his letter to Evert Duyckinck, written from Boston on April 5, 1849, joyfully reporting the event.

Ishmael's story is recounted by Pierre Bayle in his entry on Agar (Hagar). The story itself, as related in *Genesis* XVI, 1–16, XVII, 18–25, XXI, 6–12, XXV, 9–17 is the following:

Ishmael was born to Abraham when he was 86, by his wife Sarah's Egyptian maid, Hagar, whom Sarah had asked Abraham to "go in unto", as she herself had been "restrained" by the Lord "from bearing". When Hagar "conceived", Sarah became jealous and "dealt hardly with her", and Hagar "fled from her face". But the "angel of the Lord" persuaded her to return to her "mistress" and "submit" herself "under her hands". And the angel also advised Hagar to give to the son she would bear the name of Ishmael, meaning "God shall hear" and warned her that "he will be a wild man; his hand will be against every man, and every man's hand against him".

Thirteen years later, "when Abraham was ninety years old and nine" and Sarah ninety, the Lord told Abraham that he would establish a "covenant" between himself and Abraham and Abraham's "seed ... in their generations" (XVII, 7: this is the verse on which the Convenanters in both England and North America based their exclusive relationship with God), and pledged himself to give to Abraham and his seed "the land of Canaan, for an everlasting possession" (XVII, 8: this verse was meant to establish the Jews' divine right to that piece of the Middle East). Half Egyptian, Ishmael could not, of course, qualify for a covenant with God; he would nevertheless be blessed by God and made fruitful. Sarah would bear Abraham a son after all; he was to be called Isaac, and God would establish his covenant with him and his seed.

By the time Isaac "was weaned", Sarah could no longer stand the presence of Hagar and Ishmael, and asked Abraham to "cast out this bondwoman and her son: for the son of this bondwoman shall not be the heir with my son", and "God said unto Abraham, ... in all that Sarah hath said unto thee, hearken unto her voice". So "Abraham rose up early in the morning, and took bread, and a bottle of water, and gave it unto Hagar, putting it on her shoulder, and the child, and sent her away: and she . . . wandered in the wilderness . . . ".

In the "Agar" article, as in his other Biblical entries, selected for polemical purposes, sceptical Pierre Bayle does not miss the occasion to dwell on the questionable morality of the Patriarch's divinely inspired conduct.

Regarding Ishmael's character, he quotes *Genesis* XVI, 12, where the Angel warns Hagar about her son's doom and adds:

> "If it were permitted to look for Types here, as St. *Austin** did, one would think that *Ishmael* was an Emblem of certain snarling Polemical Writers, who are for snapping at every body, and who, to declare War the better against human kind, run every Moment out of their Sphere, scribling on every Subject, right or wrong, and always in a defamatory and libellous Style. All Ages and Countries produce these Copies of *Ishmael*. Some of them indeed differ from their original in this, that, tho' they cast Stones at every body, few Persons take the trouble to return them; but let them quietly enjoy a wretched Impunity, which increases their Insolence, and their Frenzy."[23]

Besides *Moby-Dick*, Melville has three other novels in which the Ishmael concept occurs: *Redburn, Pierre* and *The Confidence-Man*.

Redburn realized that under the hostile eye of Jackson, an evil and domineering sailor, the rest of the sailors

> "were afraid to speak out for me . . . ; so that at last I found myself a sort of Ishmael in the ship, without a single friend or companion; and I began to feel a hatred growing up in me against the whole crew."[24]

Pierre felt

> "entirely lonesome and orphan-like . . . driven out an infant Ishmael into the desert, with no maternal Hagar to accompany and comfort him."[25]

In Chapter 24 the Confidence-Man, masquerading as a "philanthropist", admonishes one called a misanthrope:

> "To you, an Ishmael, . . . I came ambassador from the human race, charged with the assurance that for your mislike they bore no answering grudge, but sought to conciliate accord between you and them. Yet you take me not for the honest envoy, but I know not what sort of unheard-of spy. Sir, . . . this mistaking of your man should teach you how you may mistake all men. For God's sake, . . . get you confidence. See how distrust has duped you."[26]

---

* St. Augustine

Coming from the Confidence-Man, this little harangue obviously has an inverted and satirical message. The passage is reminiscent of Pierre Bayle also in its warning against being a dupe of your trust and confidence.

In the concluding section of his Agar commentary, Pierre Bayle deals with stones worshipped by Jews, Arabs, Phrygians and Saracens. Going into a bit of comparative religious history, Bayle relishes jumbling together these different beliefs, exposing their overlappings and contradictions, until their absurdity is obvious and they discredit each other:

> "We understand by *Enthymius Zigabenus,* that the *Saracens* honoured and kissed a Stone, . . . and when they were asked the Reason of it, some answered, it was, because *Abraham* knew *Agar* on that Stone; others, that it was, because he tied his Camel to it, when he prepared to offer up his Son *Isaac.* The same Author says, that this Stone was the Head of the Statue of Venus, the Deity, which the ancient Ishmaelites worshipped. . . . On this Occasion, I shall observe, that the Stone, which was worshipped by the *Arabians,* and which they took for the God Mars, was black and unhewn . . . *The Mother of the Gods,* whom the *Phrygians* adored with a very extraordinary Zeal, was nothing more than a plain Stone . . . How absurd soever the Idolatry of those was, who worshipped the Stone which Jacob set up for a Pillar, and anointed and consecrated to God[27]; it was yet more tolerable, than That of the Saracens; for *Jacob*'s Stone served him for a Pillow, in a Night, which he past, as one may say, with God, the Dreams and Visions, with which he was entertained, representing heavenly Things in so lively a manner to him. The *Saracens* durst not have said so much, in relation to their pretended Stone of *Agar* . . . "

Pierre Bayle winds up with the following conclusion:

> "From all these Particulars we may infer, that it is very easy to deceive a Man in Matters of Religion, and very difficult to undeceive him in them. He is fond of his Prejudices, and finds Leaders, who indulge him in them, and who say within themselves, 'quando-quidem populus vult decipi, decipiatur.—*Since the People will be impos'd upon, let them be impos'd upon.'* They find their Account in this, both in point of Authority and Profit: When the Disease is become inveterate, the most disinterested fear, that the Remedy may prove worse than the Disease. These dare not cure the Wound, and it is the Interest of others, that it should not be cur'd. Thus an Abuse is perpetuated: Dishonest Men protect it; and honest Men tolerate it."[28]

Melville's Confidence-Man is one of these "Dishonest Men", masquerading in various disguises. As a herb doctor, he tells a cripple:

"Believe me that, like your crutches, confidence and hopefulness will long support a man when his own legs will not. Stick to confidence and hopefulness, then, since how mad for the cripple to throw his crutches away."

On another occasion the Confidence-Man addresses "a Missouri bachelor ... of Spartan leisure and fortune, and ... not less acquainted, in a Spartan way of his own, with philosophy and books, than with wood-craft and rifles." Previously this man had declared that he had "confidence in distrust" and warned a sick old man not to let himself be gulled by the "herb doctor". The Confidence-Man puts forward the age-old argument justifying religious deception:

"For the gulling, tell me, is it humane to talk so to this poor old man? Granting that his dependence on my medicine is vain, is it kind to deprive him of what, in mere imagination, if nothing more, may help eke out, with hope, his disease? For you, if you have no confidence, and, thanks to your native health, can get along without it, so far, at least, as trusting in my medicine goes; yet, how cruel an argument to use, with this afflicted one here."

The Missourian agrees and "eyeing the old man", says:

"Yes, it *is* pitiless in one like me to speak too honestly to one like you. You are a late sitter-up in this life; past man's usual bed-time; and truth, though with some it makes a wholesome breakfast, proves to all a supper too hearty. Hearty food, taken late, gives bad dreams."[29]*

Melville was only thirty-one, still young enough to avidly crave the "hearty food" of truth, when he created the Ishmael of *Moby-Dick*. Deriving his name from the Bible, this Ishmael however would, with Baylesque irony, reverse the Biblical story. Not expelled, but selfexiled, he enlists as a sailor on board a whaler as a "substitute for pistol and ball". Also, he is "tormented with an everlasting itch for things remote" and desirous "to sail forbidden seas, and land on barbarous coasts".[30]

Before departing, like his Biblical namesake, Ishmael is forlorn, depressed and morbid. In the course of his voyage, however, while exploring the mysteries of the whale and weathering the perils of the sea, he ceases to be an "Isolato", but feels "federated along one keel"[31] with his fellow sailors. In the end, he is the sole survivor of the final catastrophe, and is saved as "another orphan",[32] by human hands which, according to the Biblical prophecy, would be "against him".[33]

* Cf. "For unless you own the whale, you are but a provincial and sentimentalist in Truth. But clear Truth is a thing for salamander giants only to encounter; how small the chances for the provincials then?" (*Moby-Dick*, p. 336.)

4. The dense webbed bed of welded sinews

Tragic as the outcome of the narrative is, it begins on a lighthearted note. The jocular tone of the opening chapters has given rise to the "two *Moby-Dicks*" theory[34], according to which Melville first intended to write an entertaining whaling story, but, when halfway through, changed his mind and the whole purport of the novel in a "metaphysical" direction. Much external and internal evidence has been brought in support of this theory: the discrepancy between Melville's own expectations and the time he actually took to complete his book; inconsistency in style; the number of chapters dealing with cetology and the technicalities of whaling, and so on. We have, however, the written testimony of Melville's resolve never again to write such novels as *Redburn*.[35] Moreover, some of "that unwonted power" with which *Moby-Dick*, the novel, like Moby Dick, the whale, is apt "to strike the imagination" lies in the compactness of both novel and whale. For just as the tail of the whale "seems a dense webbed bed of welded sinews"[36] so the tale of the novel is closely and thoroughly interwoven with recurring metaphors, symbols, multiple cross-references and irony from "Call me Ishmael" (first three words of Chapter I) to "another orphan" (last two words of the Epilogue).

What Ishmael narrates is the story of Captain Ahab, hunting a "particular whale" to wreak vengeance upon him: "a Sperm Whale of uncommon magnitude and malignity", identified in the fishery by his "peculiar snow-white wrinkled forehead, and a high, pyramidical white hump" and named Moby-Dick. On a previous hunt this whale, with "his sickle-shaped lower jaw" had "reaped away" Captain Ahab's leg. Having sailed through 111 chapters, Ahab and his crew encounter the awe-inspiring White Whale, chase him for three days and end up at the bottom of the sea, with the sea rolling on above them, "as it rolled five thousand years ago".[37]

A peculiar story indeed of a particularly dangerous whale and a particularly single-minded captain. The climax is reached in the last three chapters, which give a dramatic account of the final chase. Throughout the preceding 132, in which Ishmael, the narrator, joins Captain Ahab's crew on board the *Pequod*[38], and the whaler and her company seek out the White Whale, Melville is at pains to establish "the natural verity of the main points", so as "to take away any incredulity".

> "So ignorant are most landsmen of some of the plainest and most palpable wonders of the world, that without some hints touching the plain facts, historical and otherwise, of the fishery, they might scout at Moby Dick as a monstrous fable, or still worse and more detestable, a hideous and intolerable allegory."[39]

In order to prove that "verity", Melville is anxious explicitly to relate his fiction to facts generally prevailing and cases frequently occurring in the sperm whale fishery. He mentions the whaleship Essex which, in 1820, was stove by a sperm whale. The case was chronicled by Owen Chase, the ship's first mate, in *Narrative of the Most Extraordinary and Distressing Shipwreck of the Whale-Ship Essex of Nantucket; Which Was Attacked & Finally Destroyed by a Large Spermaceti Whale, in the Pacific Ocean*, published in New York in 1821. Captain Ahab's chase of Moby Dick was certainly not a unique and unprecedented venture. Melville refers to two other specially ferocious whales, named, identified and "gone in quest of, systematically hunted out, chased and killed by valiant whaling captains, who heaved up their anchors with that express object in view".[40]

One of these whales, New Zealand Tom, is mentioned in both Thomas Beale's *The Natural History of the Sperm Whale* (1839) and Frederick Debell Bennett's *Narrative of a Whaling Voyage Round the Globe, from the year 1833 to 1836* (1840), Melville's chief sources of information on cetology and whaling. The other whale, Don Miguel, seems to be fictitious.[41]

With artistic discretion, Melville does not mention Mocha Dick, the renowned and dreaded ferocious white whale eventually captured in 1859, described by Jeremiah N. Reynolds in the *Knickerbocker Magazine* of May 1839. The whale derived his name from the island of Mocha, off the coast of Chile, where he had been first encountered in 1810.

When describing the second day of the final chase, Melville remarks:

> "Here be it said, that this pertinacious pursuit of one particular whale, continued through day into night, and through night into day, is a thing by no means unprecedented in the South sea fishery."[42]

In fact every single incident of the dramatic final chase is either adumbrated by a previous episode, or is explained in one of the preceding descriptive passages. There seems to be a well-designed plan here. Of the total of 135 chapters, 34 interspersed among the other 101, deal with cetology and whaling. The first 23 and the last 20 chapters are devoted entirely to the narrative. The "plain facts, historical and otherwise, of the fishery" cluster most densely around the centre, from Chapter 55 to 90. Thus, both in form and content, the narrative is firmly grounded on the facts of the mid-nineteenth century sperm whale fishery, at the time New England's chief industry one which included both extracting and processing. Thus the descriptive and narrative chapters are organically interconnected.

The result is an industrial saga. Dramatic tension escalates throughout the novel and reaches its climax—and anticlimax—in the three chapters of the final chase—itself a masterpiece and the summation of all previous chapters. Often the dramatic effect is heightened by an elevated style and dramatized diction, which might have served to raise to literary respectability a theme otherwise far below the genteel expectations of the mid-nineteenth century North-American reading public.

At the same time, Melville expands the symbolic reference of both descriptive and narrative passages so as to encompass questions of more general implication.

These concern the individual's relation to his natural and social environment; the coexistence of divine omnipotence, benevolence, providence and predestination on the one hand, and human free will, moral responsibility, physical and moral evil and indiscriminate affliction, on the other; the interpretation of the world in moral terms and the meaning of human life. No wonder Melville's wife felt "anxious about the strain on his health"[43] after *Moby-Dick* and *Pierre* had been finished and that his mother asked her brother, Peter Gansevoort, to "procure for him a foreign consulship", as "this constant working of the brain, & excitement of the imagination, is wearing Herman out".[44]

Melville, enraptured with his theme, enthused:

"Give me a condor's quill! Give me Vesuvius' crater for an inkstand! Friends, hold my arms! For in the mere act of penning my thoughts of this Leviathan, they weary me, and make me faint with their outreaching comprehensiveness of sweep, as if to include the whole circle of the sciences, and all the generations of whales, and men, and mastodons, past, present and to come, with all the revolving panoramas of empire on earth, and throughout the whole universe, not excluding its suburbs. Such, and so magnifying, is the virtue of a large and liberal theme! We expand to its bulk. To produce a mighty book, you must choose a mighty theme. No great and enduring volume can ever be written on the flea, though many there be who have tried it."[45]

With all its impassioned exuberance, this passage is intrinsically encased in one of the cetological chapters.

5. The dark Hindoo half of nature

There is one note that rings through nearly all the chapters on cetology or whaling: that of the dangers, hazards and hardships involved, so that "every individual moment ... comprises a peril".[46] What Ahab valiantly set out to do was doomed from the start by the overpowering odds he went against.

That "there is death in this business of whaling—a speechlessly quick chaotic bundling of a man into Eternity",[47]—the very fate that would meet Ahab, when caught in the line of his own harpoon,—was brought to Ishmael's understanding in the New Bedford Whaleman's Chapel at the sight of the mourners whose lost relatives clearly outnumbered the memorial tablets in the wall, as "so many are the unrecorded accidents in the fishery", for

"not one in fifty of the actual disasters and deaths by casualties in the fishery, ever finds a public record at home, however transient and immediately forgotten that record. ... For God's sake, be economical with your lamps and candles! not a gallon you burn, but at least one drop of man's blood was spilled for it."[48]

Fatal casualties were caused either by the direct onslaught of the attacked whale, or by accidents in the course of the hunt. After all, the sperm whale is "the largest inhabitant of the globe; the most formidable of all whales to encounter".

Melville is anxious to emphasize over and over again the "two-fold enormousness" of the whale, it being "an enormous creature of enormous power", and he even gives an anatomical explanation of this "measureless force". But not only is the whale powerful, and ferocious when attacked, he is also intelligent. Modern science has found the whale's intelligence (the whale belonging to the same species as the dolphin, so that what is true of the dolphin, applies also to the whale) to be second only to man's. A century earlier, Melville emphatically points out:

> "The Sperm Whale is in some cases sufficiently powerful, knowing, and judiciously malicious, as with direct aforethought to stave in, utterly destroy, and sink a large ship; and what is more, the Sperm Whale *has* done it."

Melville frequently refers to the "wilful, deliberate designs of destruction" of the stricken whale, his "cunning and malice", his "intelligent malignity"; and, regarding the most enormous and powerful of all sperm whales, Moby-Dick, Melville remarks:

> "In most instances, such seemed the White Whale's infernal aforethought of ferocity, that every dismembering or death that he caused, was not wholly regarded as having been inflicted by an unintelligent agent."

Melville, however, also points out that this "ferocity" and "malignity" is evinced by the whale when, under attack, he acts in self-defence. In fact, as a ship surgeon explains, "the digestive organs of the whale are so inscrutably constructed by Divine Providence, that it is quite impossible for him to completely digest even a man's arm ... So that what you take for the White Whale's malice is only his awkwardness. For he never means to swallow a single limb; he only thinks to terrify by feints."[49] It is significant that, whilst we read of several cases when boats and ships had been stove by whales, and crews had perished as a consequence, most casualties of the narrative are accidents due to the hunt of the whale. Moreover, in all of them the fatal agent is the sea.

Whilst Whitman exulted over the "turbulent manly cities"[50], the "Open Road" and the "earth expanding right hand and left hand"[51] before the triumphant advances of the pioneer settlers of western lands, Melville drew much of his inspiration from that "dark Hindoo half of nature", "who", as Ahab addressed it,

> "hast built thy separate throne somewhere in the heart of these unverdured seas",

the region where Ahab, in one of his remonstrative monologues, declared there were "this world's foundations". Here, Ahab expostulated

"unrecorded names and navies rust, and untold hopes and anchors rot; ...
(here) in her murderous hold this frigate earth is ballasted with bones of
millions of the drowned; ... the locked lovers when leaping from their
flaming ship; heart to heart they sank beneath the exulting wave; true to each
other, when heaven seemed false to them ... the murdered mate when tossed
by pirates from the midnight deck; for hours he fell into the deeper midnight
of the insatiate maw; and his murderers still sailed on unharmed—while swift
lightnings shivered the neighbouring ship that would have borne a righteous
husband to outstretched, longing arms ... "

There was enough here to

"split the planets and make an infidel of Abraham".

Also enough to underscore Ishmael's warning:

"To grope down into the bottom of the sea, ... to have one's hands among
the unspeakable foundations, ribs, and very pelvis of the world; this is a
fearful thing."[52]

But then, Melville loved

"all men who dive ... the whole corps of thought-divers, that have been
diving and coming up again with bloodshot eyes since the world began".[53]

And he was firmly convinced of

"that mortally intolerable truth; that all deep, earnest thinking is but the
intrepid effort of the soul to keep open independence of her sea; while the
wildest winds of heaven and earth conspire to cast her on the treacherous
slavish shore".

Yet the soul that keeps "the open independence" of her metaphorical sea, is also
aware of "the full awfulness" of the "veritable sea" which aboriginally belongs to
it". Ishmael, with sombre memory traces history back to the Biblical past:

"the most terrific of all mortal disasters have immemorially and indiscriminately befallen tens and hundreds of thousands of those who have
gone upon the waters; ...
    The first boat we read of, floated on an ocean, that with Portuguese
vengeance had whelmed a whole world without leaving so much as a widow.
That same ocean rolls now; that same ocean destroyed the wrecked ships of
last year. Yea, foolish mortals, Noah's flood is not yet subsided; two thirds of
the fair world it yet covers. ...

86

". . . not a modern sun ever sets, but in precisely the same manner the live sea swallows up ships and crews."[54]

Two-hundred and ninety-two pages later that very fate overtakes the *Pequod:*

"concentric circles seized the lone boat itself, and all its crew, and each floating oar, and every lance-pole, and spinning, animate and inanimate, all round and round in one vortex, carried the smallest chip of the *Pequod* out of sight . . .
   Now small fowls flew screaming over the yet yawning gulf; and a sullen white surf beat against its steep sides; then all collapsed, and the great shroud of the sea rolled on as it rolled five thousand years ago."

Indifferent to men and beast, the sea ruthlessly follows its own course:

"Not only is the sea such a foe to man who is an alien to it, but it is also a fiend to its own offspring . . . dashes even the mightiest whales against the rocks, and leaves them there, side by side with the split wrecks of ships. No mercy, no power but its own controls it. Panting and snorting like a mad battle steed that has lost its rider, the masterless ocean overruns the globe."

"Two thirds of the fair world it yet covers", Melville wrote a few lines earlier, and the proportion is echoed when the ocean is identified with "the dark side of this earth":

"The sun hides not Virginia's Dismal Swamp, nor Rome's accursed Campagna, nor wide Sahara, nor all the millions of miles of deserts and of griefs beneath the moon. The sun hides not the ocean, which is the dark side of this earth, and which is two thirds of this earth. So, therefore, that mortal man who hath more of joy than sorrow in him, that mortal man cannot be true—not true, or undeveloped. With books the same. The truest of all men was the Man of Sorrows, and the truest of all books is Solomon's, and Ecclesiastes is the fine hammered steel of woe. 'All is vanity.' ALL. This wilful world hath not got hold of unchristian Solomon's wisdom yet . . . There is a wisdom that is woe; but there is a woe that is madness."[55]

Thus does Melville's sea symbology allude to the universe as indifferent and dangerous to man. Melville relates this view, which discards religious teleology, to *Ecclesiastes,* that sceptical book of the Old Testament, canonized under King Solomon's name, whose anonymous author he calls "the truest of all men", and to whom he applies *Isaiah* 53:3 ("He is despised and rejected of men; a man of sorrow, and acquainted with grief . . . ") He also calls "Solomon . . . the truest man" in a letter to Hawthorne written in 1851.
   Contracting verses I, 17 and 18 of *Ecclesiastes:*

"And I gave my heart to know wisdom, and to know madness and folly: I perceived that this also is vexation of spirit.
For in much wisdom *is* much grief: and he that increaseth knowledge increaseth sorrow—"

Melville comes to his bitter conclusion:

"There is a wisdom that is woe; but there is a woe that is madness."

That wisdom and woe-begotten madness arising from his "intrepid effort" with "the open independence" of his soul to reconcile theism with awareness of "the dark Hindoo half of nature", determines the character of Ahab.

6. From storm to storm

With his great admiration for the woeful wisdom of "unchristian Solomon", Melville created "moody stricken Ahab . . . with a crucifixion in his face", and "all the nameless regal overbearing dignity of some mighty woe." Not surprisingly, pious Starbuck, the first mate, is scared:

". . . in his eyes I read some lurid woe would shrivel me up, had I it . . . Oh, life! 'tis now that I do feel the latent horror in thee! but' tis not me! that horror's out of me! . . . Stand by me, hold me, bind me, O ye blessed influences!"

And elsewhere he prays:

"Let faith oust fact; let fancy oust memory; I look deep down and do believe."

But this outcry is given a futile ring, when he later exclaims: "My God, stand by me now!" just before the White Whale, with "retribution, swift vengeance, eternal malice . . . in his whole aspect," staves the ship.
No cry for help would ever leave Ahab's lips. He believed that

"the ancestry and posterity of Grief go further than the ancestry and posterity of Joy. . . . To trail the genealogies of these high mortal miseries, carries us at last among the sourceless primogenitures of the gods; . . . the gods themselves are not for ever glad. The ineffaceable, sad birth-mark in the brow of man, is but the stamp of sorrow in the signers."

To this thought Ahab gives dramatic expression, when addressing it to his god:

"Oh, ... thou hermit immemorial, thou too hast thy incommunicable riddle, thy unparticipated grief."

And if the gods themselves are sad, what remains for men? Contemplating and interpreting the carvings on his South-American doubloon, Ahab says to himself:

"From storm to storm! So be it, then. Born in throes, 't is fit that man should live in pains and die in pangs! So be it, then! Here's stout stuff for woe to work on. So be it, then."

Melville, however, is the creator of Ahab and not his model. Taking a secular view of this "stout stuff", he is enraptured by its heroic dimensions.

In Chapter 98, where an epic description is given of how, after the killing of a whale and the trying out and casking of his oil, the whole ship and all implements are "faithfully cleansed" by "the combined and simultaneous industry of almost the entire ship's company", this is how in depicting that struggle "from storm to storm", Melville rouses admiration and compassion for all those who so relentlessly weather it:

"Many is the time, when, after the severest uninterrupted labors, which know no night; continuing straight through ninety-six hours; when from the boat, where they have swelled their wrists with all day rowing on the Line,—they only step to the deck to carry vast chains, and heave the heavy windlass, and cut and slash, yea, and in their very sweatings to be smoked and burned anew by the combined fires of the equatorial sun and the equatorial try-works; when, on the heel of all this, they have finally bestirred themselves to cleanse the ship, and make a spotless dairy room of it; many is the time the poor fellows, just buttoning the necks of their clean frocks, are startled by the cry of "There she blows!" and away they fly to fight another whale, and go through the whole weary thing again. Oh! my friends, but this is man-killing! Yet this is life. For hardly have we mortals by long toilings extracted from the world's vast bulk its small but valuable sperm; and then, with weary patience, cleansed ourselves from its defilements, and learned to live here in clean tabernacles of the soul; hardly is this done, when—*There she blows!*—the ghost is spouted up, and away we sail to fight some other world, and go through young life's old routine again."[56]

A few years later, in one of his short stories, *The Encantadas* (1856), Melville drew another picture of the "old routine", this time not heroic, but absurd and comic. One day he was watching three huge tortoises move on the deck of the ship:

"They seemed newly crawled forth from beneath the foundations of the world ... Their stupidity or their resolution was so great that they never went aside for any impediment. One ceased his movements altogether just before the mid-watch. At sunrise I found him butted like a battering ram against the immovable foot of the foremast, and still striving, tooth and nail, to force the impossible passage. That these tortoises are the victims of a penal, or malignant, or perhaps a downright diabolical, enchanter, seems in nothing more likely than in that strange infatuation of hopeless toil which so often possesses them. I have known them in their journeyings ram themselves heroically against rocks, and long abide there, nudging, wriggling, wedging, in order to displace them, and so hold on their inflexible path. Their crowning course is their drudging impulse to straightforwardness in a belittered world.

... I then pictured these three straightforward monsters, century after century, writhing through the shades, grim as blacksmiths; crawling so slowly and ponderously that not only did toadstools and all fungus things grow beneath their feet, but a sooty moss sprouted upon their backs ...

... But next evening, strange to say, I sat down with my shipmates and made a merry repast from tortoise steaks and tortoise stews; and, supper over, out knife, and helped convert the three mighty concave shells into three fanciful soup tureens, and polished the three flat yellowish calipees into three gorgeous salvers."[57]

Melville here mocks at "that strange infatuation of hopeless toil". Almost a century later, the "old routine" is mythicised and glorified by Albert Camus in *The Myth of Sisyphus* (1942):

"The gods had condemned Sisyphus to ceaselessly rolling a rock to the top of a mountain, whence the stone would fall back of its own weight. They had thought with some reason that there is no more dreadful punishment than futile and hopeless labour.

Sisyphus is the absurd hero ... the whole being is exerted towards accomplishing nothing. This is the price that must be paid for the passions of this earth ... As for this myth, one sees merely the whole effort of a body straining to raise the huge stone, to roll it and push it up a slope a hundred times over; one sees the face screwed up, the cheek tight against the stone, the shoulder bracing the clay-covered mass, the foot wedging it, the fresh start with arms outstretched, ... At the very end of his long effort measured by skyless space and time without depth, the purpose is achieved. Then Sisyphus watches the stone rush down in a few moments towards that lower world whence he will have to push it up again towards the summit. He goes back down to the plain ...

If his myth is tragic, that is because its hero is conscious. Where would his torture be, indeed, if at every step the hope of succeeding upheld him? The workman of to-day works every day in his life at the same tasks and this fate is no less absurd. But it is tragic only at the rare moments when it becomes conscious. Sisyphus, proletarian of the gods, powerless and rebellious, knows the whole extent of his wretched condition; ... The lucidity that was to

90

constitute his torture at the same time crowns his victory. There is no fate that cannot be surmounted by scorn.

If the descent is thus sometimes performed in sorrow, it can also take place in joy. . . .

Happiness and the absurd are two sons of the same earth. They are inseparable." This "makes of fate a human matter, which must be settled among men.

All Sisyphus' silent joy is contained therein. His fate belongs to him. His rock is his thing. Likewise, the absurd man, when he contemplates his torment, silences all the idols. . . . he knows himself to be the master of his days. . . . Thus, convinced of the wholly human origin of all that is human, . . . he is still on the go. The rock is still rolling."[58]

In *Moby-Dick*, neither Ahab nor Ishmael ever share in what Camus imagines to by "Sisyphus' silent joy" at becoming conscious of an absurd fate in a masterless universe.

Ahab seeks to wreak vengeance for the absurd enormity of his own and of all mankind's suffering and strikes out at a transcendental power he presumes to exist and to be malicious. Ishmael, on the other hand, views with compassionate admiration the prowess and ingenuity of the company of men, who jointly and recklessly brave the forces of nature. Old as the routine is, it is not presented as "accomplishing nothing". What becomes clear is that the fruits of the sailors' relentless exertions go to their Gospel-preaching exploiters.

"Not ignoring what is good, I am quick to perceive a horror", Melville writes in Chapter 1. Moreover when describing human suffering, he makes sure that it is demythicized Ishmael rails at, Ahab expostulates about the absurdity of "man-killing" life. But because of its secular presentation, located in specific time and space, this existence, for all its absurdity, seems neither immutable, nor futile.

In Chapter 97, entitled "The Lamp", Melville gleefully remarks:
"The whaleman as he seeks the food of light, so he lives in light. He makes his berth an Aladdin's lamp, . . . so that in the pitchiest night the ship's black hull still houses an illumination."

7. The vast practical joke

Endless repetition is not the only bane of the "old routine". The routine may be old, but the men might never be! They are at constant risk, indiscriminately exposed to hazards that threaten them with "demoniac indifference" whether sinning or sinned against.

The dangers of the whale hunt are eloquently described in chapters 48, 49, 54, 58, 60, 62, 63, 93, 100, 128 and the final three. Ironically barring a direct onslaught by the whale, it seems that the line attached to the darted harpoon was the main source of accidents. It nearly strangled Pip, the Negro cabin boy, when, in his fright, he leapt out of the boat and got entangled in the slack whale line as "the stricken whale started on a fierce run". The "swiftly straightened" line almost choked him by the time it was cut. But there was no time to save Ahab's life when he darted his harpoon in the final encounter, "the stricken whale flew forward; with igniting velocity the line ran through the groove;—ran foul. Ahab stooped to clear it; he did clear it; but the flying turn caught him round the neck, and voicelessly as Turkish mutes bowstring their victim, he was shot out of the boat, ere the crew knew he was gone".[59]

Two-hundred and eighty-eight pages earlier, "for the better understanding of all similar scenes elsewhere presented", Melville devotes a complete chapter (60) to "the magical, sometimes horrible whale-line". When out of use, it is "spirally coiled away" with utmost care, as "the least tangle or kink in the coiling would, in running out, infallibly take somebody's arm, leg, or entire body off". A clear adumbration of what was to be Ahab's fate! Then follows a dramatic description of the line when in use:

> "The whale-line folds the whole boat in its complicated coils, twisting and writhing around it in almost every direction. All the oarsmen are involved in its perilous contortions; so that to the timid eye of the landsman, they seem as Indian jugglers, with the deadliest snakes sportively festooning their limbs. Nor can any son of mortal woman, for the first time, seat himself amid those hempen intricacies, and while straining his utmost at the oar, bethink him that at any unknown instant the harpoon may be darted, and all these horrible contortions be put in play . . . ; he cannot be thus circumstanced without a shudder that makes the very marrow in his bones to quiver in him like a shaken jelly. Yet habit—strange thing! what cannot habit accomplish?—Gayer sallies, more merry mirth, better jokes, and brighter repartees, you never heard over your mahogany than you will hear over the half-inch white cedar of the whale-boat, when thus hung in hangman's nooses; and, like the six burghers of Calais before King Edward, the six men composing the crew pull into the jaws of death, with a halter around every neck, as you may say.
>
> Perhaps a very little thought will now enable you to account for those repeated whaling disasters—some few of which are casually chronicled—of this man or that man being taken out of the boat by the line, and lost. For, when the line is darting out, to be seated then in the boat, is like being seated in the midst of the manifold whizzings of a steam-engine in full play, when every flying beam, and shaft, and wheel, is grazing you. It is worse; for you cannot sit motionless in the heart of these perils, because the boat is rocking like a cradle, and you are pitched one way and the other, without the slightest warning; and only by a certain self adjusting buoyancy and simultaneousness of volition and action, can you escape being made a Mazeppa of, and run away with where the all-seeing sun himself could never pierce you out."

As if all that was not enough to make "the very marrow" in the oarsman's "bones to quiver in him like a shaken jelly", there is another harpoon attached to this line (mark the dramatic escalation in Melville's description):

"It is a doubling of the chances. But it very often happens that owing to the instantaneous, violent, convulsive running of the whale upon receiving the first iron, it becomes impossible for the harpooneer, however lightninglike in his movements, to pitch the second iron into him. Nevertheless, as the second iron is already connected with the line, and the line is running, hence that weapon must, at all events, be anticipatingly tossed out of the boat, somehow and somewhere; else the most terrible jeopardy would involve all hands. Tumbled into the water, it accordingly is in such cases; ... But this critical act is not always unattended with the saddest and most fatal casualties. ... When the second iron is thrown overboard, it thenceforth becomes a dangling, sharp-edged terror, skittishly curvetting about both boat and whale, entangling the lines, or cutting them, and making a prodigious sensation in all directions. Nor, in general, is it possible to secure it again until the whale is fairly captured and a corpse.

Consider, now, how it must be in the case of four boats all engaging one unusually strong, active, and knowing whale; when ... eight or ten loose second irons may be simultaneously dangling about him. For, of course, each boat is supplied with several harpoons to bend on to the line should the first one be ineffectually darted without recovery. All these particulars are faithfully narrated here, as they will not fail to elucidate several most important, however intricate passages, in scenes hereafter to be painted."[60]

And elucidate they do the following two scenes:
   When the *Pequod* gams with the *Samuel Enderby,* Captain Boomer relates how he had lost an arm in an ecounter with Moby-Dick. With his tail the White Whale had cut his boat in two and he was cast into the sea. For a moment, he seized hold of his harpoonpole, stuck in the whale, but then was dashed off by the sea:

"'At the same instant, the fish ... went down like a flash; and the barb of that cursed second iron towing along near me caught me here' (clapping his hand just below his shoulder)."

Again, on the second day of the final chase, it was these "cursed second irons" that presented "a sight more savage than the embattled teeth of sharks":

"Caught and twisted—corkscrewed in the mazes of the line, loose harpoons and lances, with all their bristling barbs and points, came flashing and dripping up to the chocks in the bows of Ahab's boat. ... Seizing the boat-knife, he critically reached within—through—and then, without—the rays of steel; ... twice sundering the rope ..."[61]

After his first lowering Ishmael asks Stubb, the second mate, if "going plump on a flying whale with your sail set in a foggy squall is the height of a whaleman's discretion". Stubb answers: "Certain. I've lowered for whales from a leaking ship in a gale off Cape Horn."[62] Note that the ship is leaking throughout "The Town-Ho's Story", the pumps being worked all the time, all trouble starting when Radney, the mate, maliciously orders Steelkilt, head of one of the whalemen's gangs, to sweep down the planks of the ship, after several hours' "toiling at the pump". "You must know"—Melville explains—that

> "in a settled and civilized ocean like our Atlantic, for example, some skippers think little of pumping their whole way across it; though of a still, sleepy night, should the officer of the deck happen to forget his duty in that respect, the probability would be that he and his shipmates would never again remember it, on account of all hands gently subsiding to the bottom. Nor in the solitary and savage seas . . . to the westward, . . . is it altogether unusual for ships to keep clanging at their pump-handles in full chorus even for a voyage of considerable length."[63]

This demonstration of the unsparing and ruthless profit-making drive of the whaling industry is subsequently, in true Melvillean style, expanded into a symbol of universal implications.

In Chapter 109 Starbuck, the first mate reports to Captain Ahab that "the oil in the hold is leaking" and that the casks ought to be brought up and the leak found and plugged. At first, Ahab would not hear of stopping in order "to tinker a parcel of old hoops" and exclaims:

> "Let it leak! I'm all aleak myself. Aye! leaks in leaks! not only full of leaky casks, but those leaky casks are in a leaky ship; and that's a far worse plight than the Pequod's, man. Yet I don't stop to plug my leak; for who can find it in the deep-loaded hull; or how hope to plug it, even if found, in this life's howling gale?"[64]

But it is not only the odds facing the whalemen that are breathtaking; the exertions they are expected to make are no less so. Chapter 62 elaborates this point:

> "According to the invariable usage of the fishery, the whale-boat pushes off from the ship, with the headsman or whale-killer as temporary steersman, and the harpooneer or whale-fastener pulling the foremost oar . . . But however prolonged and exhausting the chase, the harpooneer is expected to pull his oar meanwhile to the uttermost; indeed, he is expected to set an example of superhuman activity to the rest, not only by incredible rowing, but by repeated loud and intrepid exclamations; and what it is to keep shouting at the top of one's compass, while all the other muscles are strained

and half started—what that is none know but those who have tried it. For one, I cannot bawl very heartily and work very recklessly at one and the same time. In this straining, bawling state, then, with his back to the fish, all at once the exhausted harpooneer hears the exciting cry—"Stand up, and give it to him!" He now has to drop and secure his oar, turn round on his centre half way, seize his harpoon from the crotch, and with what little strength may remain, he essays to pitch it somehow into the whale. No wonder, taking the whole fleet of whalemen in a body, that out of fifty fair chances for a dart, not five are successful; no wonder that so many hapless harpooneers are madly cursed and disrated; no wonder that some of them actually burst their blood-vessels in the boat; no wonder that some sperm whalemen are absent four years with four barrels; no wonder that to many ship owners, whaling is but a losing concern; for it is the harpooneer that makes the voyage, and if you take the breath out of his body how can you expect to find it there when most wanted! ...

To insure the greatest efficiency in the dart, the harpooneers of this world must start to their feet from out of idleness, and not from out of toil."

Nor is that call the only general conclusion Melville draws from the jeopardy into which the whaleboats rush; for:

"the graceful repose of the line, as it silently serpentines about the oarsmen before being brought into actual play—this is a thing which carries more of true terror than any other aspect of this dangerous affair ... All men live enveloped in whale-lines. All are born with halters round their necks; but it is only when caught in the swift, sudden turn of death, that mortals realize the silent, subtle, ever-present perils of life. And if you be a philosopher, though seated in the whale-boat, you would not at heart feel one whit more of terror, than though seated before your evening fire with a poker, and not a harpoon, by your side."[65]

Considering all these things, Ishmael bursts into a hyena-like laughter—in a chapter appropriately called "The Hyena", dwelling on the terrors of whaling, Melville uses black humour to underscore to dichotomy of life indiscriminately blighted by disaster and suffering in a world claimed to be divinely created and governed:

"There are certain queer times and occasions in this strange mixed affair we call life when a man takes this whole universe for a vast practical joke, though the wit thereof he but dimly discerns, and more than suspects that the joke is at nobody's expense but his own ... There is nothing like the perils of whaling to breed this free and easy sort of genial, desperado philosophy; and with it I now regarded this whole voyage of the Pequod, and the great White Whale its object."

When Ishmael asked Flask, the third mate,

> "whether it is an unalterable law in this fishery, . . . for an oarsman to break his own back pulling himself back-foremost into death's jaws?",

Flask assured him, that "Yes, that's the law". Then Ishmael was satisfied that he had "a deliberate statement of the entire case":

> "Considering . . . that squalls and capsizings in the water and consequent bivouacs on the deep, were matters of common occurrence in this kind of life; . . . I thought I might as well go below and make a rough draft of my will. 'Queequeg', said I, 'come along, you shall be my lawyer, executor, and legatee.'
>
> It may seem strange that of all men sailors should be tinkering at their last wills and testaments, but there are no people in the world more fond of that diversion. This was the fourth time in my nautical life that I had done the same thing. After the ceremony was concluded upon the present occasion, I felt all the easier; a stone was rolled away from my heart. Besides, all the days I should now live would be as good as the days that Lazarus lived after his resurrection; a supplementary clean gain of so many months or weeks as the case might be. I survived myself; my death and burial were locked up in my chest. I looked round me tranquilly and contentedly, like a quiet ghost with a clean conscience sitting inside the bars of a snug family vault.
>
> Now then, thought I, unconsciously rolling up the sleeves of my frock, here goes a cool, collected dive at death and destruction, and the devil fetch the hindmost."[66]

8. Hyena chuckle

Ishmael's lugubrious chuckle underlies the novel from the very beginning. In search of an inn in New Bedford, Ishmael is appalled by

> "Such dreary streets! blocks of blackness, not houses, on either hand, and here and there a candle, like a candle moving about in a tomb."

Inadvertedly, he steps into "a negro church", that

> "seemed the great Black Parliament sitting in Tophet. A hundred black faces turned round in their rows to peer; and beyond, a black Angel of Doom was beating a book in a pulpit . . . the preacher's text was about the blackness of darkness, and the weeping and wailing and teethgnashing there."

He finally comes to his inn and reads the words on the sign: "The Spouter-Inn:— Peter Coffin." He thinks the name rather ominous, but then reassures himself by considering that it is common in Nantucket, and "this Peter here" might be "an emigrant from there."

It is with this macabre chuckle anticipating the later "The Hyena" chapter that Ishmael first raises the problem of a divine creation with built in evil. When, trying to find a place to put up at, short of money, freezing and "comparing the gloom towards the north with the darkness towards the south"[67], Ishmael, in sportive mood, pretends to acquiesce in a faulty creation:

> "It's too late to make any improvements now. The universe is finished; the copestone[68] is on, and the chips were carted off a million years ago."

But with the copestone on, there was left

> "poor Lazarus . . . , chattering his teeth against the curbstone for his pillow, and shaking off his tatters with his shiverings . . .
> Now, that Lazarus should lie stranded there on the curbstone before the door of Dives, this is more wonderful than that an iceberg should be moored to one of the Moluccas. Yet Dives himself, he too lives like a Czar in an ice palace made of frozen sighs, and being a president of a temperance society, he only drinks the tepid tears of orphans."[69]

Melville refers to the parable of Lazarus, as narrated in *Luke* XVI, 19—31 also in *Redburn, The Encantadas, Poor Man's Crumbs,* and *The Confidence-Man.* Invariably, he invokes the case of Lazarus when wishing to expose undeserved suffering and destitution.

This theme of a defective creation, "that intangible malignity which has been from the beginning; to whose dominion even the modern Christians ascribe one-half of the worlds; . . . all that most maddens and torments; all that stirs up the lees of things; all truth with malice in it; all that cracks the sinews and cakes the brain"[70], all of which Ahab saw incarnate in the white Whale, is amply elaborated throughout the novel. In Chapter 69, Ishmael reflects on the indiscriminate and "horrible vultureism of earth".[71] Chapter 58 points to "the universal cannibalism of the sea; all whose creatures prey upon each other, carrying on eternal war since the world began"[72], so that Ahab rightly wonders in the final chase "whether these sharks swim to feast on the whale or on Ahab?"[73] and in Chapter 64, the pagan "savage" remarks: "Queequeg no care what god made him shark, wedder Fejee god or Nantucket god; but de god wat made shark must be one dam Ingin."[74]

Of this "universal cannibalism" Chapter 64 on "Stubb's Supper" contains a striking symbol. Refuting the divine argument implied in the rhetorical question put to Job in XLI, 6 regarding Leviathan: "Shall the companions make a banquet of him?" Stubb, the second mate, feasts on a whale that has previously been killed and fastened to the ship, contrary to God's other arguments in *Job* XLI, 1, 2, 7, and 10.[75] During Stubb's repast, in the meantime "mingling their mumblings with his own mastications, thousands on thousands of sharks, swarming round the dead leviathan, smackingly feasted on its fatness ... yet, Stubb heeded not the mumblings of the banquet that was going on so nigh him, no more than the sharks heeded the smacking of his epicurean lips".

Melville reinforces this symbol of "universal cannibalism" and "voltureism" by evoking three other "sharkish" scenes: a battleship, a slave-ship and a meat-market:

"While the valiant butchers over the deck-table are ... cannibally carving each other's live meat with carving-knives all gilded and tasselled, the sharks, also, with their jewel-hilted mouths, are quarrelsomely carving away under the table at the dead meat; and though, were you to turn the whole affair upside down, it would still be pretty much the same thing, that is to say, a shocking sharkish business enough for all parties; ... sharks also are the invariable outriders of all slave ships crossing the Atlantic, systematically trotting alongside, to be handy in case a parcel is to be carried anywhere, or a dead slave to be decently buried;"[76]

or else:

"Go to the meat-market of a Saturday night and see the crowds of live bipeds staring up at the long rows of dead quadrupeds. Does not that sight take a tooth out of the cannibal's jaw? Cannibals? who is not a cannibal? I tell you it will be more tolerable for the Fejee that salted down a lean missionary in his cellar against a coming famine; it will be more tolerable for that provident Fejee, I say, in the day of judgment, than for thee, civilized and enlightened gourmand, who nailest geese to the ground and feastest on their bloated livers in thy paté-de-foie-gras."[77]*

In this context, when bullied about by Stubbs, the negro cook's remark sounds quite pertinent:

"Wish, by gor! whale eat him, 'stead of him eat whale. I'm bressed if he ain't more of shark dan Massa Shark hisself."[78]

But it is tongue in cheek that Melville has the cook sermonize to the sharks and exhort them to "govern" their "wicked nature":

* Note the recurrence of the "ee" sound in the last sentence: Fejee, lean, thee, geese, featest; as if to underscore the comparableness of the two processes.

98

"Your woraciousness, fellow-critters[79], I don't blame ye so much for; dat is natur, and can't be helped; but to gobern dat wicked natur, dat is the pint. You is sharks, sartin; but if you gobern the shark in you, why den you be angel; for all angel is not'ing more dan de shark well goberned."[80]

Which seems to point in the same direction of divinely created evil as Melville's admonition in *Mardi:*

"As well hate a seraph, as a shark, Both were made by the same hand ... he who hates is a fool",

followed somewhat later by this remark:

"Oh, believe me, God's creatures fighting, fin for fin, a thousand miles from land, and with the round horizon for an arena, is no ignoble subject for a masterpiece."[81]

Not exactly Carlyle's exultation in *Sartor Resartus:*

"This fair Universe, were it in the meanest providence thereof, is in very deed the star-domed City of God; ... through every star, through every grass-blade, and most through every Living Soul, the glory of a present God still beams. But Nature, which is the Time-vesture of God, and reveals Him to the wise, hides Him from the foolish."[82]

Melville's approach is more reminiscent of the satirical device of refutation by defence used by Montaigne when writing *In Defense of Raymond Sebond:*

"It is not likely or believable that this mechanism that is the world does not have some traces of the hand of the great architect, that there are no signs in the things of this world that speak of the worker who designed them and gave them form. He has left the mark of his divinity imprinted in his admirable works, and it is only because of our imbecility that we do not recognize them. He himself has told us that he manifests his invisible actions through visible ones.[83] Sebond has worked at this worthy study, and showed us how there is not one piece of the world that denies its creator. If the universe did not bear out our faith, it would be an offense to divine goodness. The heavens, the earth, the elements, our bodies and souls, all things point to that faith; the only question is how to use it all. If we are capable of understanding, the world can instruct us. For the world is a sacred temple of statues, not worked by mortal hands but by the divine mind: the sun, the stars, the waters, the earth, as signs of what can be understood, have been placed there for us to contemplate them. The invisible things of God, says Saint Paul, appear in the creation of the world, reflecting the infinite wisdom and holiness of God."[84]

Elsewhere however, Melville is more explicit. "There! the ringed horizon", on board the *Pequod* the old Manx sailor says. "In that ring Cain struck Abel. Sweet work, right work, No? Why then, God, mad'st thou the ring?"[85]

9. Sunshine

Not only is there "universal cannibalism" in "this whaling world", there also seems to be deceit: the "most dreaded creatures glide under water, unapparent for the most part, and treacherously hidded beneath the loveliest tints of azure."[86]

Throughout the novel, except in the case of the *Jeroboam,* whenever a whale encounter is depicted, the horrors of the scene are intensified by "the contrasting serenity of the weather", for invariably, they happen under a serene, blue, sunlit sky. (Obviously, whales were more likely to be spotted in clear weather.) When the *Town Ho*'s crew first perceived "the snowy whale", they were appalled by the "beauty of the vast milky mass, that lit up by a horizontal spangling sun, shifted and glistened like a living opal in the blue morning sea."[87] "It was a beautiful, bounteous, blue day; the spangled sea calm and cool"[88], when Pip, the Negro cabin boy fell overboard and "the sea ... drowned the infinite of his soul."[89] When one of the sailors fell from the masthead, there was "a little tossed heap of white bubbles in the blue of the sea". When on the first day of the final chase Moby Dick suddenly emerged from under the sea, and his "glittering mouth yawned beneath the boat like an open-doored marble tomb", "his vast, shadowed bulk" was "still half blending with the blue of the sea". On the second day, they were chasing Moby-Dick "through that infinite blueness", when he suddenly "burst into view ... in the blue plain of the sea, and relieved against the still bluer margin of the sky".[90] On the third day the air was "cloven blue", it was "a lovely day again". As Ahab said to himself: "A fairer day could not dawn upon that world. Here's food for thought, had Ahab time to think."

This recurring "contrasting serenity of the weather"[91] indicates Nature's aloofness from human woe: the sun that shines on some thirty pages recalls the indifferent sun that "also ariseth, and ... goeth down, and hasteth to his place where he arose", whilst "one generation passeth away, and another generation cometh: buth the earth abideth for ever"—as Ecclesiastes says in I, 5 and 4.

The manifestation of the indifference of nature to human affairs runs counter to the protagonist, Ahab's belief in "linked analogies" and the "cunning duplicate in mind" of anything that "stirs or lives on matter".[92] Ahab's belief, in its turn, is a duplicate of Emerson's philosophy of nature: "Every natural fact is a symbol of some spiritual fact",[93] Emerson writes in *Nature,* and this in *its* turn derives from Schelling's theory in *System des Transzendentalen Idealismus* (1800): "Jede Organisation in der Natur symbolisiert den Geist. Daher ist jede Organisation etwas Symbolisches."

But underlying the adoption of this piece of German idealist philosophy by Emerson and his followers, was the North-American Calvinist habit of regarding nature, the creation of God, as a kind of sign system of divine revelation. In this sense "the dark side of this earth, ... which is two thirds of this earth"[94] dramatically depicted by Melville, reveals, if anything, a god lacking either omnipotence or benevolence, and calls into question the traditional Judaeo–Christian god image.

By presenting nature as morally neutral, independent of and indifferent or inimical to man, Melville radically dissociates himself from, and, in the context of the novel, condemns those traits of Ahab's character that epitomize the religious and philosophical idealism of Emerson and North-American Transcendentalism.

10. Fishy fundamentals of jurisprudence

With "universal cannibalism" and "vultureism",[95] and an indifferent or deceptive universe in view, it is not surprising that in spite of occasional displays of sportiveness, a baneful atmosphere hovers over the scene throughout the novel. At the outset it forebodes the woe and disaster to come. Yet when those occur, for all their likelihood, they are not inevitable. The dangers of the universe are transmitted and condensed by social factors.

When Ishmael enters the New Bedford Spouter Inn, he is struck by the hoary weirdness of the place. There is an old oil-painting hung on one side, "besmoked and ... defaced", where in the "masses of shades and shadows" a whale can be vaguely discerned "in the enormous act of impaling himself upon the three mast-heads" of a ship. "Rusty old whaling lances and harpoons ... broken and deformed" are hung on the opposite wall. The whole place is old, cold, "dusky" and "dark-looking", with "low ponderous beams above, and ... old wrinkled planks beneath". A "vast arched bone of the whale's jaw" forms the entrance to the bar, where "old decanters, bottles, flasks" are ranged on "shabby shelves"

"and in those jaws of swift destruction,
like another cursed Jonah
(by which name indeed they call him), bustles a little withered old man,
who, for their money, dearly
sells the sailors deliriums and death."

(Written in prose, this is one of Melville's rhythmic sentences.)

The spirit that serves to keep the sailors' body and soul together and help them to put up with their miserable lot is poured into "abominable ... tumblers, ... villainous green goggling glasses" and is quickly consumed when sailors burst on the scene: a whole shipload of them, straight from a three-year voyage, making directly for the bar and not much later "capering about most obstreperously".[96]

In fact the Spouter Inn adumbrates the complexion of the *Pequod,* the whaleship Ishmael is to board, appropriately named after the Indian tribe practically exterminated by the New England colonists in 1637, a feat subsequently attributed by the New England chroniclers to divine providence. That ship will be "long seasoned", "weather-stained" and "darkened", with "ancient decks ... worn and wrinkled". She will have her bulwarks "garnished like one continuous jaw, with the long sharp teeth of the sperm whale", and a tiller "carved from the long narrow lower jaw"[97] of a whale.

Foreboding as the opening chapters are, they are embedded in an ingratiating texture of humour. This rouses compassion and affection for the characters involved in the predicament and reinforces the tragic impact.

There is a slippery* fishiness all over the place. The more so the closer we get to the time of embarkation. Especially on the island of Nantucket, whence Ishmael is to set sail. Using the device of the hyperbole, Melville gives an extremely graphic picture of the absolute sterility of this island that lies just off the shores of Cape Cod, and its reliance on the sea for its livelihood:

> "Look at it—a mere hillock, and elbow of sand; all beach, without a background. ... Some gamesome wights will tell you that they have to plant weeds there, they don't grow naturally; that they import Canada thistles; ... that pieces of wood in Nantucket are carried about like bits of the true cross in Rome; that people there plant toadstools before their houses, to get under the shade in summer time; that one blade of grass makes an oasis, three blades in a day's walk a prairie; ...
> What wonder, then, that these Nantucketers, born on a beach, should take to the sea for a livelihood!"[98]

In Nantucket, Ishmael puts up at the Try Pots Inn, and leaves no doubt regarding its neighbourhood:

> "Fishiest of all fishy places was the Try Pots, which well deserved its name; for the pots there were always boiling chowders. Chowder for breakfast, and chowder for dinner, and chowder for supper, till you began to look for fish-bones coming through your clothes. The area before the house was paved with clam-shells. Mrs. Hussey wore a polished necklace of codfish vertebra; and Hosea Hussey had his account books bound in superior old shark-skin. There was a fishy flavor to the milk, too, which I could not at all account for, till one morning happening to take a stroll along the beach among some fishermen's boats, I saw Hosea's brindled cow feeding on fish remnants, and marching along the sand with each foot in a cod's decapitated head, looking very slip-shod, I assure ye."[99]

But there is more to the seaboard than fishiness. There also are "patrician-like houses" and "flowery gardens". And Ishmael, who in his wanderings, observes in

---

* Cf. Ahab to the Carpenter: "I like a good grip; I like to feel something in this slippery world that can hold, man." *Moby-Dick*, p. 466.

102

the New Bedford Whaleman's Chapel the "bleak" marble tablets commemorating only a few of the "many . . . unrecorded accidents in the fishery"[100] cannot fail to see the connection:

> "New Bedford is a queer place. Had it not been for us whalemen, that tract of land would this day perhaps have been in as howling condition as the coast of Labrador. As it is, parts of her back country are enough to frighten one, they look so bony. The town itself is perhaps the dearest place to live in, in all New England. It is a land of oil, true enough: but not like Canaan; a land, also, of corn and wine. The streets do not run with milk; nor in the spring-time do they pave them with fresh eggs. Yet, in spite of this, nowhere in all America will you find more patrician-like houses; parks and gardens more opulent, than in New Bedford. Whence came they? how planted upon this once scraggy scoria of a country?
> Go and gaze upon the iron emblematical harpoons round yonder lefty mansion, and your question will be answered. Yes; all these brave houses and flowery gardens came from the Atlantic, Pacific, and Indian oceans. One and all, they were harpooned and dragged up hither from the bottom of the sea."[101]

And what did the whalemen get for harpooning and dragging "up hither from the bottom of the sea" those "brave houses and flowery gardens?" What *lay* was their share? "In the whaling business they paid no wages"—as we are informed in Chapter 16—"but all hands, including the captain, received certain shares of the profits called *lays,* and . . . these lays were proportioned to the degree of importance pertaining to the respective duties of the ship's company." Contemporary figures are quoted in J. Ross Browne's *Etchings of a Whaling Cruise* (1846):

> "The captain's *lay* is generally one seventeenth of the whole; the first officer's, one twentieth; the second officer's, one forty-fifth; the third officer's one sixtieth; the boatsteerer's, from one eightieth to 120th; and the common sailor's, from 120th to 150th."

In Chapter 16, Melville gives an impassioned and satirical picture of the monstrous exploitation of sailors in the whaling industry. Through an ingenious pun he also exposes the way in which the Gospel is put to profitable use.

Enlisting on board the *Pequod*, Ishmael encounters the two principal part owners: Captain Bildad and Captain Peleg. In New England, it was customary to use Scriptural names and in Nantucket there were numerous Pelegs, but no Bildads.[102] Peleg's name is mentioned in *Genesis* X, 25, where a marginal note indicates that it means "division". Bildad is one of Job's three friends and questionable comforters, who in *Job* VIII, XVIII and XXV keep mouthing conventional teachings of religious orthodoxy, irrespective of Job's actual plight. In XLII, 7, God repudiates them: "Ye have not spoken of me the thing which is right, like my servant Job".

Both captains were "well-to-do, retired" whalemen, who had worked their way up in the whaling industry: rising from cabin-boy to chief-mate, to captain and finally to ship-owner. Like many other Nantucketers, both captains were Quakers, "the island having been originally settled by the sect". They were, moreover, "fighting Quakers; . . . Quakers with a vengeance".

In Bildad, Melville creates a marvellously chiselled type of the Quaker taskmaster. The characterization is so exquisite, that nothing short of a full quotation could do it justice:

> "For a pious man, especially for a Quaker, he was certainly rather hard-hearted, to say the least. He never used to swear, though, at his men, they said; but somehow he got an inordinate quantity of cruel, unmitigated hard work out of them. When Bildad was a chief-mate, to have his drab-colored eye intently looking at you, made you feel completely nervous, till you could clutch something—a hammer or a marling-spike, and go to work like mad, at something or other, never mind what. Indolence and idleness perished from before him. His own person was the exact embodiment of his utilitarian character. On his long, gaunt body, he carried no spare flesh, no superfluous beard, his chin having a soft, economical nap to it, like the worn nap of his broad-brimmed hat . . .
>
> The space between the decks was small; and there, bolt-upright, sat old Bildad, who always sat so, and never leaned, and this to save his coat tails."

Bildad was absorbed in reading a "ponderous" Bible, when Peleg introduced Ishmael to him:

> "'He says he's our man, . . . he wants to ship.'
> 'Dost thee?' said Bildad, in a hollow tone,
> and turning round to me.
> 'I *dost,*' said I unconsciously, he was so intense
> a Quaker.
> 'What do ye think of him, Bildad?' said Peleg.
> 'He'll do,' said Bildad, eyeing me, and then
> went on spelling away at his book in a mumbling
> tone quite audible."

Ishmael expected to be offered the 275th lay; though "a rather *long lay*", yet it would have been better than nothing,

> "and if we had a lucky voyage, might pretty nearly pay for the clothing I would wear out on it".

But he was not to be so fortunate:

> "Bildad never heeded us, but went on mumbling to himself out of his book,
> '*Lay* not up for yourselves treasures upon earth, where moth—*
> 'Well, Captain Bildad,' interrupted Peleg,
> 'What d'ye say, what lay shall we give this young man?'
> 'Thou knowest best,' was the sepulchral reply,
> 'the seven hundred and seventy-seventh wouldn't be too much, would it?—
> 'where moth and rust do corrupt, but *lay*—'
>   *Lay,* indeed, thought I, and such a lay! the seven hundred and seventy-
> seventh! Well, old Bildad, you are determined that I, for one, shall not *lay* up
> many *lays* here below, where moth and rust do corrupt. . . .
> 'Why, blast your eyes, Bildad,' cried Peleg, 'thou dost not want to swindle
> this young man! he must have more than that.'
> 'Seven hundred and seventy-seventh,' again said Bildad, without lifting his
> eyes; and then went on mumbling—'for where your treasure is, there will
> your heart be also.'
> 'I am going to put him down for the three hundredth,' said Peleg, 'do ye hear
> that, Bildad! The three hundredth lay, I say.'"[103]

And down he went for the three hundredth lay. Nor was this in any way incongruous with the "universal cannibalism" of this God-created earth, or with the fact, that "man is a money-making animal, which propensity often interferes with his benevolence or, for that matter, with "the fundamentals of all human jurisprudence": the "two laws touching Fast-Fish and Loose-Fish".[104]

For, in Chapter 89, a masterpiece in itself, in brief sequences, Ishmael comes to understand that once private acquisition has become the aim and purpose of the whale fishery, it is unavoidable that its pursuit should be regulated by one single consideration: possession. Whales are then bound to fall into two categories, regarded either as "Fast-Fish", or as "Loose-Fish":

> "I. A Fast-Fish belongs to the party fast to it.
> II. A Loose-Fish is fair game for anybody who can soonest catch it."[105]

But then, these two laws seem to transcend the boundaries of the whaling industry, for

> "Is it not a saying in every one's mouth, Possession is half of the law: that
> is, regardless of how the thing came into possession? But often possession is
> the whole of the law. What are the sinews and souls of Russian serfs and
> Republican slaves** but Fast-Fish, whereof possession is the whole of the
> law? ... What is the Archbishop of Savesoul's income of £ 100,000 seized

* Bildad keeps mumbling *Matthew* VI, 19–21.
** Note the alliteration.

from the scant bread and cheese of hundreds of thousands of broken-backed laborers (all sure of heaven without any of Savesoul's help) what is that globular 100,000 but a Fast-Fish? What are the Duke of Dunder's hereditary towns and hamlets but Fast-Fish? What to that redoubted harpooneer, John Bull, is poor Ireland, but a Fast-Fish? What to that apostolic lancer, Brother Jonathan, is Texas a Fast-Fish? And concerning all these, is not Possession the whole of the law?

But if the doctrine of Fast-Fish be pretty generally applicable, the kindred doctrine of Loose-Fish is still more widely so. That is internationally and universally applicable.

What was America in 1492 but a Loose-Fish, in which Columbus struck the Spanish standard by way of waifing* it for his royal master and mistress? What is Poland to the Czar? What Greece to the Turk? What India to England? What at last will Mexico be to the United States? All Loose-Fish.

What are the Rights of Man and the Liberties of the World but Loose-Fish? What all men's minds and opinions but Loose-Fish? What is the principle of religious belief in them but a Loose-Fish? What to the ostentatious smuggling verbalists are the thoughts of thinkers but Loose-Fish? What is the great globe itself but a Loose-Fish? And what are you, reader, but a Loose-Fish and a Fast-Fish, too?"[106]

Aware of cosmic indifference and not mythicizing the "human condition", Melville was quick to perceive that what extends the "horrible vultureism of earth" to social affairs is that all jurisprudence is based on the law of possession.

The impassioned "Fast Fish and Loose Fish" chapter, seldom considered by critics, was widely out of pace with the mentality of most of Melville's contemporaries, spell-bound by the triumphant growth of North-American capitalism. The most eloquent spokesman of the 19th century North-American bourgeoisie, R. W. Emerson, in his essay on *Wealth* in fact glorified what Melville deplored:

> "Wealth is mental; wealth is moral . . . a dollar goes on increasing in value with all the genious and all the virtue of the world. . . . In a free and just commonwealth, property rushes from the idle and imbecile to the industrious, brave, and persevering."

* "The waif is a pennoned pole", which is "inserted upright into the floating body of a dead whale, both to mark its place on the sea, and also as token of prior possession." *Moby-Dick*, p. 389.

106

CHAPTER 2

Striking at pasteboard masks:
Ahab's sound and fury

1. Ahab's "Everlasting No"

Melville calls both Moby Dick and Ahab indomitable.[1] The White Whale would not be a Fast Fish and would break loose from the *Pequod,* and so would Ahab from the owners of the ship. Unlike Carlyle's Professor Teufelsdröckh in *Sartor Resartus* Ahab would not find "all contradiction ... solved" in "the EVERLASTING YEA"[2] of loving God. Conscious of being "madness maddened"[3] Ahab "says NO! in thunder"*—and strikes out.

Disregarding "how many barrels" his action would "yield" and what these would "fetch" on the "Nantucket market"[4], or what the owners would say[5], Ahab, with another obsession in his mind, sets out to take revenge for

"that intangible malignity which has been from the beginning; ... all that most maddens and torments; ... all truth with malice in it; all that cracks the sinews and cakes the brain"[6],

for his own pointless

"forty years of continual whaling ... of privation, and peril, and storm-time"

and for all "the piled centuries since Paradise".[7]

Goaded by all these, Ahab is determined to strike. But in what direction? "I'd strike the sun if it insulted me"—he tells Starbuck. As it happened, the direct insult came from a sperm whale "of uncommon magnitude" and "unwonted power", distinguished by "a peculiar snow-white wrinkled forehead, and a high, pyramidal white hump", and identified in the sperm-whale fishery as Moby-Dick. Upon that whale's white hump Ahab "piled ... the sum of all the general rage and hate felt by his whole race from Adam down".[8]

Ahab had been a-whaling ever since he was eighteen. The shipowners thought very well of him. "Ahab's above the common"—Peleg, in an early chapter,

---

* "There is the grand truth about Nathaniel Hawthorne. He says NO! in thunder; but the Devil himself cannot make him say *yes*. For all men who say *yes*, lie; and all men who say *no*, ... cross the frontier into Eternity with nothing but ... the Ego." Melville's letter to Hawthorne, April 16, 1851, *Letters,* p. 125.

107

explains to Ishmael. An excellent harpooner: "His lance! aye, the keenest and the surest that out of all our isle!"; undaunted: "used to deeper wonders than waves" and "mightier, stranger foes than whales". Ahab is also an absolute master of his men: "Oh he's a hard driver"—the ship's carpenter remarks in a later chapter, and Peleg also describes him to Ishmael as "a grand, ungodly god-like man, ... doesn't speak much; but, when he does speak, then you may well listen".[9]

Even when Moby-Dick "had reaped away" his leg, and Ahab showed signs of moodiness,

> "far from distrusting his fitness for another whaling voyage, on account of such dark symptoms, the calculating people of that prudent isle were inclined to harbor the conceit, that for those very reasons he was all the better qualified and set on edge, for a pursuit so full of rage and wildness as the bloody hunt of whales. Gnawed within and scorched without, with the infixed, unrelenting fangs of some incurable idea; such an one, could he be found, would seem the very man to dart his iron and lift his lance against the most appalling of all brutes. Or, if for any reason thought to be corporeally incapacitated for that, yet such an one would seem superlatively competent to cheer and howl on his underlings to the attacks."

But "the calculating people of that prudent isle" were unaware of the real purport of Ahab's moodiness. Mad as were his "motive and ... object", he had a "great natural intellect", a "predominating brain and heart"; and was shrewd enough to conceal from his employers that, embarking on his last expedition, his "one only and all-engrossing object" was what he told his men when already "plunged" far ahead in "the lone Atlantic": to chase Moby-Dick "round Good Hope, and round the Horn, and round the Norway Maelstrom, and round perdition's flames ... on both sides of land, and over all sides of earth, till he spouts black blood and rolls fin out." And it was just as well that before setting sail he kept his own counsel, for,

> "Had any one of his old acquaintances on shore but half dreamed of what was lurking in him then, how soon would their aghast and righteous souls have wrenched the ship from such a fiendish man! They were bent on profitable cruises, the profit to be counted down in dollars from the mint. He was intent on an audacious, immitigable, and supernatural revenge."[10]

Intent he was indeed, and relentless. When, in a dramatic confrontation, Starbuck, the first mate, virtuously identifying himself with his employers, remonstrates with his captain that

> "I am game for his* crooked jaw, and for the jaws of Death too, Captain Ahab, if it fairly comes in the way of the business we follow; but I came here

* Moby Dick's

to hunt whales, not my commander's vengeance. How many barrels will thy vengeance yield thee ven if thou gettest it, Captain Ahab? it will not fetch thee much in our Nantucket market,"

he meets with Ahab's outright rebuff:

"Nantucket market! Hoot!"

Then, realizing that Starbuck requires "a little lower layer", Ahab explains:

"If money's to be the measurer, man, and the accountants have computed their great counting-house the globe, by girdling it with guineas, one to every three parts of an inch; then, let me tell thee, that my vengeance will fetch a great premium *here!*"—meaning his heart.[11]

Nor would Ahab on a subsequent occasion heed Starbuck's warning that they ought to heave to for a few days to detect the cask from which oil was leaking; and when Starbuck, by way of persuasion, interjected: "What will the owners say, sir?", Ahab burst out:

"Let the owners stand on Nantucket beach and outyell the Typhoons. What cares Ahab? Owners, owners? Thou art always prating to me, Starbuck, about those miserly owners, as if the owners were my conscience. But look ye, the only real owner of anything is its commander; and hark ye, my conscience is in this ship's keel."

And at Starbuck's further remonstration

"Ahab seized a loaded musket from the rack . . ., and pointing it towards Starbuck, exclaimed: 'There is one God that is Lord over the earth, and one Captain that is lord over the Pequod.—On deck!'"[12]

Subsequently, however, temper gave way to prudence, and in order to avoid giving "the slightest symptom of open disaffection", Ahab ordered the casks to be hoisted on deck and the leak searched for.

But he would not change course. "Not reasoning; not remonstrance; not entreaty"[13] would "swerve" Ahab from the "path" of his "fixed purpose".[14]

Nor would the hints, messages, warnings and entreaties that came from the nine whaleships the *Pequod* met on her route.

2. Gamming

"When two whalers meet on any of the whaling grounds, it is usual to have 'a gam', or mutual visit, for the purpose of interchanging the latest news, comparing reckoning, discussing the prospects of whales, and enjoying a general chit-chat," writes J. Ross Browne in his *Etchings of a Whaling Cruise*.[15] Melville, in his definition of the term adds that the whaleships first exchange hails and then visits, and points out that it is not accidental that "of all ships separately sailing the sea" this custom is only practised by the whalers, they being the most sociable, sharing as they do a peculiar congeniality "arising from a common pursuit and mutually shared privations and perils".[16]

Interspersed in the course of the novel, Melville uses these gams as an ingenious device to relate Ahab and his single-minded pursuit to the whole fraternity of the sperm-whale fishery. Against this background, the odd contours of Ahab's character stand out in all the more sharp relief. "Ahab's above the common", Ishmael had been warned by co-owner Captain Peleg even before boarding ship, "he ain't Captain Bildad; no, and he ain't Captain Peleg; he's *Ahab*, boy".

From the very start of the voyage Ahab showed himself "socially ... inaccessible. Though nominally included in the census of Christendom, he was still an alien to it. He lived in the world, as the last of the Grisly Bears lived in settled Missouri ... burying himself in the hollow of a tree, lived out the winter there, sucking his own paws; so, in his inclement, howling old age, Ahab's soul, shut up in the caved trunk of his body, there fed upon the sullen paws of its gloom".[17]

That Ahab's obsession has led to his isolation becomes all the more conspicuous in the conventionally sociable gam situation. "He cared not to consort, even for five minutes, with any stranger captain, except he could contribute some of that information he so absorbingly sought."

From five ships (the *Town-Ho*, the *Jeroboam*, the *Samuel Enderby*, the *Rachel*, and the *Delight*) he does not get such information.

At one gam, the gathering storm prevents reciprocal visits; the wind intercepts communication through loud-hailers and, with ominous undertones, leaves Ahab's bold introduction: "This is the Pequod, bound round the world!"[18] without reply. Three other gams tell us of German ill-success (the "clean" *Virgin*); of French incompetence (the *Rosebud*); and of American plenary success (the *Bachelor*), and present Ahab's and the crew's respective reactions to them.

The messages obtained from each of the whale-ships gammed with ought either to deter Ahab from his dangerous hunt, or urge him in the direction of a more profitable course. But Ahab remains unaffected. Nor will his men take alarm or be diverted. *Moby-Dick* is, in fact, an epic monument to the undaunted prowess and ingenuity of all whalemen. Moreover, Melville uses some of the gam-chapters to extol the superior competence and efficiency of the American whalers over their English, German and French rivals. Seventy years after political sovereignty had been achieved, at a time when the federated states were striving to emancipate their trade and industry from dependence on England, literary manifestations of national pride were both incited and welcomed. In Melville's national assurance there is relish and cheer. It is the triumphant assertion of the ingenuity and daring of the American common man:

> "The English whalers sometimes affect a kind of metropolitan superiority over the American whalers; regarding the long, lean Nantucketer, with his nondescript provincialisms, as a sort of sea-peasant. But where this superiority in the English whalemen does really consist, it would be hard to say, seeing that the Yankees in one day, collectively, kill more whales than all the English, collectively, in ten years."[19]

The chapter on the gam with the *Virgin* describes a race with a German rival. This ship, as Melville points out, well deserved the name of "Jungfrau or Virgin"; she "was indeed what in the Fishery is technically called a *clean* one (that is, an empty one), being so "out of oil", that the captain came over to the *Pequod* a-begging for some to feed his lamp. (On the other hand, Melville names the extremely successful ship the *Pequod* gams with later, where "indeed everything was filled with sperm"[20]—the *Bachelor*.) With back-breaking speed the Americans outrowed the Germans and harpooned the whale they had both been chasing.

The French rivals, in their turn, are not outrowed, but outwitted. Their ship is pertinently called the *Rosebud,* being "aromatic" with the stench of two carrions of whales they had found floating on the sea and had fastened alongside their ship.

Stubb, the second mate, experienced and endowed with daring and initiative, knew that one of the corpses, that of an exceptionally lean whale, if "entirely bankrupt of anything like oil", might "contain something worth a good deal more, ... ambergris." With cunning ingenuity he diddled the French dandy of a captain into letting loose the two carrions; then, swooping down on the lean one, opened up its body with a boat-spade, "thrust both hands in, and drew out handfuls of ... ambergris, worth a gold guinea an ounce to any druggist." Yet the lure of treasure would not affect Ahab:

> "Some six handfuls were obtained; ... and still more, perhaps, might have been secured were it not for impatient Ahab's loud command to Stubb to desist, and come on board, else the ship would bid them good bye."[21]

Nor would Ahab be enticed by the spectacular success of the *Bachelor*. This homeward-bound ship

> "had met with the most surprising success; all the more wonderful, for that while cruising in the same seas numerous other vessels had gone entire months without securing a single fish. Not only had barrels of beef and bread been given away to make room for the far more valuable sperm, ... the sailors had actually caulked and pitched their chests, and filled them; ... the stewart had plugged his spare coffee-pot and filled it; ... the harpooneers had headed the

sockets of their irons and filled them; . . . indeed everything was filled with sperm, except the captain's pantaloons pockets, and those he reserved to thrust his hands into, in selfcomplacent testimony of his entire satisfaction."

What a marvellous picture of the essentials of life being "given away to make room for" a commodity deemed "far more valuable"! Worth remembering in our days of polluted air and waters. Melville, unique in his perspicacity and foresight in the period of the triumphant ascendancy of American capitalism, would, four generations later, have much in common with many a doomwatcher of modern monopoly capitalism.

At the sight of the ship bearing all the signs of rejoicing and jubilation, Ahab stood "shaggy and black, with a stubborn gloom". Without caring even to answer an invitation to board the "glad ship of good luck", he would only ask the "gay Bachelor's commander" about the White Whale:

> "'Hast seen the White Whale?' gritted Ahab . . .
> 'No; only heard of him; but don't believe in him at all,' said the other good-humoredly.
> 'Come aboard!'
> 'Thou are too damned jolly. Sail on. Hast lost any men?'
> 'Not enough to speak of—two islanders, that's all;—but come aboard, old hearty, come along. I'll soon take that black from your brow. Come along, will ye (merry's the play); a full ship and homeward-bound.'
> 'How wondrous familiar is a fool!' muttered Ahab; then aloud, 'Thou art a full ship and homeward bound, thou sayst; well, then, call me an empty ship, and outward bound. So go thy ways, and I will mine. Forward there! Set all sail, and keep her to the wind!'
> And thus, while the one ship went cheerily before the breeze, the other stubbornly fought against it."[22]

And if material success would not "swerve" Ahab, neither would the accounts given by the *Town-Ho* and the *Jeroboam* of disastrous encounters with Moby Dick, their impact on the "ignorance and superstitiousness hereditary to all sailors" notwithstanding.

To many on board the *Pequod,* the story of Radney, the *Town-Ho*'s cruel mate who was carried off by Moby Dick, "seemed obscurely to involve . . . a certain wondrous, inverted visitation of one of those so called judgments of God."[23]

In the gam with the *Jeroboam,* Ahab resists the imposture of a Shaker "scaramouch"* who "had gained a wonderful ascendancy over almost everybody" by posing as the archangel Gabriel and "announcing the speedy opening of the seventh vial, which he carried in his vest-pocket". When in *The Revelation of*

* A rascal, a scamp.

St. John, XVI, 17; 18, "the seventh angel poured out his vial into the air, . . . there were voices, and thunders, and lightnings; and there was a great earthquake". Significantly, the vial of Melville's self-styled archangel, "instead of containing gunpowder, was supposed to be charged with laudanum."* "The sailors, mostly poor devils, cringed, and some of them fawned", before this Gabriel. Living at the time of the mid-nineteenth century religious revivals which swept through the United States, Melville remarks at this juncture:

> "Such things may seem incredible; but, however wondrous, they are true. Nor is the history of fanatics half so striking in respect to the measureless self-deception of the fanatic himself, as his measureless power of deceiving and bedevilling so many others."

Gabriel had pronounced "the White Whale to be . . . the Shaker God incarnated". He was "hurling forth prophecies of speedy doom to the sacrilegious assailants of his divinity", when Macey, the chief mate, unheedful of "the archangel's denunciations and forewarnings", attacked the White Whale "with all the reckless energy of his tribe". But "the luckless mate, so full of furious life, was smitten . . . into the air" by the tail of the whale and then fell to his death in the sea, an accident, as Melville remarks, "as frequent as any" in the sperm-whale fishery.

> "This terrible event clothed the archangel with added influence; because his credulous disciples believed that he had specifically fore-announced it, instead of only making a general prophecy, which any one might have done, and so have chanced to hit one of many marks in the wide margin allowed. He became a nameless terror to the ship."

But not to Ahab. Unperturbed he inquired about the White Whale, at which

> "Gabriel once more started to his feet, glaring upon the old man, and vehemently exclaimed, with downward pointed finger—'Think, think of the blasphemer—dead, and down there!—beware of the blasphemer's end!'"

At which "Ahab stolidly turned aside".[24]

As the *Pequod* nears the haunts of Moby-Dick, she gams with three whale-ships, all bearing fresh scars of recent encounters with the ferocious whale. Far from disheartening Ahab, these only serve to inspirit him. When he speaks with the *Rachel*, a ship "weeping for her children, because they were not",[25] Ahab is "throttling with joy"[26] to hear the captain answer his query regarding Moby-Dick with the unambiguous: "Have ye seen a whale-boat adrift?" Fired with impatient eagerness to come to grips at last with what for him was the incarnation of "all that most maddens and torments"[27], Ahab "but icily" receives the entreaty of the

---

* The most popular narcotic drug of the Victorian era, containing opium.

"stranger Captain" to interrupt the chase for two days and help recover two boats the *Rachel* had lost in their recent struggle with Moby-Dick, with the captain's two sons among their crew.

Standing "like an anvil, receiving every shock, but without the least quivering of his own", Ahab has only this to say: "I will not do it. Even now I lose time."[28] He had "stolidly turned aside"[29] from Gabriel's execrations; he "averted" his face from the beseeching captain. Pity would prevail with him no more than fear.

Wilfully identifying not only his own woes with that one White Whale, but also piling "upon the whale's white hump the sum of all the general rage and hate felt by his whole race from Adam down"[30], Ahab, bent on a personal and single-handed vengeance, paradoxically excludes himself from the community of that "whole race". Yet it is for the "mighty woe" of that race that he, "with a crucifixion in his face"[31], divests himself of all joy ("Gifted with the high perception, I lack the low, enjoying power"[32]) and dashes forth to avenge it in a suicidal assault on what he deems to be the incarnation of its cause.

If the *Rachel's* captain, standing "transfixed at this unconditional and utter rejection of his so earnest suit" is pathetic, so is Ahab in his isolation.

> "Ahab stands alone among the millions of the peopled earth, nor gods nor men his neighbors! Cold, cold—I shiver!"[33]

are his words to Starbuck.

In the course of the gams with the *Delight* and the *Samuel Enderby,* the captains of both ships warn Ahab that what he is after cannot be done. The *Delight,* "miserably misnamed" (elsewhere: "the dejected *Delight''*) had a whale-boat wrecked and five men killed in an encounter with Moby-Dick the previous day, and the "hollow-cheeked" captain, in answer to Ahab's anxious question if he had killed the whale, says: "The harpoon is not yet forged that will ever do that."[34]

The jovial English captain of the *Samuel Enderby* has had his arm ript off by that dangerous "second iron" in a battle with Moby Dick; he now has an ivory arm, matching Ahab's ivory leg. "No more White Whales" for him:

> " 'I've lowered for him once, and that has satisfied me. There would be great glory in killing him, I know that; and there is a shipload of precious sperm in him, but, hark ye, he's best let alone; don't you think so, Captain?'—glancing at the ivory leg."

To which Ahab says:

> "He is. But he will still be hunted, for all that. What is best let alone, that accursed thing is not always what least allures."[35]

3. The wondrous old man

It is in dauntlessly hunting "that accursed thing" that the tragic grandeur of Ahab, "the wondrous old man",[36] lies. This is also where he most differs from his fellow protagonists in his creator's other narratives. Pierre tries to comply both with "terrestrial (chronometrical)" and "celestial (horological)" principles and realizes that: "Lo! I leave corpses wherever I go!"[37] Bartleby "prefers not to" live his pointless, humdrum, scrivener's life, opts out, and in his death sleeps "with kings and counselors", as the narrator remarks, quoting *Job,* III, 14 and referring—in tune with that inquisitive Biblical patriarch and also with the sceptical Ecclesiastes, or Preacher—to the pointlessness or "vanity" of human striving. Billy Budd submits to "this incomputable[38] world of ours", where "innocence" earns "infamy", and "spiritual depravity" is rewarded with "fair repute"; and in conventional fashion blesses the captain who sentences him to be hanged.

"Gifted with the high perception" Ahab's heart was one of those that

> "sometimes condense to one deep pang, the sum total of those shallow pains kindly diffused through feebler men's whole lives. And ... such hearts ... in their life-time aggregate a whole age of woe, ... for even in their pointless centres, those noble natures contain the entire circumferences of inferior souls."[39]

This "moody" captain, this "Man of Sorrows", whom nothing will scare or soothe[40], does not comply, submit or opt out. He defies and challenges. This makes him a hero, however suicidal his act. Melville loves and respects him so much that he must reach for symbols from outer space to find adequate trappings:

> "Ahab, my Captain, still moves before me in all his Nantucket grimness and shagginess; ... I must not conceal that I have only to do with a poor old whalehunter ... and, therefore, all outward majestical trappings and housings are denied me. Oh, Ahab! what shall be grand in thee, it must needs be plucked at from the skies, and dived for in the deep, and featured in the unbodied air!"[41]

No king or emperor Ahab is, but a whale-hunter. Yet his "intellectual superiority", his "mortal indomitableness" and a "certain sultanism of his brain"[42] give him majestic bearing. When Melville jubilantly exclaims:

> "For a Khan of the plank, and a king of the sea, and a great lord of Leviathans was Ahab",[43]

the effect of the anapaestic meter bedwarfs conventional royalty in the presence of the moody, shaggy captain.

4. Blasphemous Ahab

How did this grim, "poor old whale-hunter" become "a grand, ungodly, god-like man"[44], and why was his purpose called "blasphemous" and "heaven-insulting" by Starbuck, his first mate? What "invested" his hunt with a "strange imaginative impiousness"?[45]

> "'Forty—forty—. . .—Forty years of continual whaling! forty years of privation, and peril, and storm-time! forty years on the pitiless sea!'"—

Ahab pathetically exclaims to Starbuck on the eve of his final engagement with the White Whale, looking back on his "whole foregone life":

> "'Aye and yes, Starbuck, out of those forty years I have not spent three ashore. When I think of this life I have led; the desolation of solitude it has been; the masoned, walled-town of a Captain's exclusiveness, which admits but small entrance to any sympathy from the green country without—. . . when I think of all this; only half-suspected, not so keenly known to me before—and how for forty years I have fed upon dry salted fare—fit emblem of the dry nourishment of my soul—when the poorest landsman has had fresh fruit to his daily hand, . . . away, whole oceans away, from that young girl-wife I wedded past fifty, . . . and then, the madness, the frenzy, the boiling blood and the smoking brow, with which, for a thousand lowerings old Ahab has furiously, foamingly chased his prey—more a demon than a man!—aye, aye! what a forty years' fool—fool—old fool, has old Ahab been! Why this strife of the chase? why weary, and palsy the arm at the oar, and the iron, and the lance? how the richer or better is Ahab now.* Behold. Oh, Starbuck! is it not hard, that with this weary load I bear, one poor leg should have been snatched from under me?'"[46]

That "one poor leg" had been "snatched from under" Ahab by Moby Dick's "sickle-shaped lower jaw", when, in a previous encounter, his mind was "impelled" to such "pitches of inflamed, distracted fury" at the sight of "the chips of chewed boats, and the sinking limbs of torn comrades", all in a "serene, exasperating sunlight", that "seizing the line-knife" he "dashed at the whale" . . . blindly seeking with a six inch blade to reach the fathom-deep life of the whale."

After this accident, he at first "probably but felt the agonizing bodily laceration". But during the months of the homeward voyage "Ahab and anguish" lying "stretched together in one hammock", "his torn body and gashed soul bled into one another; and so interfusing, made him mad".

---

* Mark the lamenting dactylic-trochaic meter of the two sentences from "Why this strife" to "Ahab now?"

116

From that time on Ahab had identified with the White Whale "not only all his bodily woes, but all his intellectual and spiritual exasperations". And that made out a long list indeed:

"The White Whale swam before him as the monomaniac incarnation of all those malicious agencies which some deep men feel eating in them, ... That intangible malignity which has been from the beginning; to whose dominion even the modern Christians ascribe one-half of the worlds; which the ancient Ophites of the east reverenced in their statue devil;—Ahab did not fall down and worship it like them; but deliriously transferring its idea to the abhorred white whale, he pitted himself, all mutilated, against it. All that most maddens and torments; all that stirs up the lees of things; all with malice in it; all that cracks the sinews and cakes the brain; all the subtle demonisms of life and thought; all evil, to crazy Ahab, were visibly personified, and made practically assailable in Moby Dick. He piled upon the whale's white hump the sum of all the general rage and hate felt by his whole race from Adam down; and then, as if his chest had been a mortar, he burst his hot heart's shell upon it."[47]*

The Ophites were a second century gnostic sect who glorified Satan for having helped Adam and Eve liberate themselves from serving a malicious God. Melville's reference to them might seem to imply a kind of Manicheanism on Ahab's part.

But when Ahab expounds this "intangible malignity which has been from the beginning", far from being dualistic, his explanation to Starbuck is clearly monotheistic:

"All visible objects, man, are but as pasteboard masks. But in each event—in the living act, the undoubted deed—there, some unknown but still reasoning thing puts forth the mouldings of its features from behind the unreasoning mask. If man will strike, strike through the mask! How can the prisoner reach outside except by thrusting through the wall? To me, the white whale is that wall, shoved near to me. Sometimes I think there's naught beyond. But 'tis enough. He tasks me; he heaps me; I see in him outrageous strength, with an inscrutable malice sinewing it. That inscrutable thing is chiefly what I hate; and be the white whale agent or be the white whale principal, I will wreak that hate upon him."[48]

Actually Ahab's fatal epistemology is a near replica of the philosophy of Carlyle's Professor Teufelsdröckh, who, strongly reminiscent in his views of E. W. J.

---

* Note the heroic iambic pentameter followed by iambic tetrameter in the final two clauses of this passage.

Schelling's *System of Transcendental Idealism*, dresses his Platonic thoughts in a similar garb of metaphors in Chapter XI of *Sartor Resartus*:

> "All visible things are emblems; what thou seest is not there on its own account; strictly taken, is not there at all: Matter exists only spiritually, and to represent some Idea, and *body* it forth. Hence Clothes ... are emblematic."[49]

It should be noted that in Melville's time German idealist philosophy was transmitted to North America through the works of Coleridge and Carlyle.

The direction of Ahab's hints and appeals are even more explicit in the three instances where he either addresses "ye great gods", or "thou clear spirit of clear fire", or invokes that "nameless, inscrutable, unearthly thing".[50]

In all three cases almighty, supreme divinity is involved, upbraided and defied.

It is characteristic of Melville that in his philosophical allusions he mixes Christian doctrine, complete with sectarian and so-called heretical views, Platonic, neo-Platonic, German idealist philosophy, and Greek and Near Eastern mythology. In doing so, he underscores both their affinities and their conflicting affirmations, thus challenging religious idealism manifested in whatever form.

In the dramatic "The Candles" chapter addressing the "clear spirit of clear fire," in the midst of a typhoon, with the "tri-pointed lightning-rod-ends" of the three mainmasts "silently burning in that sulphurous air", and himself standing "before the lofty tri-pointed trinity of flames", Ahab, in the way *Ecclesiastes* does in III, 19–20, when remonstrating about indiscriminate death awaiting man and beast, expostulates:

> "To neither love nor reverance wilt thou be kind; and e'en for hate thou canst but kill; and all are killed."

Then he pays full homage to that omnipotent divine power:

> "No fearless fool now fronts thee. I own thy speechless, placeless power; ... of thy fire thou madest me."

But he inverts the conventional attitude of submission into blasphemous defiance:

> "Thy right worship is defiance ... defyingly I worship thee!"

He also inverts the traditional Judaeo–Christian guilt-ridden humiliation of the individual before divinity into the assertion of the individual emancipated from the tutelage of that transcendental authority:

> "I own thy speechless, placeless power; but to the last grasp of my earthquake life will dispute its unconditional, unintegral mastery in me. In

the midst of the personified impersonal, a personality stands here. Though but a point at best; whencesoe'er I came; wheresoe'er I go; yet while I earthly live, the queenly personality lives in me, and feels her royal rights ... Oh, thou clear spirit, of thy fire thou madest me, and like a true child of fire, I breathe it back to thee ... ... Thou canst blind; but I can then grope. Thou canst consume; but I can then be ashes ... The lightning flashes through my skull; mine eye-balls ache and ache; my whole beaten brain seems as beheaded, and rolling on some stunning ground. Oh, oh! Yet blindfold, yet will I talk to thee!"

But in his address in "The Candles" chapter Ahab does not merely defy the divine principle. He also questions its very essence. He refers to the light symbology of the Zoroastrian religion:

"Light though thou be, thou leapest out of darkness; but I am darkness leaping out of light, leaping out of thee!"[51]

There had been a time when Ahab had himself embraced Parsism, the creed of the Persian followers of Zoroaster, Iranian prophet of the 6th century B. C. The leader of Ahab's private crew of five, Fedallah, too, was a Parsee. Melville probably drew most of his information on Parsism from Pierre Bayle's *Dictionary Historical and Critical*. In his article on Zoroaster, Pierre Bayle, with his usual ingenuity, makes full use of the basic dichotomy inherent in Zoroastrianism's ambivalence regarding the existence of evil. Professing to be monotheistic, the heterogeneous tradition of Zoroastrianism also uphold belief in a dualistic system of a Good Spirit, symbolized by light and fire, and an Evil Spirit, symbolized by darkness, the two contending with each other for the domination of the world. Pierre Bayle argues in such a way as to underscore the affinity of Zoroastrianism with Christian belief, after which he points out the absurdity of either supposing the co-existence of two uncreated, eternal and supreme principles, or of hypothesizing one almighty good God being the creator both of good and evil, for how could "Arimanius, the evil principle, have been produced by a cause infinitely good"? Subsequently he remarks: "The Magi ... differ concerning the manner and cause of the production of darkness; since from light nothing can proceed but light, ... how then was the principle of evil ... produced?"[52]

The incompatibility of an almighty and infinitely good divine creator with the existence of physical and moral evil is argued and stressed by Bayle in article after article. In those dealing with the Manicheans and the Paulicians, religious sects founded in the 3rd and the 7th century respectively, influenced by Zoroastrianism, Platonism and Christianity and upholding dualistic beliefs in two uncreated,—co-eternal—, creative principles, a good spirit and an evil spirit, contending with each other for control over the world, Bayle uses the following stratagem: first he proves that the Manichean–Paulician premise of two principles is logically untenable. Having thus exploded the very foundation of religious dualism and so discredited all its doctrines, Bayle changes position. On page after page there follow endless quotations of orthodox Christian monotheistic arguments directed against dualistic doctrines only to be refuted by Bayle under the pretence of defending the Zoroastrian–Manichean–Paulician dualism view he himself had previously invalidated. The outcome of this argumentation, of course, is the questioning of any kind of divine principle, single or plural.

In his article on the Paulicians, Bayle avails himself of the fire and light symbology of Zoroastrianism. According to Zoroastrian cosmogony, when creating the material world, Ormazd, the good lord of all things, first produced from infinite light a form of fire out of which all things were to be born. In one place, Bayle persistently wonders "how evil came into the world, ... since ... man is the workmanship of a being infinitely holy, and infinitely powerful ... ought not the work of such a cause to be good?" and adds: "Is it not more impossible, that darkness should proceed from light, than that the product of such a principle should be bad?"[53]

When Ahab adopts the same symbology in his speech in "The Candles" chapter, in true Baylesque spirit and manner, he raises the questions of the genesis of and the responsibility for evil.

He then attempts to penetrate the very mystery of "that inscrutable thing", the divine principle:

> "Oh, thou magnanimous! now I do glory in my genealogy. But thou art but my fiery father; my sweet mother, I know not. Oh, cruel! What hast thou done with her? There lies my puzzle; but thine is greater. Thou knowest not how came ye, hence callest thyself unbegotten; certainly knowest not thy beginning, hence callest thyself unbegun. I know that of me, which thou knowest not of thyself, oh, thou omnipotent. There is some unsuffusing thing beyond thee, thou clear spirit, to whom all thy eternity is but time, all thy creativeness mechanical. ... Oh, thou foundling fire, thou hermit immemorial, thou too hast thy incommunicable riddle, thy unparticipated grief. Here again with haughty agony, I read my sire."[54]

Within a few months of writing these lines, Melville wrote to Hawthorne, monologizing as was his wont ("I know little about you, but something about myself. So I write about myself,—at least to you. Don't trouble yourself, though, about writing; and don't trouble yourself about visiting; and when you *do* visit, don't trouble yourself about talking. I will do all the writing and visiting and talking myself."[55]):

> "By visable truth, we mean the apprehension of the absolute condition of present things as they strike the eye of the man who fears them not, though they do their worst to him,—the man who, like Russia or the British Empire, declares himself a sovereign nature (in himself) amid the powers of heaven, hell, and earth. He may perish; but so long as he exists he insists upon

120

treating with all Powers upon an equal basis. If any of those other Powers choose to withhold certain secrets, let them; that does not impair my sovereignty in myself; that does not make me tributary. And perhaps, after all, there is *no* secret. We incline to think that the Problem of the Universe is like the Freemason's mighty secret, so terrible to all children. It turns out, at last, to consist in a triangle, a mallet, and an apron,—nothing more! We incline to think that God cannot explain His own secrets, and that He would like a little information upon certain points Himself."[56]

Ahab certainly would, and in one of the final chapters, after an escalation of doubts and queries throughout the novel, he questions the congruity of divine providence with free will, moral responsibility and the existence of evil. When this happens, devout Starbuck becomes "blanched to a corpse's hue with despair".

As in other similar instances, in this scene, too, Melville accentuates the challenge of Biblical doctrine by mocking Biblical imagery:

"Ahab . . . like a blighted fruit tree he shook, and cast his last, cindered apple to the soil."

Then Ahab blazes forth his woeful questionnaire:

"What is it, what nameless, inscrutable, unearthly thing is it; what cozzening, hidden lord and master, and cruel, remorseless emperor commands me; that against all natural lovings and longings, I so keep pushing, and crowding, and jamming myself on all the time; recklessly making me ready to do what in my own proper, natural heart, I durst not so much as dare? Is Ahab, Ahab? Is it I, God, or who, that lifts this arm? But if the great sun move not of himself; but is as an errand-boy in heaven; nor one single star can revolve, but by some invisible power; how then can this one small heart beat; this one small brain think thoughts; unless God does that beating, does that thinking, does that living, and not I. By heaven, man, we are turned round and round in this world, like yonder windlass, and Fate is the handspike. And all the time, lo! that smiling sky, and this unsounded sea! Look! see yon Albicore! who put it into him to chase and fang that flying-fish? Where do murderers go, man! Who's to doom, when the judge himself is dragged to the bar?"[57]

And it was towards this bar the *Pequod* was heading, with "nearly all Islanders" on board,

"*Isolatoes* too, I call such, not acknowledging the common continent of men, but each *Isolato* living on a separate continent of his own. Yet now, federated along one keel, what a set these Isolatoes were! . . . from all the isles of the sea, and all the ends of the earth, accompanying Old Ahab in the Pequod to lay the world's grievances before the bar from which not very many of them ever come back."[58]

5. Ahab's madness

In April, 1849, Melville wrote to Evert A. Duyckinck:

"I bought a set of Bayle's Dictionary the other day, & on my return to New York intend to lay the great old folios side by side & go to sleep on them thro' the summer, with the Phaedon in one hand & Tom Browne in the other."[59]

As mentioned before, of the many sections of Pierre Bayle's *Dictionary Historical and Critical* that influenced Melville, those dealing with Manicheanism are of special significance. In a chapter entitled "An Explanation Concerning the Manichees" Bayle writes:

"Calvin might thus have defended himself against those who disliked his hypothesis of Predestination; he might have told them, You are preposterously squeamish, after having digested the difficulties of one God in three persons, and those of Transubstation ... Why then do ye attack the mystery of Predestination by human arguments? Why do not ye believe that the power of God extends even to the reconciling the liberty of creatures with the necessity of his decrees, and his justice with the punishment of a sin necessarily committed? Be it how it will, it cannot be denied that the introduction of moral evil, with the doctrines annexed to it, is one of the most impenetrable mysteries which God has revealed to men."[60]

In his entry on the Manichees, Bayle confronts their heretic views of supreme power shared by two principles, a good and an evil one, which "two contrary Creators concurred to the production of man, and that man received from the good principle, whatever good he has; and from the bad principle, whatever he has of evil"[61] with the Scriptural thesis of a single and good divine principle. Here, as in the entries confronting Protestant with Catholic doctrine, Bayle arranges the contrary arguments so that they mutually expose each other's absurdity, implying that all efforts are bound to be absurd that try to reconcile the existence of evil and of undeserved suffering with an omnipotent, good and just divine principle.

"If man is the creature of one principle perfectly good, most holy and omnipotent, can he be exposed to diseases, to heat and cold, hunger and thirst, pain and grief? can he have so many bad inclinations? can he commit so many crimes? can perfect holiness produce a criminal creature? can perfect goodness produce an unhappy creature? would not omnipotence, joined with infinite goodness, furnish his own work plentifully with good things, and secure it from every thing that might be offensive or vexatious?"

Bayle refutes the attempt to find a way out of this paradox through the doctrine of original sin, for

122

"if man were the work of a principle infinitely good and holy, he ought to have been created not only without any actual evil, but also without any inclination to evil, ... hindered ... from sinning, ... determined ... to . moral good".

Bayle expounds the Manichean theory of "two principles" as a seeming solution to the problem, as it provides "an open way to come at the explication of the origin of evil". But the inherent weakness of the Manichean argument is easily exposed even in the light of its dogmatic and inconclusive orthodox refutation, which, in the process, reveals its own weakness. With simulated orthodoxy, Pierre Bayle writes:

"Reason ... can only discover to man his ignorance and weakness, and the necessity of another revelation, which is that of the Scripture. There we find what is sufficient to refute unanswerably the hypothesis of two principles ... We find there the unity of GOD, and his infinite perfections; the fall of man, and the consequences of it. Let any one tell us with a pompous shew of arguments, that it was not possible, that moral evil should introduce itself into the world by the work of a principle infinitely good and holy; we shall answer, that this was nevertheless done, and consequently that it is very possible. There is nothing more foolish than to reason against matter of fact; this maxim, *Ab actu ad potentiam valet consequentia,* is as clear as this proposition, two and two make four. The Manichees were sensible of what I have just now observed, and therefore they rejected the Old Testament; but what they retained of the Scripture supplied the orthodox with sufficient arms against them. And so it was not very difficult to confound those Heretics, who otherwise childishly entangled themselves when they came to particulars."[62]

How those "heretics" "enlarged themselves" is made more explicit in the entry on the Paulicians:

"The Old and New Testament are two parts of revelation, which mutually confirm one another; since therefore these Heretics acknowledged the Divine authority of the New, it was no difficult matter to prove to them the Divine authority of the Old ... According to Scripture there is but one good principle, and yet moral and physical evil have been introduced among mankind: it is not therefore contrary to the nature of a good principle, to permit the introduction of moral evil, and to punish crimes."[63]

Having artfully exposed the absurdity of both the orthodox and the Manichean argument, Bayle winds up his critique of the two doctrines with the following cunning statement:

"Now since the Scripture affords us the best solutions, I cannot be blamed for saying, that it would be difficult to gain the victory over a Heathen Philosopher in this cause."[64]

123

The extent to which Melville was likely to be receptive to Bayle's scepticism can be measured by *Mardi,* which Melville had completed before purchasing Bayle's *Dictionary.* In a discussion, Babbalanja, the philosopher, asserts himself as a champion of reason:

> "Nor is there any impiety in the right use of our reason, whatever the issue. Smote with superstition, shall we let it wither and die out, a dead limb to a live trunk . . . ? Or shall we employ it but for a paw, to help us to our bodily needs, as the brutes use their instinct? . . . Can we starve that noble instinct in us, and hope that it will survive? Better slay the body than the soul; and if it be the direst of sins to be the murderers of our own bodies, how much more to be a soul suicide . . . What shall appall us? If eagles gaze at the sun, may not men at the gods?"

Then Babbalanja gives vent to his speculations:

> "Oro* is not merely a universal on-looker, but occupies and fills all space; and no vacancy is left for any being or any thing but Oro. Hence, Oro is *in* all things, and himself *is* all things—the time-old creed. But since evil abounds, and Oro is all things, then he can not be perfectly good; wherefore, Oro's omnipresence and moral perfection seem incompatible. Furthermore, . . . those orthodox systems which ascribe to Oro almighty and universal attributes every way, those systems . . . destroy all intellectual individualities but Oro, and resolve the universe into him. But this is heresy; wherefore, orthodoxy and heresy are one."[65]

Ahab is no heretic and no Manichean. He accepts the authority of Scripture and the principle that there is but one Creator and Lord of both good and evil. Yet in accepting what is against reason, Ahab fails to do something Bayle slyly warns his readers is essential:

> "All this serves to admonish us, that we must not engage with the Manichees, till we have before all things laid down the doctrine *of the exaltation of faith, and the abasing of reason.*"[66]

In "An Explanation Concerning the Manichees" Bayle ironically quotes Calvinistic doctrines that recommend "the sacrificing of our reason, and the captivating of our understanding to the authority of God with respect to the most incomprehensible mysteries" and warns against examining "a heavenly mystery by earthly reason".[67]

* God, in *Mardi's* terminology

124

But Ahab's "queenly personality" refuses to abase or sacrifice his reason, and therefore his reason clashes with his faith and becomes unbalanced. Melville's reference to the dichotomy between "moral reason" and "heaven's sense"

> "So man's insanity is heaven's sense; and wandering from all mortal reason, man comes at last to that celestial thought, which, to reason, is absurd and frantic",[68]

is a sly echo of what St. Paul says in his First Letter to the Corinthians:

> "... hath not God made foolish the wisdom of this world?" (I, 20)
> "Let no man deceive himself. If any man among you seemeth to be wise in this world, let him become a fool, that he may be wise.
> For the wisdom of this world is foolishness with God ..." (III, 18, 19)

Meticulously careful and deliberate an artist as Melville was, it is no accident that in *Moby-Dick* he contrasted "heaven's sense" with man's "*insanity*" and not *folly*, which would have been the Pauline term in this context. But St. Paul's self-abasing acquiescence could never be Melville's meat. Much rather would he go along with the only writer of the Bible whose authority he acknowledged: sceptical Ecclesiastes. Ecclesiastes would not sacrifice his reason, either, "to the authority of God", but gave his heart

> "to seek and search out by wisdom concerning all *things* that are done under heaven",

only to "behold" that "all is vanity and vexation of spirit". This turns wisdom into sorrow:

> "And I gave my heart to know wisdom, and to know madness and folly: I perceived that this also is vexation of spirit.
> For in much wisdom *is* much grief: and he that increaseth knowledge increaseth sorrow."[69]

Melville reduces these verses of "unfathomable wondrous Solomon" to one sentence:

"There is a wisdom that is woe; but there is a woe that is madness."

Ahab calls himself "madness maddened", and tells the much afflicted blacksmith:

> "In no Paradise myself, I am impatient of all misery in others that is not mad. Thou should'st go mad, blacksmith; say, why dost thou not go mad? How can'st thou endure without being mad? Do the heavens yet hate thee, that thou can'st not go mad?"

125

Melville remarks, that in Ahab's "lunacy" "not one jot of his great natural intellect had perished".[70] The remark that had been made of King Lear also applies to Ahab:

"O! matter and impertinency mix'd; Reason in madness!"[71]

Ahab's madness stems from his attempt to reconcile faith in a divine creation and providence, with his own reason and experience, and it manifests itself, when he tries to act accordingly. His intent is absurd and bound to fail. So is his conduct— to the point of destroying both his crew and himself.

6. Ahab's transcendentalism

It certainly is absurd for Ahab "to be enraged" with and to seek to wreak "vengeance on a dumb brute"—Starbuck calls it "blasphemous"—and to identify the White Whale with "not only all his bodily woes, but all his intellectual and spiritual exasperations".[72] However justified and heroic his protest, it is obvious that Ahab is striking in the wrong direction.

On a peaceful day, Ahab would lean over the deckside and watch

"how his shadow in the water sank and sank to his gaze, the more and the more that he strove to pierce the profundity."[73]*

So would at the outset of the novel, the New York "crowds of water-gazers", whom Melville describes standing along "the extremest limit of the land", "fixed in ocean reveries".—This scene that reminds Ishmael "of that story of Narcissus", who, because he could not grasp the tormenting, mild image he saw in the fountain, plunged into it and was drowned.[74] Lost in pantheistic reveries on top of a masthead, such an end threatens many "young Platonists", who, "disgusted with the carking cares of earth, and seeking sentiment in tar and blubber", enlist in the whale fishery. Melville's warning against the fatal delusion inherent in neo-Platonism and German philosophical and religious idealism, the two sources of Emerson's eclectic philosophy of nature, is quite explicit in Chapter 35, "The Mast-Head", where he relates how a "romantic, melancholy, and absent-minded" young man would be

"lulled into such an opium-like listlessness of vacant, unconscious reverie ..., that at last he loses his identity; takes the mystic ocean at his feet for the visible image of that deep, blue, bottomless soul, pervading mankind and nature; ...

There is no life in thee, now, except that rocking life imparted by a gently rolling ship; by her, borrowed from the sea; by the sea, from the inscrutable

* Another example of Melville's metric prose: the first line is trochaic-iambic, the second: iambic-anapaestic, pertinently evoking first the sense of descent and then that of intent exertion.

tides of God. But while this sleep, this dream is on ye, move your foot or hand an inch; slip your hold at all; and your identity comes back in horror. Over Descartian vortices you hover. And perhaps, at mid-day, in the fairest weather, with one half-throttled shriek you drop through that transparent air into the summer sea, no more to rise for ever. Heed it well, ye Pantheists!"[75]

Ishmael himself once nearly fell victim to such "drowsiness", as he stood at the helm one night and was looking into the fire of the try-works:

"Starting from a brief standing sleep, I was horribly conscious of something fatally wrong. ... Uppermost was the impression, that whatever swift, rushing thing I stood on was not so much bound to any haven ahead as rushing from all havens astern. A stark, bewildered feeling, as of death, came over me. Convulsively my hands grasped the tiller, but with the crazy conceit that the tiller was, somehow, in some enchanted way, inverted. My God! what is the matter with me? thought I. Lo! in my brief sleep I had turned myself about, and was fronting the ship's stern, with my back to her prow and the compass. In an instant I faced back, just in time to prevent the vessel from flying up into the wind, and very probably capsizing her. How glad and how grateful the relief from this unnatural hallucination of the night, and the fatal contingency of being brought by the lee!"

As a counterpart to his warning to "young Platonists . . . lulled into . . . reverie" whilst watching the ocean waters, Melville here issues a warning to those, who, by looking into fire too long, allow themselves to be disorientated by "unnatural hallucination":

"Look not too long in the face of the fire, O man! Never dream with thy hand on the helm! Turn not thy back to the compass; accept the first hint of the hitching tiller; believe not the artificial fire, when its redness makes all things look ghastly.... The natural sun, ... the only true lamp—all others but liars!"[76]

There is a third warning in the book addressed to the same quarters. While baling out the whale's spermaceti, Tashtego, the Indian harpooner, accidentally falls into the whale's head, and almost sinks in the "fragrant sperm". He is dexterously delivered by Queequeg. Ishmael remarks:

"Now, had Tashtego perished in that head, it had been a very precious perishing; smothered in the very whitest and daintiest of fragrant spermaceti; ... Only one sweeter end can readily be recalled—the delicious death of an Ohio honey-hunter, who seeking honey in the crotch of a hollow tree; found such exceeding store of it, that leaning too far over, it sucked him in, so that he died embalmed. How many, think ye, have likewise fallen into Plato's honey head, and sweetly perished there?"[77]

Ahab certainly did not perish sweetly. But the how and the why of his death justify all three of Melville's warnings.

With all his blasphemy and neo-Platonic, Schellingian–Emersonian philosophy, Ahab was also a faithful follower of the Judaeo–Christian tradition in assuming the existence of an "inscrutable, unearthly thing", "some unknown but still reasoning thing", behind "all visible objects". His concept diverged from the Judaeo–Christian god-image only in that he substituted malice, which seemed more in harmony with his personal experiences, for goodness. Accordingly, his relation to this "inscrutable, unearthly thing . . . hidden lord and master"[78] was one of hatred, not of love.

Even in piling "upon the whale's white hump the sum of all the general rage and hate felt by his whole race from Adam down" Ahab was in keeping with Biblical tradition. In the Old Testament several mentions are made of a huge aquatic animal, alternatively translated into English as sea-monster, whale, or leviathan. In *Moby-Dick,* Melville identifies them all as whales, and conversely, some forty times refers to the whale as leviathan.

With the exception of *Genesis* I, 21, where it is stated that "God created great whales" (quoted in the first Extract), "and every living creature that moveth, which the waters brought forth . . . and every winged fowl . . . : and God saw that it was good", and *Jonah* I, 17 (quoted in the second Extract), where "a great fish" had been "prepared" by the Lord to rescue the prophet, all Biblical references to the leviathan–whale–sea-monster represent him as a daunting superpower, whom only God can control (*Job* VII, 12, XLI, 1–33); only God can break his head (*Psalms* LXXIV, 13, 14); wound (*Isaiah* LI, 9); punish and slay ("the piercing serpent . . . that crooked serpent", *Isaiah* XXVII, 1, quoted in the fifth Extract). He is likened to the Pharaoh of Egypt, public enemy number one in the Old Testament context and said to be opposed by God (*Ezekiel* XXIX, 3 and XXXII, 2). In *Leviticus* XI, 12, God will not have the children of Israel eat "whatsoever hath no fins nor scales in the waters" and wants these to be regarded as "an abomination".

Saint Augustine takes special note of this Biblical prejudice against whales. Melville, on the other hand, registers his personal protest against the belief "that all whales always smell bad"[79] and in his *Confessions* writes:

"See now, you have given us for food every herb bearing seed . . . and every tree, in which is the fruit of a tree yielding seed.[80] And this is not only to us, but also to all the fowls of the air, and to the beasts of the earth, and to all creeping things. But you did not give these things to the fishes and to the great whales."

Undisturbed by *Genesis* I, 21, St. Augustine believed this carried the following figurative sense:

"What is meant by the fishes and whales are the ignorant and the infidels."[81]

The whale, playing as it did an important role in New England's economy, could not fail to become a handy symbol in New England theology. Jonathan Edwards, the famous 18th century New England Puritan theologian, wrote about the whale with the rage of an Ahab:

"There are three sorts of inhabitants of this world inhabiting its three regions, viz., the inhabitants of the earth, and the animals that inhabit the waters under the earth, and the fowls of heaven that inhabit the air or firmament of heaven. In these is some faint shadow of the three different sorts of inhabitants of the three worlds, viz., earth, heaven, and hell. The birds represent the inhabitants of heaven. . . . The fishes in the waters under the earth represent the inhabitants of hell. The waters in Scripture is represented as the place of the dead, the Rephaim, the destroyers; and whales and sea monsters that swim in the great deep are used in Scripture as emblems of devils and the wrath of God, and the miseries of death and God's wrath are there compared to the sea, to the deeps, to floods and billows and the like."[82]

Melville could never have read this passage, as it was only published in 1948, together with 211 other entries, under the title of *Images or Shadows of Divine Things by Jonathan Edwards,* edited by Perry Miller. Yet many of the Images are contained in Edward's other works, published during his lifetime (1703–1758) and in the following century, and they probably also went into his unpublished sermons. There is no evidence whatsoever of Melville having read Jonathan Edwards. Yet that celebrated theologian's enunciations were symptomatic of the spirit which permeated Melville's religious heritage.

Speaking of the North American Protestant heritage, it is important to note that Ahab, a Quaker, was quite within this tradition: in an effort to bring home the teachings of Christianity to a people absorbed in the overpowering task of procuring the prime necessities of life in a newly settled continent, American Protestantism was at special pains to relate everyday life and experience to the Bible, by extending Biblical metaphors and parables to the practical experiences of the settlers; and conversely, to relate any occurrence or phenomenon of their lives to direct divine intention. Ahab was specially inclined to this sort of interpretation, as "to any monomaniac man, the veriest trifles capriciously carry meanings".[83]

Moreover, Ahab can be regarded as the exponent of an inverted Emersonian neo-Platonic idealism, or "transcendentalism", as it came to be labelled, in his concept of a divine spirit permeating the world. He believed it to be not a benevolent, but a malevolent spirit, one that he defined even as he worshipped it: "Defyingly I worship thee!"[84]

Like Emerson, Ahab, as we have seen, regards matter as the manifestation of some transcendental spirit, and thinks in terms of "linked analogies" between the two:

> "O Nature, and O soul of man! how far beyond all utterance are your linked analogies! not the smallest atom stirs or lives on matter, but has its cunning duplicate in mind."

Analogies can always move in both directions and can be arbitrarily established. Ahab, with a subjective outlook on life relates everything to himself. This is how he interprets the carvings on the South American doubloon:

> "The firm tower, that is Ahab; the volcano, that is Ahab; the courageous, the undaunted, and victorious fowl, that, too, is Ahab; all are Ahab; and this round gold is but the image of the rounder globe, which, like a magician's glass, to each and every man in turn but mirrors back his own mysterious self."

Believing in an analogical correspondence between the outside world and the human mind, this is how Ahab orders the ship's carpenter to make "a complete man after a desirable pattern":

> "Shall I order eyes to see outwards? No, but put a sky-light on top of his head to illuminate inwards."[85]

Following such inward illumination, Ahab fared no better than either the "young Platonist" falling from the masthead, or than Ismael might have, had he not at the last moment "faced back", or than many others who had "sweetly perished" in "Plato's honey head".

Like the young Platonist, who "takes the mystic ocean at his feet for the visible image of that deep, blue, bottomless soul, pervading mankind and nature"[86], and like Emerson, who maintained that "Nature is the symbol of spirit" and that "there seems to be a necessity in spirit to manifest itself in material forms" so that "a fact is the end or last issue of spirit" and the visible creation is the terminus or the circumference of the invisible world"[87], Ahab regarded "all visible objects . . . as pasteboard masks", beyond which "some unknown but still reasoning thing puts forth the mouldings of its features from behind the unreasoning mask". This obsession proved to be Ahab's and his crew's doom.

Significantly, Ahab, who himself once recognized, as his own puffs "blew back . . . into his face", that he was "ignorantly smoking to windward all the while"; who, "consumed with one unachieved revengeful desire" slept "with clenched hands" and woke "with his own bloody nails in his palms"; who had "created . . . a vulture" in himself, which was feeding upon his heart; who chased the White Whale for three days to get at close quarters with him, and even then nearly missed him, for the whale "seemed swimming with his utmost velocity, ... only intent upon pursuing his own straight path in the sea", while Ahab's ship was inadvertently "sailing in the contrary direction",—Ahab was not killed by the whale. He was "caught ... round the neck, and voicelessly as Turkish mutes bowstring their victim, ... was shot out of the boat"[88] by the line of his own harpoon.

His religio-philosophical delusions waxed into frenzy through his "intense thinking"[89], Ahab fell victim to his own obsession.

7. Providence

"Befooled!" Ahab exclaimed at the sight of Fedallah's dead body pinioned to the White Whale by involuted harpoon-lines, and realizing that the first of Fedallah's three prophecies had come true.

Fedallah, the Parsee, had reassured Ahab that he would not die before having seen two hearses on the sea: "The first not made by mortal hands; and the visible wood of the last one must be grown in America." He also predicted that death could not overtake Ahab ere he, Fedallah, had "gone before" and then reappeared. Fedallah's third assurance to Ahab was: "Hemp only can kill thee."[90]

Ahab himself too, dabbled in oracular ambiguity, when, playing on three different meanings of the verb "raise" (to lift; to restore a dead person or animal to life; to come in sight of something and loudly announce it) and on the equivocal reference of the personal pronouns "he" and "him", as pointing to the South-American doubloon nailed to the mainmast he thus harangued his men:

"Men, this gold is mine, for I earned it; but I shall let it abide here till the White Whale is dead; and then, whosoever of ye first raises him, upon the day he shall be killed, this gold is that man's; and if on that day I shall again raise him, then ten times its sum shall be divided among all of ye!"[91]

Yet, in Fedallah's prophecy, Ahab, in his *hubris,* did not detect the equivocation and exulted "with a laugh of derision". "I am immortal then, on land and on sea!"[92] Macbeth, whose tragedy might have inspired Melville, a great admirer of Shakespeare, was less immoderate in his certainty when augurially assured that

"none of woman born/Shall harm" Macbeth, nor would he "vanquish'd be, until / Great Birnam wood to high Dunsinane hill / Shall come against him."

Triumphantly, he merely rejoiced that

"Macbeth / Shall live the lease of nature, pay his breath / To time and mortal custom."[93]

Though shocked at the way Fedellah's first prediction materialized, Ahab never fully understood the purport of the Parsee's ambiguous warnings. The "hemp"— not that of "the gallows", as Ahab had interpreted Fedallah's augury, but that of the whale-line, made "of the best hemp", as Melville emphatically remarked in the earlier "The Line" chapter—this hemp killed him "ere the crew", or ere himself "knew he was gone".[94] Macbeth, on the other hand, was aware of his imminent doom when he was told that Birnam wood had in fact been seen moving. He then began

> "To doubt the equivocation of the fiend/That lies like truth;"

But when the rest of the weird oracle invoked by the witches exploded, he exclaimed:

> "And be these juggling fiends no more believ'd,
> That palter with us in a double sense;
> That keep the word of promise to our ear,
> And break it to our hope."

Yet even then would Macbeth not yield:

> "Though Birnam wood be come to Dunsinane,
> And thou oppos'd, being of no woman born,
> Yet I will try the last: before my body
> I throw my warlike shield."[95]

Nor would Ahab surrender, when he realized that his stove ship was Fedellah's "second hearse":

> "Towards thee I roll, thou all-destroying but unconquering whale; to the last I grapple with thee; from hell's heart I stab at thee; for hate's sake I spit my last breath at thee. .... *Thus*, I give up the spear!"[96]

In which act he much differs from his Biblical namesake, who disguised himself before going into the battle of Ramoth-gilead, and when accidentally wounded, tried to get "out of the host", but was "stayed up in his chariot against the Syrians, and died at even" and "the dogs licked up his blood", which happened "according unto the word of the Lord which he spake."

This word the Lord spake in *I. Kings* XXI, 19 to the prophet Elijah.

Ahab, king of Israel, had, as narrated in *I. Kings* XVI, 28–XXII, 40, invited God's wrath by marrying out of the faith, a prime sin in an endogamous society, and by worshipping Baal. To bring about his perdition, the Lord, according to the prophet Micaiah's warning, "hath put a lying spirit in the mouth" of four hundred prophets, who then proceeded to persuade king Ahab to "go against Ramoth-

132

gilead to battle"[97]. Unheedful of the solitary warning of the one prophet Micaiah, Ahab fell into the divine trap and met defeat and death as planned by Providence.

Thus Ahab's very name in *Moby-Dick* contains ironic allusion to a deceitful Old Testament god and to the incongruity of divine Providence with responsible and punishable human free will a dichotomy often reverted to by Pierre Bayle in his *Dictionary*.

Whilst working on *Moby-Dick*, Melville is likely to have read these passages. In Explanation Concerning the Manichees, this is Bayle's ironic rendition of Calvin's doctrine:

> "It is true he every where affirms, that nothing is done but by the will of God; and yet he maintains, that the wicked actions of men are so directed and governed by the secret judgment of God, that he has no communication with their vices. The sum of his doctrine is, that God directs all things, by means wonderful and unknown to us, to what end he pleases, so that his eternal will is the first cause of all things. And he confesses it to be an incomprehensible mystery, that God should will what to us appears unreasonable; and nevertheless he affirms, that we are not to enquire too curiously or audaciously into his conduct, since the judgements of God are a profound abyss, and that it is better to adore with all reverence the mysteries and secrets which exceeded our capacity, than to scan them, or intrude too far into them. You see how he advises us not to approach this abyss, but with a spirit of submission and reverence for this great and incomprehensible mystery."[98]

Whatever Melville approached this mystery with, it certainly was neither submission, nor reverence, but much rather impish mockery:

> "Doubtless, my going on this whaling voyage, formed part of the grand programme of Providence that was drawn up a long time ago."

Ishmael observes in the opening chapter, and then reflects:

> "Now that I recall all the circumstances, I think I can see a little into the springs and motives which being cunningly presented to me under various disguises, induced me to set about performing the part I did, besides cajoling me into the delusion that it was a choice resulting from my own unbiased freewill and discriminating judgment."

When it comes to selecting the whaling craft to sign on with, Ishmael is asked by his cannibal friend, Queequeg, to decide for both of them. This, Queequeg explained, was the desire of Yojo, his self-made "black little god":

"Yojo earnestly enjoined that the selection of the ship should rest wholly with me, inasmuch as Yojo purposed befriending us; and, in order to do so, had already pitched upon a vessel, which, if left to myself, I, Ishmael, should infallibly light upon, for all the world as though it had turned out by chance; and in that vessel I must immediately ship myself, for the present irrespective of Queequeg.

... in many things, Queequeg placed great confidence in the excellence of Yojo's judgment and surprising forecast of things; and cherished Yojo with considerable esteem, as a rather good sort of god, who perhaps meant well enough upon the whole, but in all cases did not succeed in his benevolent designs."[99]

This certainly was written with tongue in cheek. But elsewhere a more sombre note underlies the apparent mirth: "Ha! ha! ha! ha!"—Stubb, the jolly and commonsensical second mate begins his soliloquy and then explains the cause of his hilarity:

"I've been thinking over it ever since, and that ha, ha's the final consequence. Why so? Because a laugh's the wisest, easiest answer to all that's queer; and come what will, one comfort's always left—that unfailing comfort is, it's all predestinated. ... I know not all that may be coming, but be it what it will, I'll go to it laughing. Such a waggish leering as lurks in all your horribles! I feel funny. Fa, la! lirra, skirra! What's my juicy little pear at home doing now? Crying its eyes out?—Giving a party to the last arrived harpooneers, I dare say, gay as a frigate's pennant, and so am I—fa, la! lirra, skirra!"[100]

Most often, however, divine providence and predestination are related to tragedy in a grim style weighted with ominous past participles, such as "fated", "doomed", and "predestinated".

Radney, the vicious "predestinated mate" of "The Town-Ho's Story", was from the start "doomed and made mad"; "a strange fatality pervades" that whole story of cruelty and revenge, as if it had been "verily mapped out before the world itself was charted." The *Pequod* "duly" gammed with the *Jungfrau* on the "predestinated day". By the second day of the final chase, it seemed that the crew had their souls "snatched" by "the hand of Fate, ... and ... enslaved ... to the race" and "all the spars" were "in full bearing of mortals, ready and ripe for their fate". The *Pequod* herself was a "predestinated", "doomed" and "fated" craft.

Underscoring the paradox involved, in two instances predestination is referred to by a present participle. In "The Town-Ho's Story", when Steelkilt was just on the point of killing Radney, the first mate, "in the *fore-ordaining** soul of Steelkilt, the mate was already stark and stretched as a corpse, with his forehead crushed

* My italics

134

in". The other predestinating agent is the White Whale's head, as it staves the *Pequod:*

> "The Whale, ... from side to side strangely vibrating his predestinating head, sent a broad band of overspreading semicircular foam before him as he rushed. Retribution, swift vengeance, eternal malice were in his whole aspect, and spite of all that mortal man could do, the solid white buttress of his forehead smote the ship's starboard bow, till men and timbers reeled."[101]

But predestination and Providence are perhaps most dramatically called to account in Pip's tragedy.

Scared by the recklessness of the whale-chase, Pip jumped out of the boat, but was saved by Stubb and warned that he would not be picked up a second time.

> "But we are all in the hands of the Gods; and Pip jumped again ... Alas! Stubb was but too true to his word,"

and turned his "inexorable back" upon Pip, who was left in the "intense concentration of self in the middle of ... a heartless immensity". "By the merest chance" he was rescued by the ship, "but from that hour the little negro went about the deck an idiot; such, at least, they said he was. The sea had jeeringly kept his finite body up, but drowned the infinite of his soul." For that very reason Ahab calls Pip "holiness" and exclaims:

> "Oh, ye frozen heavens! look down here. Ye did beget this luckless child, and have abandoned him, ye creative libertines."[102]

Melville did not attempt to resolve the paradox of God's children suffering and sinning under His Providence, but he passionately dramatized this incongruity in Ahab's character and absurd pursuit.

Paradoxically, Ahab believed in the predetermining power of that "inscrutable, unearthly thing" yet challenged, defied and "pitted himself ... against it". On the other hand he confirmed his own authority by relating it to predestinating Providence:

> "There is one God that is Lord over the earth, and one Captain that is lord over the Pequod.—On deck!"

he commanded Starbuck, when that mate tried to persuade him to heave to and search for a suspected leak. And when, in the final chase, the first mate implored Ahab, "in Jesus' name" to stop it:

> "Never, never wilt thou capture him, old man ... Impiety and blasphemy to hunt him more!"

135

Ahab retorted with the self-righteousness of a Cromwell:

> "Ahab is for ever Ahab, man. This whole act's immutably decreed. 'Twas rehearsed by thee and me a billion years before this ocean rolled. Fool! I am the Fates' lieutenant; I act under orders. Look thou, underling! that thou obeyest mine."[103]

Ahab's conviction prompted him to his own and his company's pointless destruction. Was that irremediably foreordained? Or was it rather Ahab's belief that it was, that caused his miscarriage? Dangerous, as whaling was, did not faith in the divine direction of the world prod Ahab, in his defiance, recklessly to enhance the hazards? And had he baptized his harpoon "in nomine patris" instead of "in nomine diaboli"[104], would his enterprise, in the context of the novel, have been less absurd, or fatal?

8. Indifferent as his God

"No thanks, but curses, will you get for your earnestness."—King Media tells Babbalanja, the philosopher, in *Mardi*.—"You yourself you harm most. Why not take creeds as they come? It is not so hard to be persuaded; never mind about believing."

"True, my lord;"—Babbalanja answers—"not very hard; no act is required; only passiveness. Stand still and receive. Faith is to the thoughtless, doubts to the thinker."

"Then, why think at all?"—King Media asks. "Is it not better for you mortals to clutch error as in a vice, than have your fingers meet in your hand?* And to what end your eternal inquisitions? You have nothing to substitute. You say all is a lie; then out with the truth."

But Babbalanja, no more than Melville, would "out with the truth":

"Ah! My lord, think not that in aught I've said . . . I would assert any wisdom of my own. I but fight against the armed and crested Lies of Mardi, that like a host, assail me. I am stuck full of darts; but tearing them from out me, gasping, I discharge them whence they come."

Himself doing the same, Melville left more questions than answers. Exposing the absurdity of Ahab's Judaeo–Christian theism reinforced by neo-Platonic and German philosophical idealism, and the disaster it might lead to if taken to its logical conclusion, he never substituted any other philosophy for it. "My lord!"—Babbalanja tells King Media—sick with the spectacle of the madness of men, and broken with spontaneous doubts, I sometimes see but two things in all Mardi to believe:—that I myself exist, and that I can most happily, or least miserably exist,

---

* Cf. "He sleeps with clenched hands; and wakes with his own bloody nails in his palms." (Referring to Ahab) *Moby-Dick*, p. 199.

by the practice of righteousness. All else is in the clouds; and naught else may I learn, till the firmament be split from horizon to horizon."[105]

Melville does not deny the existence of a divinity. But in his narrative he does not hypothesize it either. His theism is ambivalent, and his references to a potential divine power indicate that he believes it would be morally indifferent, unrevealed and unknowable to man. This leaves "chance, free will, and necessity—nowise incompatible—all interweavingly working together".[106]

The final catastrophe, when the *Pequod,* together with her crew is caught up in a vortex and sinks to the bottom of the ocean, takes place amidst universal indifference, with "the great shroud of the sea" rolling on "as it rolled five thousand years ago".

Foreshadowing this event, the sight of innocent Pip, the cabin boy, nearly drowning, makes the author wonder, if human reason and "heaven's sense" did not contradict and mutually refute each other, driving man eventually to feel "uncompromised, indifferent as his God".[107]

The moral indifference of divine power and of the universe is also hinted at in attributes ascribed to the ship's carpenter and to the whale, and in the very blankness of "the Albino whale".

The whole of Chapter 107, entitled "The Carpenter", is undiluted reference to divinity and, with all its intricate complexities, worth a special study:

> "This carpenter was prepared at all points, and alike indifferent and without respect in all. ... remarkable ... for a certain impersonal stolidity ... impersonal, I say;* for it so shaded off into the surrounding infinite of things, that it seemed one with the general stolidity discernible in the whole visible world; which while pauselessly active in uncounted modes, still eternally holds its peace, and ignores you, though you dig foundations for cathedrals. Yet was this half-horrible stolidity in him, involving, too, as it appeared, an all-ramifying heartlessness;**—yet was it oddly dashed at times, with an old, crutch-like, antediluvian, wheezing humorousness;*** not unstreaked now and then with a certain grizzled wittiness; such as might have served to pass the time during the midnight watch on the bearded forecastle of Noah's ark. ... He was a stript abstract; an unfractioned integral; uncompromised as a new-born babe; ... You might almost say, that this strange uncompromised-ness**** in him involved a sort of unintelligence; for in his numerous trades, he did not seem to work so much by reason or by instinct, or simply because he had been tutored to it, or by any intermixture of all these, even or uneven; but merely by a kind of deaf and dumb, spontaneous literal process."

* Cf. Ahab's exclamation: "In the midst of the personified impersonal, a personality stands here." (p. 500.)
** Cf. the "heartless immensity" of the ocean, p. 159.
*** Cf. Chapter 49, "The Hyena".
**** Cf. "uncompromised, indifferent as his God." (p. 413).

137

Ahab tells him that he is "as unprincipled as the gods, and as much of a jack-of-all-trades". To this the carpenter answers with a meaningful pun: "But I do not mean anything, sir." And adds with Biblical exactitude: "I do as I do."—a clear replica of God's self introduction to Moses in *Exodus* III, 14: "I AM THAT I AM." Ahab duly remarks: "The gods again."[108]

When Moby Dick first comes into the view of the *Pequod*'s crew, "not Jove, not that great majesty Supreme! did surpass the glorified White Whale as he so divinely swam".

Previously, Melville devotes seven consecutive chapters (74–80) to describe the "predestinating" head of the whale. He established that the whale has "no external nose"—a sly hint at God's taunting question regarding Leviathan in *Job* XLI, 2: "Canst thou put an hook into his nose?"—and that "his eyes and ears are at the sides of his head, nearly one third of his entire length from the front". Nor are there any bones in the head, "so that this whole enormous boneless mass is as one wad". Therefore: "the front of the Sperm Whale's head is a dead, blind wall, without a single organ or tender prominence of any sort whatsoever" . . . and it is unlikely "that any sensation lurks in it".

Having said this, three chapters later Melville asserts: "in the great Sperm Whale, this high and mighty god-like dignity inherent in the brow is so immensely amplified, that gazing on it, in that full front view, you feel the Deity and the dread powers more forcibly than in beholding any other object in living nature." But nothing "in that full front view" is seen by the whale, as "from this peculiar sideway position of the whale's eyes, it is plain that he can never see an object which is exactly ahead". Radney, "the predestinated mate" of "The Town-Ho's Story", knew this, for when tossed by the sea to the flank of the White Whale, he was "wildly seeking to remove himself from the eye of Moby Dick". And in the final chase of Moby Dick, Ahab intended to pull straight to the Whale's forehead for "such a course excludes the coming onset from the Whale's sidelong vision".

Completing the delineation of the divine sublimity of the sperm whale's head, Melville observes:

> "You see no one point precisely: not one distinct feature is revealed; no nose, eyes, ears, or mouth; no face; he has none, proper; nothing but that one broad firmament of a forehead, pleated with riddles; dumbly lowering with the doom of boats, and ships, and men."[109]

Reflecting the moral indifference of the universe, the blind and dumb obtuseness of the whale's forehead is underscored and made more hideous by "the visible absence of color".

In his chapter on "The Whiteness of the Whale" Melville enumerates various contrary interpretations of whiteness by different social conventions. In the longest period of the novel, containing 15 clauses and 460 words, he gives a long list of the uses of white to symbolize gladness, innocence, honour, justice, royal and imperial majesty, the white man's "ideal mastership over every dusky tribe" and "divine spotlessness and power" in the "higher mysteries of the most august religions", like those of "the Persian fire worshippers, . . . the Greek mythologies, . . . the noble Iroquois, . . . all Christian priests, . . . the Romish faith", and ends it with a sudden anticlimax:

> "though among the holy pomps of the Romish faith, white is specially employed in the celebration of the Passion of our Lord; though in the Vision of St. John, white robes are given to the redeemed, and the four-and-twenty elders stand clothed in white before the great white throne, and the Holy One that sitteth there white like wool; yet for all these accumulated associations, with whatever is sweet, and honorable, and sublime, there yet lurks an elusive something in the innermost idea of this hue, which strikes more of panic to the soul than that redness which affrights in blood."

Here follow six pages of examples, where whiteness seems "ghastly", "abhorrent", "more loathsome than terrific", hideous, appalling, spectral, like in the cases of "the white-shrouded bear or shark", "the albatross", "the Albino man", "the dead", etc.

Winding up, Melville unites the two contrary interpretations of whiteness in a symbol that deftly perpetuates the ambiguity:

> "But thou sayest, methinks this white-lead chapter about whiteness is but a white flag hung out from a craven soul; thou surrenderest to a hypo, Ishmael."

In conclusion Melville tries to find the reason why whiteness "is at once the most meaning symbol of spiritual things, nay, the very veil of the Christian's Deity; and yet should be as it is, the intensifying agent in things the most appalling to mankind."

> "Is it"—he wonders—"that by its indefiniteness it shadows forth the heartless voids and immensities* of the universe, and thus stabs us from behind with the thought of annihilation, when beholding the white depths of the milky way?"[110]

Five or six years after having written this, in November, 1856, on his way to the Middle East, Melville visited Hawthorne, who was then American consul in Liverpool. This is how Hawthorne recorded this meeting in his journal:

> ". . . We took a pretty long walk together, and sat down in a hollow among the sand hills . . . and smoked a cigar. Melville, as he always does, began to reason of Providence and futurity, and of everything that lies beyond human

---

* Cf. the "heartless immensity" of the ocean, (p. 159) and the carpenter's "heartlessness", (p. 166).

ken, and informed me that he had 'pretty much made up his mind to be annihilated;' but still he does not seem to rest in that anticipation; and, I think, will never rest until he gets hold of a definite belief. It is strange how he persists—and has persisted ever since I knew him, and probably long before—in wandering to and fro over these deserts, as dismal and monotonous as the sand hills amid which we were sitting. He can neither believe, nor be comfortable in his unbelief; and he is too honest and courageous not to try to do one or the other."[111]

Previously, in 1849, Melville had written in *Mardi:* "Eternity is not ours by right; and, alone, unrequited sufferings here, form no title thereto, unless resurrections are reserved for maltreated brutes. Suffering is suffering; be the sufferer man, brute, or thing."[112] *In Moby-Dick,* Father Mapple ended his sermon on a similar note: "O, Father!—. . . I have striven to be Thine, more than to be this world's, or mine own. Yet this is nothing; I leave eternity to Thee; for what is man that he should live out the lifetime of his God?"

When Melville was writing *Moby-Dick,* ready "to be annihilated", he seems to have been aware of the "dumb blankness" not only in the sperm-whale's forehead, but in the universe as well. Moreover, he had the courage to say what he saw, as did Pip, emerging from the "heartless immensity" of the ocean, "wherefore his shipmates called him mad".[113] So was Melville regarded by several of his contemporary critics.

Yet all he did was merely to reject "colouring glasses"; for

"is it, that as in essence whiteness is not so much a color as the visible absence of color, and at the same time the concrete of all colors; is it for these reasons that there is such a dumb blankness, full of meaning, in a wide landscape of snows—a colorless, all-color of atheism from which we shrink? And when we consider that other theory of the natural philosophers, that all other earthly hues . . . are but subtile deceits, not actually inherent in substances, but only laid on from without; . . . that . . . light, for ever remains white or colorless in itself, and if operating without medium upon matter, would touch all objects, even tulips and roses, with its own blank tinge—pondering all this, the palsied universe lies before us a leper; and like wilful travellers in Lapland, who refuse to wear colored and coloring glasses upon their eyes, so the wretched infidel gazes himself blind at the monumental white shroud that wraps all the prospect around him. And of all these things the Albino whale was the symbol. Wonder ye then at the fiery hunt?"[114]

Melville faced up to the implications of a morally blank universe. The nonexistence of divine providence was one of them. An Epicurean denial of life after death was another. But equally implied was, that Ahab's disastrous chase in order to strike at what he believed to be beyond the pasteboard mask of the White Whale was void, pointless and futile.

9. The Voice of God

"Pyramidical silence" is another aspect through which Melville relates the whale to divinity:

> "had the great Sperm Whale been known to the young Orient World, he would have been deified by their child-magian thoughts. They deified the crocodile of the Nile, because the crocodile is tongueless; and the Sperm Whale has no tongue, or at least it is so exceedingly small, as to be incapable of protrusion."

Another chapter explains that the whale's windpipe

> "solely opens into the tube of his spouting canal", which "is furnished with a sort of locks (that open and shut) for the downward retention of air or the upward exclusion of water, therefore the whale has no voice;* unless you insult him by saying, that when he so strangely rumbles, he talks through his nose. But then again, what has the whale to say?"

Ahab acknowledges the "speechless, placeless power" of the "clear spirit of clear fire"[115] whom he defyingly worships, but Pierre is more perplexed. Lying under a huge "mass of rock", which he had named the "Terror Stone", he exclaims:

> "'. . . if to vow myself all Virtue's and all Truth's, be but to make a trembling, distrusted slave of me; if Life is to prove a burden I can not bear without ignominious cringings; if indeed our actions are all foreordained, and we are Russian serfs to Fate; if invisible devils do titter at us when we most nobly strive; if Life can be a cheating dream, and Virtue as unmeaning and unsequeled with any blessing as the midnight mirth of wine; if by sacrificing myself for Duty's sake, my own mother re-sacrifices me; if Duty's self be but a bugbear, and all things are allowable and unpunishable to man;—then do thou, Mute Massiveness, fall on me! Agnes thou hast waited; and if these things be thus, then wait no more; for whom better canst thou crush than him who now lies here invoking thee?'
> A down-darting bird, all song, swiftly lighted on the unmoved and eternally immovable balancings of the Terror Stone, and cheerfully chirped to Pierre. . . . slowly Pierre crawled forth, and stood haughtily upon his feet, as he owed thanks to none, and went his moody way."

---

* With all due respect to Melville's symbol, one should be aware that it has been recently found that the whale does communicate with other members of the species. His beautiful baritone has been recorded and its frequency made audible to human ears.

Later in *Pierre* Melville is quite explicit:

> "Silence is the general consecration of the universe. Silence is the invisible laying on of the Divine Pontiff's hands upon the world. Silence is at once the most harmless and the most awful thing in all nature. It speaks of the Reserved Forces of Fate. Silence is the only Voice of our God."[116]

10. Undecipherable hieroglyphics

Divinely silent and indifferent to human affairs, the whale, as presented by Melville, is also "inscrutable".

The "mystic-marked whale remains undecipherable". "Champollion deciphered the wrinkled granite hieroglyphics", but how could "unlettered Ishmael hope to read" the hieroglyphical marks of the sperm whale's brow, as long as "there is no Champollion to decipher the Egypt of every man's and every being's face"?

Melville's "hieroglyphics" imply that both divine and earthly truth are ultimately unknowable to man. They can only be approached, never reached.* But in one instance he infers the former from the latter, with a somewhat unorthodox twist. At the end of his chapter on "The Tail" of the whale, after having analysed every bit of it, he exclaims:

> "Dissect him how I may, then, I but go skin deep; I know him not, and never will. But if I know not even the tail of this whale, how understand his head? much more, how comprehend his face, when face he has none? Thou shalt see my back parts, my tail, he seems to say, but my face shall not be seen. But I cannot completely make out his back parts; and hint what he will about his face, I say again he has no face."[117]

Here Melville follows the sly reasoning of Sir Thomas Browne, who in his *Religio Medici* writes:

> "Our understanding is dimmer then Moses' eye; we are ignorant of the backparts of God and the lower side of his divinity; therefore to pry into the maze of his counsels is not only folly in man, but presumption even in angels. There is no thread or line to guide us in that labyrinth."[118]

---

* Cf. "And since Oro is past finding out, and mysteries ever open into mysteries beyond; so, though these beings will for aye progress in wisdom and in good; yet will they never gain a fixed beatitude." (*Mardi*, p. 634.)

"Fellow-men; the ocean we would sound is unfathomable; and however much we add to our line, when it is out, we feel not the bottom." (*Mardi*, pp. 576-7.)

142

Both passages refer to *Exodus* XXXIII, 20, 22 and 23, where the Lord tells Moses:

> "Thou canst not see my face: for there shall no man see me, and live. . . .
> And . . . I will put thee in a clift of the rock, and will cover thee with my hand while I pass by:
> And I will take away mine hand, and thou shalt see my back parts: but my face shall not be seen."

The latter verse was put to good use by St. Paul in arguing the possibility of knowing God, in *Romans*, I, 20:

> "For the invisible things of him from the creation of the world are clearly seen, being understood by the things that are made, *even* his eternal power and Godhead."

When Calvin referred to the same *Exodus* verse, he interpreted it as setting forth the limits of man's ability to know God. Melville probably read Pierre Bayle's version of Calvin's thesis:

> "The Mysteries of God belong unto God, but the things which are revealed, to us and our children. Moses heard the voice of God, but did not see his face, because we walk by faith, and not by sight, and of that God the glory of whose majesty we are not able to bear, we behold, with Moses, the works, only as it were in their back parts."[119]

But in *Moby-Dick*, using combined biblico-whaling terminology, Melville declares that because he does not and never will know the tail, or the "back parts" of the whale, he cannot "comprehend his face" either, nor is he sure that there is one.

Elsewhere in the novel Melville follows Pierre Bayle's stratagem and ironically infers a controversial God image from what a defective creation reveals. But in Chapter "The Tail" he uses Sir Thomas Browne's device of interpreting the ambiguous Biblical argument of the possibility of knowing God from the created world, by turning affirmation into negation.

11. If

"Undecipherable" as the "hieroglyphics" on the whale's brow are, they are also wrinkles of antiquity, harking back to "all the generations of whales, and men, and mastodons".[120]

In the course of the novel, such wrinkles often appear.

The planks of the Spouter Inn are "wrinkled". So are the *Pequod*'s "ancient decks . . . worn and wrinkled"; so is the "snow-white wrinkled forehead", which, together with his "high, pyramidical white hump" distinguishes Moby Dick from other sperm whales—"all crows feet and wrinkles" he appeared to the captain of the *Samuel Enderby;* it is to "systematically" hunt out that "white-headed whale with a wrinkled brow", that with "wrinkled brow" Ahab marks out new courses "over spaces that before were blank" on "wrinkled . . . yellowish sea charts" and doggedly and relentlessly continues doing so 272 pages later "with his snow-white ivory leg braced against the screwed leg of his table, . . . wrinkling his brow, and tracing his old courses again". By page 533 Ahab is gnarled and knotted with wrinkles; haggardly firm and unyielding", no wonder if the blacksmith can "smoothe . . . all seams and dents", but not Ahab's "ribbed brow", for, as Ahab explains: "it is unsmoothable; . . . it has worked down into the bone of my skull—*that* is all wrinkles!" And when, on the first day of the final chase, Ahab "practically" assails in Moby Dick "all evil", "all that most maddens and torments; . . . all truth with malice in it; all that cracks the sinews and cakes the brain", and the White Whale bites his craft "in twain", then Ahab is "spilled" into the sea and dragged into another boat, "with blood-shot, blinded eyes" and "the white brine caking in his wrinkles".[121]

All these deep-seated wrinkles point in one direction: the "antemosaic", "antediluvian", "pre-adamite" and "unsourced existence of the unspeakable terror of the whale, which, having been before all time, must needs exist after all humane ages are over".[122]

Ahab, who had "piled upon the whale's white hump the sum of all the general rage and hate felt by his whole race from Adam down", tells Starbuck, the day before the final chase begins, how "intolerably old" he feels: "deadly faint, bowed, and humped as though I were Adam, staggering beneath the piled centuries since Paradise", and exclaims when facing the white forehead for the third time: "An old, old sight, and yet somehow so young; . . . The same!—the same!—the same to Noah as to me"—a note struck by the narrator several chapters earlier: "That same ocean rolls now; that same ocean destroyed the wrecked ships of last year. . . . Noah's flood is not yet subsided."[123]

Yet the antiquity of the whale goes far beyond Biblical Noah.

Melville has a special chapter on "The Fossil Whale", which shows that he was fairly well read in contemporary geology and paleontology:

"While in the earlier geological strata there are found the fossils of monsters now almost completely extinct; the subsequent relics discovered in what are called the Tertiary formations seem the connecting, or at any rate intercepted links, between the antichronical creatures, and those whose remote posterity are said to have entered the Ark; all the Fossil Whales hitherto discovered belong to the Tertiary period, which is the last preceding the superficial formations. And though none of them precisely answer to any known species of the present time, they are yet sufficiently akin to them in general respects, to justify their taking rank as Cetacean fossils.

Detached broken fossils of pre-adamite whales, fragments of their bones and skeletons, have within thirty years past, at various intervals, been found at the base of the Alps, in Lombardy, in France, in England, in Scotland, and in the States of Louisiana, Mississippi, and Alabama."

Then science gives way to rhapsody:

"When I stand among these mighty Leviathan skeletons, skulls, tusks, jaws, ribs, and vertebrae, all characterized by partial resemblances to the existing breeds of sea-monsters; but at the same time bearing on the other hand similar affinities to the annihilated antichronical Leviathans, their incalculable seniors; I am, by a flood, borne back to that wondrous period, ere time itself can be said to have begun; for time began with man. Here Saturn's grey chaos rolls over me, and I obtain dim, shuddering glimpses into those Polar eternities; when wedged bastions of ice pressed hard upon what are now the Tropics; and in all the 25,000 miles of this world's circumference, not an inhabitable hand's breadth of land was visible. Then the whole world was the whale's; and, king of creation, he left his wake along the present lines of the Andes and the Himmalehs. Who can show a pedigree like Leviathan? Ahab's harpoon had shed older blood than the Pharaoh's. Methuselah seems a schoolboy. I look round to shake hands with Shem. I am horror-struck at this antemosaic, unsourced existence of the unspeakable terrors of the whale, which, having been before all time, must needs exist after all humane ages are over."[124]

Whilst these passages contain some inaccuracies, they certainly assume the idea of evolution and self-creation, as does Pip's vision in the depths of the ocean of "the multitudinous, God-omnipresent, coral insects, that out of the firmament of waters heaved the colossal orbs."[125]

In the latter case it is interesting to note the deliberate poetic use to which Melville puts the planet-creating image of the coral insects. The contemporary popular belief here represented, that coral islands and atolls were built up from the bottom of the ocean, was exploded by Charles Darwin in his *Journal and Remarks* (1839), showing that corals cannot live more than twenty fathoms below the surface.[126] Melville was aware of this as early as 1847, when *Omoo* was published. For in *Omoo*, too, he wrote about the coral insects, using them to carry the same message as in *Moby-Dick*, even more explicitly so:

"The island turned out to be one of the ... Coral Islands ... The origin of the entire group is generally ascribed to the coral insect.

According to some naturalists, this wonderful little creature, commencing its erections at the bottom of the sea, after the lapse of centuries, carries them up to the surface, where its labors cease. Here, the inequalities of the coral collect all floating bodies; forming, after a time, a soil, in which the seeds carried thither by birds, germinate, and cover the whole with vegetation. Here and there, all over this archipelago, numberless maked, detached coral formations are seen, just emerging, as it were, from the ocean. These would appear to be islands in the very process of creation—at any rate one involuntarily concludes so, on beholding them."

But here Melville added the following footnote:

"The above is the popular idea on the subject. But of late, a theory directly the reverse has been started. Instead of regarding the phenomena last described as indicating any thing like an active, creative power now in operation, it is maintained, that, together with the entire group, they are merely the remains of a continent, long ago worn away, and broken up by the action of the sea."[127]

No footnote would dim the image of evolution and natural self-creation in *Moby-Dick!*

It took the western churches some four decades to absorb the theory of evolution and interpret *Genesis* in its terms. At the time when Melville was writing *Moby-Dick,* they still maintained that the theory of evolution was incompatible with the Biblical doctrine.

But if the whale is "unsourced", and "must needs exist after all humane ages are over", then why "the fiery hunt"?[128] If there is no "reasoning thing . . . behind the unreasoning mask" of the White Whale, then why strike and "wreak . . . hate upon him"? Why Ahab's "sound and fury"?*

The awareness of this "If"** is what separates Ishmael from Ahab:

"There is no steady unretracing progress in this life; we do not advance through fixed gradations, and at the last one pause:—through infancy's unconscious spell, boyhood's thoughtless faith, adolescence' doubt (the common doom), then scepticism, then disbelief, resting at last in manhood's pondering repose of If. But once gone through, we trace the round again; and are infants, boys, and men, and Ifs eternally, Where lies the final harbor, whence we unmoor no more? In what rapt ether sails the world, of which the weariest will never weary? Where is the foundling's father hidden? Our souls

---

* "Life's but a walking shadow, a poor player.
That struts and frets his hour upon the stage,
And then is heard no more; it is a tale
Told by an idiot, full of sound and fury,
Signifying nothing."
(*Macbeth,* Act V, Scene V, 24–28.)
** EI, the Greek word engraven over the gate of Apollo's temple at Delphi, one of the meanings of which is "if". "If" is the title of Plotinus Plinlimmon's pamphlet in *Pierre*. The pamphlet comes "to a most untidy termination" with "if—". (*Pierre,* p. 215.)

are like those orphans whose unwedded mothers die in bearing them: the secret of our paternity lies in their grave, and we must there to learn it."

Thus does Ishmael meditate, eighty pages before he calls himself, the sole survivor of the *Pequod*'s company, "another orphan".[129]

12. Artistic reflections

Ultimate truth being out of the reach of men, how çan it be reflected in art? Translating the answer into whaling terminology, Melville writes:

"The great Leviathan is that one creature in the world which must remain unpainted to the last. True, one portrait may hit the mark much nearer than another, but none can hit it with any very considerable degree of exactness. So there is no earthly way of finding out precisely what the whale really looks like. And the only mode in which you can derive even a tolerable idea of his living contour, is by going a whaling yourself; but by so doing, you run no small risk of being eternally stove and sunk by him. Wherefore, it seems to me you had best not be too fastidious in your curiosity touching* this Leviathan."[130]

Melville intensifies his warning with regard to the whale's spout:

"You might almost stand in it, and yet be undecided as to what it is precisely. . . .
Nor is it at all prudent for the hunter to be over curious touching the precise nature of the whale spout. It will not do for him to be peering into it, and putting his face in it. You cannot go with your pitcher to this fountain and fill it, and bring it away."[131]

In two chapters on the pictorial representation of whales, Melville points out that they are all misleading and some are even "monstrous".[132]
So far as "the English and American whale draughtsmen" are concerned, the trouble with them is that "for the most part" they seem

"entirely content with presenting the mechanical outline of things, such as the vacant profile of the whale; . . . Even Scoresby[133], the justly renowned Right whaleman, after giving us a stiff full length of the Greenland whale, and three or four delicate miniatures of narwhales and porpoises, treats us to a series of classical engravings of boat hooks, chopping knives, and grapnels; and with the microscopic diligence of a Leuwenhoeck submits to the inspection of a

* Mark the pun

shivering world ninety-six fac-similes of magnified Arctic snow crystals. I mean no disparagement to the excellent voyager (I honor him for a veteran), but in so important a matter it was certainly an oversight not to have procured for every crystal a sworn affidavit taken before a Greenland Justice of the Peace."[134]

In contrast to his ironic references to these "microscopic" and lifeless representations, Melville extols two French engravings, "taken from paintings by one Garnery". They are "by far the finest, though in some details not the most correct, presentations of whales and whaling scenes". Both depict an attack on a whale: "the foreground is all raging commotion", "the heads of the swimming crew are scattered about the whale in contrasting expressions of affright" and "the action of the whole thing is wonderfully good and true . . . conveying the real spirit of the whale hunt".[135] In a similar vein Melville elsewhere remarks: "Only in the heart of quickest perils; only when within the eddyings of his angry flukes; only on the profound unbounded sea, can the fully invested whale be truly and livingly found out."[136]

Melville seems to have believed that truth can be best approached through art, and art for him begins where there is "the real spirit" of human pursuits and of the odds they confront. He was also convinced that a whaling narrative could epitomize just that. "But if", he exclaims in Chapter 24, ("The Advocate"), "you still declare that whaling has no aesthetically noble associations connected with it, then am I ready to shiver fifty lances with you there, and unhorse you with a split helmet every time".

Moby-Dick does certainly not lack "aesthetically noble associations", proliferating in their own turn, as witness their numerous interpretations, so that Melville's assertion in the same chapter, that "whaling may well be regarded as that Egyptian mother, who bore offspring themselves pregnant from her womb" (a reference to the Isis–Osiris myth), applies with equal force to "the high and mighty business of whaling" and to its "aesthetically noble associations". Yet whatever the multifarious symbolic implications of *Moby-Dick,* they are solidly founded upon the carefully established authenticity of both action and characters. It is from this basic "truth of the thing" that perpetuates the pervasive magic and fascination of the novel.

13. Mythology

Believing ultimate truth to be out of reach, Melville would accept no one's contrary assumption, and like Babbalanja in *Mardi,* would passionately "discharge" the "darts" of "crested lies" in the direction whence they came.[137] Heated with the same passion in creating *Pierre,* Melville wrote in that book:

"... the enthusiast youth ... unless he can find the talismanic secret, to reconcile this world with his own soul, then there is no peace for him ... in this life. Now without doubt this Talismanic Secret has never yet been found; and in the nature of human things it seems as though it never can be. Certain philosophers have time and again pretended to have found it; but if they do not in the end discover their own delusion, other people soon discover it for themselves, and so those philosophers and their vain philosophy are let glide away into practical oblivion. Plato, and Spinoza, Goethe, and many more belong to this guild of self-impostors, with a preposterous rabble of Muggletonian[138] Scots and Yankees, whose vile brogue still the more bestreaks the stripedness of their Greek or German Neoplatonical originals. That profound Silence, that only Voice of our God, ... from that divine thing without a name, those impostor philosophers pretend somehow to have got an answer; which is as absurd, as though they should say they had got water out of stone; for how can a man get a Voice out of Silence?"[139]

In *Moby-Dick*, with ample evidence of "that profound Silence", the "speechless ... power" of the "clear spirit of clear fire" and the "pyramidical silence" of the whale, Melville exposes the fallacy of all allegorical interpretations. In the scene in front of the South American doubloon riveted on the mainmast, a prize for the man who first raises Moby Dick, the different ways in which the same carvings on the doubloon are interpreted cast little light on the meaning of the carving, but all the more on the interpreting characters. Pip in his wise insanity pertinently remarks:

"I look, you look, he looks; we look, ye look, they look ... And I, you, and he; and we, ye, and they, are all bats."[140]

In Melville's view the same applies to all creeds that claim to interpret the world. No one has a "warrant, with Oro's sign manual"[141]. With all its inaccuracies, self-contradictions and the highly questionable morality it purports, Melville rejects the belief in the divine inspiration of the Bible, and treats the Old Testament and the religions based on it on equal footing with other religions and mythologies of the world, regarding them all as equally fallacious and misleading.

In the chapter on "The Honor and Glory of Whaling", meant to heighten the respectability of whalemen, Melville traces their genealogy back to "demi-gods and heroes, prophets of all sorts". Having identified all aquatic monsters of the Bible as leviathans or whales, and then, on basis of *Ezekiel* XXXII, 2, Leviathan with the Dragon, Melville lumps together Biblical, legendary and mythical heroes and hails them as equally authentic ancestors of the whaling fraternity:

"Perseus, St. George, Hercules, Jonah, and Vishnoo! there's a member-roll for you! What club but the whaleman's can head off like that?"

And if the heroes are equally authentic, so ought the creeds be that celebrate them. However, as each creed vindicate divine and exclusive revelation, they must be equally inauthentic.

For obvious reasons, the Jonah story had special fascination for Melville:

> "By the best contradictory authorities, this Grecian story of Hercules and the whale is considered to be derived from the still more ancient Hebrew story of Jonah and the whale; and vice versa; certainly they are very similar. If I claim the demi-god then, why not the prophet?"[142]

Which he did all the more so, as Pierre Bayle had a special entry on Jonah in his *Dictionary Historical and Critical*. Melville took parts of this over almost verbatim in his chapter entitled "Jonah Historically Regarded".

Both Pierre Bayle and Melville dwell on the obvious absurdities of *Jonah* I, 17; II, 10 and III, 3 and its similarities with the Greek mythological stories of Hercules and of Arion, implying that the Biblical story is no more authentic or divinely inspired than its heathen opposite numbers. Both Bayle and Melville use the same device of refuting apologetic exegesis under the pretence of advocating it.

In his entry on "Jonas", Pierre Bayle is quite explicit in emphasizing the organic relationship between the Jonah story, the Bible, and Christology, so that once the authenticity of the Jonah story is exploded, so is that of the Bible and of the divinity of Jesus.

As is his custom, Bayle argues by alternating his own reflections with well-tailored quotations from and indirect reports of orthodox authorities, mixing the three, until his own heretical opinions assume the respectability of those authorities whose views he refutes. It is in this vein that he refers to Saint Augustine's letter to a pagan friend:

> "Either", says he, "we must deny all the miracles of God, or acknowledge we have no reason to reject this*. Should we believe the resurrection of Jesus Christ, if we were afraid of the railleries of the infidels? And since our friend has not supposed any doubts about our admitting the resurrection of Lazarus and that of Jesus Christ, I very much wonder he should look upon the adventure of Jonas as incredible. Is it easier to raise a dead man from the grave, than to preserve a man alive in the belly of a great fish? Will it be said that the digestive faculty of the stomach cannot be suspended?"

Here Bayle expounds the basic idea of his argument:

> "Either believe or reject in general all the facts of the same nature, even those that appear still more incredible."[143]

---

* I.e. the story of Jonah

Bayle in fact sets up a tripodal equation, the elimination of either leg of which will topple the whole edifice Pagans, who believe their own legendary miracles, must, by the same token, also give credit to the miracles recorded in the Bible. Those who give credit to some Scriptural miracles (like the resurrection of Lazarus and of Jesus Christ), must believe all. Conversely: disbelief in either the pagan miracles or any of the Biblical ones should raise doubts regarding all others: pagan ones, and those narrated in the Old and New Testament alike. All the more so as the miracles of the Old Testament are supposed to adumbrate those in the New, with Jonah's delivery from the whale's belly, for instance, regarded as an adumbration of the resurrection of Jesus Christ.

Whilst Pierre Bayle in his *Jonas* entry refers to St. Augustine, Melville's chief authority on whaling mythology is "one old Sag-Harbor whaleman" who questions "the Hebrew story" on three accounts: the whale's swallowing Jonah without choking; Jonah resisting "the whale's gastric juices"; and being "vomited up somewhere within three days' journey of Nineveh".[144] As regards the last of these three, the relevant passage in Pierre Bayle's *Dictionary* reads as follows:

"Note, that Nineveh was built upon the river Tigris, which has no immediate communication with the Mediterranean Sea. Besides, there is not water enough for such a fish in this river at the port of Nineveh. This reason, together with the surprising miracle, we must suppose, ... that the whale went into the ocean, and doubled the cape of Good Hope, and entered into the mouth of the Tigris, and made that prodigious compass in three days."[145]

This is Melville's version:

"Jonah was swallowed by the whale in the Mediterranean Sea, and after three days he was vomited up somewhere within three days' journey of Nineveh, a city on the Tigris, very much more than three days's journey across from the nearest point of the Mediterranean coast. How is that?
... The Whale ... might have carried him round by the way of the Cape of Good Hope. But not to speak of the passage through the whole length of the Mediterranean, and another passage up the Persian Gulf and Red Sea, such a supposition would involve the complete circumnavigation of all Africa in three days, not to speak of the Tigris waters, near the site of Nineveh, being too shallow for any whale to swim in."

Tongue in cheek, Melville concludes the chapter in the following Baylesque manner:

"But all these foolish arguments of old Sag-Harbor only evinced his foolish pride of reason—a thing still more reprehensible in him, seeing that he had but little learning except what he had picked up from the sun and the sea. I say it only shows his foolish, impious pride, and abominable, devilish

151

rebellion against the reverend clergy. For by a Portuguese Catholic priest, this very idea of Jonah's going to Nineveh via the Cape of Good Hope was advanced as a signal magnification of the general miracle. And so it was. Besides, to this day, the highly enlightened Turcs devoutly believe in the historical story of Jonah. And some three centuries ago, an English traveller in old Harris's Voyages, speaks of a Turkish Mosque built in honor of Jonah, in which mosque was a miraculous lamp that burnt without any oil."[146]

It is interesting to mark how, "with a view to popular conservatism"[147]. Melville carefully kept sceptical Bayle out of the picture. For although John Harris's *Navigantium atque Itinerantium Bibliotheca* (London, 1705) does refer to "a Mosque, in the place where, they say, Jonas is buried", and remarks that "the Turks have a mighty Veneration for it"[148], it makes no mention whatever of the "miraculous lamp", the source for which reads thus:

"The Turks have built a very fine mosque to the honour of Jonas, in which there is a miracuolus lamp, that burns continually without any oil or other liquor",

and can be found on p. 579, Vol. III. of Pierre Bayle's *Dictionary*.

In his drive to explode the myth of the divine authority of the Scriptural religions, Melville draws a parallel between them and primitive religious beliefs and practices and points out that in all cases men make their own gods and therefore no religion can claim divine authenticity.

On one of the Arsacide Islands in the Pacific near the southern tip of the Solomon Islands, Ishmael visits a temple, where the skeleton of a great sperm whale is worshipped.

"The ribs were hung with trophies; the vertebrae were carved with Arsacidean annals, in strange hieroglyphics; in the skull, the priests kept up an unextinguished aromatic flame, so that the mystic head again sent forth its vapory spout; while, suspended from a bough, the terrific lower jaw vibrated over all the devotees, like the hair-hung sword that so affrighted Damocles."

Here follows a passage that graphically brings home the irrelevance of the lifeless object of worship in the midst of the unceasing activity of the natural environment:

"It was a wondrous sight. The wood was green as mosses of the Icy Glen; the trees stood high and haughty, feeling their living sap; the industrious earth beneath was as a weaver's loom, with a gorgeous carpet on it, whereof the ground-vine tendrils formed the warp and woof, and the living flowers the figures. All the trees, with all their laden branches; all the shrubs, and ferns, and grasses; the message-carrying air; all these unceasingly were active.

152

Through the lacings of the leaves, the great sun seemed a flying shuttle weaving the unwearied verdure. Oh, busy weaver! unseen weaver!—pause!—one word!—whither flows the fabric? what palace may it deck? wherefore all these ceaseless toilings? Speak, weaver!—stay thy hand!—but one single word with thee! Nay—the shuttle flies—the figures float from forth the loom; the freshet-rushing carpet for ever slides away. The weaver-god, he weaves; and by that weaving is he deafened, that he hears no mortal voice; and by that humming, we, too, who look on the loom are deafened; and only when we escape it shall we hear the thousand voices that speak through it.

. . .

Now amid the green, life-restless loom of that Arsacidean wood, the great, white, worshipped skeleton lay lounging—a gigantic idler! Yet, as the ever-woven verdant warp and woof intermixed and hummed around him, the mighty idler seemed the cunning weaver; himself all woven over with the vines; every month assuming greener, fresher verdure; but himself a skeleton. Life folded Death; Death trellised Life; the grim god wived with youthful Life, and begat him curly-headed glories."[149]

This passage also shows how Melville's religious scepticism would at times mix with some of Plato's thoughts.

The model of the deafened weaver-god is the ambiguous demiurge (artificer) of Plato's *Timaeus,* who, in a continuous and eternal process constructs the physical body of the universe, "weaving" the soul into it, whilst we mortals, too, are deafened by the humming of the loom. A few years after *Moby-Dick,* the personal impression that might have been behind Melville's deafening loom symbol inspired one of his short stories: *The Tartarus of Maids.* In a New England paper-mill he visited,

"Not a syllable was breathed. Nothing was heard but the low, steady overruling hum of the iron animals. The human voice was banished from the spot."[150]

In *Moby-Dick,* the mortals deafened by the humming loom can expect, as Socrates does in Plato's *Phaedo,* their souls, distinct from their bodies, to survive physical death and, freed from the body and thus released from its evils, to enter into a better state and attain a fuller and richer life. "Oh God! that man should be a thing for immortal souls to sieve through!"[151] Ahab exclaims contemplating deranged Pip. And Ishmael reassures himself before signing on for the expedition in a similar Platonic vein:

"Methinks my body is but the lees of my better being. In fact take my body who will, take it I say, it is not me. And therefore three cheers for Nantucket; and come a stove boat and stove body when they will, for stave my soul, Jove himself cannot."[152]

153

Although Christianity in its formative centuries absorbed much of Platonism and Greek philosophy, the cosmogony referred to in the passages quoted above, it did not. The Platonic cosmogony lacks the concept of instant creation out of nothing, which was an element of Jewish folklore. The Demiurge constructs out of eternally existing material and does not create that material at a certain instant, as does the Judaeo–Christian God. Nor is he the supreme or only divine principle, and he is limited in his power by the imperfections of eternally existing matter. Nor does Plato's system of thought attempt to explain away the imperfections of the world with the theory of original sin committed by the first man and woman in eating the fruit of "the tree of the knowledge of good and evil"[153], which God had planted, but forbidden man to eat of. With no deliberately inspired feelings of inherent guilt, Platonism is not concerned with redemption either. The Christian concept of a divine Redeemer was based on the Jewish historical expectation of a Messiah, or "anointed one", who would deliver his people from captivity and restore them to their patrimony.

The indifferent and deaf weaver-god also appears to Pip, when the sea drowns "the infinite of his soul".

> "Carried down alive to wondrous depths, ... among the joyous, heartless, ever-juvenile eternities, Pip saw ... God's foot upon the treadle of the loom."[154]

The whale skeleton god had no relation whatsoever to life, and however Ishmael "paced" "to and fro ... before this skeleton—brushed the vines aside—broke through the ribs", he "saw no living thing within; naught was there but bones".

But it was all the more closely related to the priests, who swore that "the artificial smoke ascending from where the real jet had issued, ... was genuine". And they were adamant when they saw that Ishmael intended to take the measurements of the skeleton:

> "'How now!' they shouted; 'Dar'st thou measure this our god! That's for us.'"

At which Ishmael retorted with a marvellous pun:

> "'Aye, priests—well, how long do ye make him, then?'"

Without going into the ambiguity of the predicate, the priests instantly fell out with each other and

> "a fierce contest rose among them, concerning feet and inches; they cracked each other's sconces with their yard-sticks—the great skull echoed—and seizing that lucky chance",

154

Ishmael "quickly concluded" his "own admeasurements".[155] "The great skull echoed" and all institutionalized religions claiming unique and exclusive divine revelation might just as well have reverberated. It was in the light of this paradox of men variously worshipping and extolling their self-made gods that in an earlier chapter Ishmael referred to "the infallible Presbyterian Church".

This was when Queequeg, a South-Sea islander, his heathen room-mate in the New Bedford inn, invited Ishmael to join him in the worship of Yojo. Yojo was Queequeg's little black idol which he had carved out of wood and was improving all the time, "with a jack-knife gently whittling away at its nose",—a pertinent symbol of the origin and history of all religions. When Queequeg motioned Ishmael to join him in his prayers, Ishmael made his decision after some deliberation:

> "I was a good Christian; born and bred in the bosom of the infallible Presbyterian Church. How then could I unite with this wild idolator in worshipping his piece of wood?"

The paradox of the infallibility of any particular church is here followed by a correspondingly paradoxical logical sequence, leading to a conclusion that equates Christian worship with idolatry:

> "But what is worship? thought I. Do you suppose now, Ishmael, that the magnanimous God of heaven and earth—pagans and all included—can possibly be jealous of an insignificant bit of black wood? Impossible! But what is worship?—to do the will of God—*that* is worship. And what is the will of God?—to do to my fellow man what I would have my fellow man to do to me—*that* is the will of God. Now, Queequeg is my fellow man. And what do I wish that this Queequeg would do to me? Why, unite with me in my particular Presbyterian form of worship. Consequently, I must then unite with him in his; ergo, I must turn idolator. So I kindled the shavings; helped prop up the innocent little idol; offered him burnt biscuit with Queequeg; salamed before him twice and thrice; kissed his nose; and that done, we undressed and went to bed, at peace with our own consciences and all the world."

Queequeg's outlandish habits are held up to ridicule even while they are shown to reflect Euro-American conventions—a device common to social travesty. Queequeg puts on his boots in private and his pantaloons in public view, which, for all its oddity, is not presented as any more absurd than our customary choice of things to be done privately or in public. The same applies to Queequeg's religious practices.

In one of these religious exercises Ishmael refused to cooperate. This was when Queequeg shut himself up for a whole day and night and was "squatting on his hams" in the middle of the room "and holding Yojo on top of his head" and "going too without his regular meals", as if it was "some sort of Lent or Ramadan" (periods of fasting prescribed by the Christian and Mohammedan religions, respectively). To bring the point even closer home, Ishmael heaps likeness upon likeness:

"*how* it was I never could find out, for, though I applied myself to it several times, I never could master his liturgies and XXXIX Articles"[156]

a clear hint at the Forty-Two Articles on which the authoritative creed of the Anglican Church and of all Episcopal churches has been based since 1563.[157]

Yet however he disagreed with this practice, Ishmael would not disturb Queequeg,

"for I cherish the greatest respect towards everybody's religious obligations, never mind how comical, and could not find it in my heart to undervalue even a congregation of ants worshipping a toad-stool."

But there is a point where Ishmael would raise an objection:

"as I before hinted, I have no objection to any person's religion, be it what it may, so long as that person does not kill or insult any other person, because that other person don't believe it also. But when a man's religion becomes really frantic; when it is a positive torment to him; and, in fine, makes this earth of ours an uncomfortable inn to lodge in; then I think it high time to take that individual aside and argue the point with him."

Which is what Ishmael did with Queequeg:

"Beginning with the rise and progress of the primitive religions, and coming down to the various religions of the present time", Ishmael "labored to show Queequeg that all these Lents, Ramadans, and prolonged ham-squattings in cold, cheerless rooms were stark nonsense; bad for the health; useless for the soul; opposed, in short, to the obvious laws of Hygiene and common sense."

Ishmael's next argument was bowdlerized from the first English edition in 1851:

"I told him, too, that he being in other things such an extremely sensible and sagacious savage, it pained me . . . to see him now so deplorably foolish about this ridiculous Ramadan of his. Besides, argued I, fasting makes the body cave in; hence the spirit caves in; and all thoughts born of a fast must necessarily be half-starved.* This is the reason why most dyseptic religionists

* Cf. "Alma forbid! We never fast; our aspirations are our prayers, our lives are worship." (*Mardi*, p. 628.)

156

cherish such melancholy notions about their hereafters. In one word, Queequeg, said I, rather digressively; hell is an idea first born on an undigested apple-dumpling; and since then perpetuated through the hereditary dyspepsias nurtured by Ramadans."[158]

This irreverent and satirical reference to Chapter III of *Genesis* compares strangely with the metaphor Carlyle uses in the opening chapter of *Sartor Resartus*. As in the case of Ahab's "pasteboard masks" and Professor Teufelsdröckh's "emblematic clothes", the two writers use much the same metaphor in contexts that carry contrary implications. Whilst in the passage quoted above, Melville's "apple-dumpling" connotes the human origin and the fallacy of the *Genesis* story, Carlyle's satirical remarks and his reference to "dumplings" and "apples" are meant to denigrate the achievements of science and confirm the credibility of divine creation as imparted in *Genesis*:

"Of Geology and Geognosy we know enough: what with the labours of our Werners and Huttons, what with the ardent genius of their disciples, it has come about that now, to many a Royal Society, the Creation of the World is little more mysterious than the cooking of a dumpling; concerning which last, indeed, there have been minds to whom the question, *How the apples were got in,* presented difficulties."[159]

Melville borrowed Carlyle's *Sartor Resartus* from Evert Duyckinck in June or July of 1850.[160]

But argue as he will, Ishmael was to get no other response from Queequeg than what he would have from anyone else holding religious views:

"He somehow seemed dull of hearing on that important subject, . . . and . . . no doubt thought he knew a good deal more about the true religion than I did. He looked at me with a sort of condescending concern and compassion, as though he thought it a great pity that such a sensible young man should be so hopelessly lost to evangelical pagan piety."

Firm in his own belief, Queequeg did not wish to become a Christian, or be "converted", as Captain Bildad, the sanctimonious part-owner of the *Pequod* expected him to be.

Son of "a High Chief, a King" and "actuated by a profound desire to learn among the Christians, the arts whereby to make his people still happier than they were; and more than that, still better than they were", Queequeg had "sought a passage to Christian lands" by enlisting on board a whaler as a harpooner.

"But, alas! the practices of whalemen soon convinced him that even Christians could be both miserable and wicked; infinitely more so, than all his father's heathens. Arrived at last in old Sag Harbor; and seeing what the

157

sailors did there; and then going on to Nantucket, and seeing how they spent their wages in *that* place also, poor Queequeg gave it up for lost. Thought he, it's a wicked world in all meridians; I'll die a pagan."

Nevertheless he would not yet dare go back to his native island, for

"he was fearful Christianity, or rather Christians, had unfitted him for ascending the pure and undefiled throne of thirty pagan Kings before him. But by and by, ... he would return,—as soon as he felt himself baptized again."

But he was never to be baptized or re-baptized. Nor would that have made any difference in the final catastrophe, when the crew, Christians and non-Christians alike, were wrapped forever in "the great shroud of the sea."[161] With the single exception of the narrator, they all perished in a universe devoid of providence and blankly indifferent to human aspirations and misgivings and to the myths men create for others or themselves to believe in.

CHAPTER 3

Counterpoint

1. What makes a good voyager

When Queequeg died in the final catastrophe, he had no time to prepare for death. Some time earlier, however, he had been "seized with a fever", so that "not a man of the crew but gave him up"; it was then that Queequeg, showing no sign whatever of any fear or tribulation, prepared for the termination of his life with an initiative befitting his conduct of it, whilst lunatic Pip kept repeating: "Queequeg dies game! ... Queequeg dies game! ... Queequeg dies game!"

For Queequeg, death was an inherent part of life, and thus something to take charge of. He asked for a coffin to be made to his measurements; it had to be brought to him, and he had to be lifted into the coffin to try it out, with Yojo, "his little god" on his breast between his crossed arms. When dead, he was to be floated on the sea, as was customary among his people, who held that the dead, laid in their canoes, would be carried away "far beyond all visible horizons", where "their own mild, uncontinented seas, interflow with the blue heavens".

> "There lay Queequeg in his coffin with little but his composed countenance in view. Rarmai (it will do; it is easy), he murmured at last, and signed to be replaced in his hammock."

Then suddenly he changed his mind:

> "But now that he had apparently made every preparation for death; now that his coffin was proved a good fit, Queequeg suddenly rallied; ... he had just recalled a little duty ashore, which he was leaving undone; and therefore had changed his mind about dying: he could not die yet, he averred. They asked him, then, whether to live or die was a matter of his own sovereign will and pleasure. He answered, certainly. In a word, it was Queequeg's conceit, that if a man made up his mind to live, mere sickness could not kill him: nothing but a whale, or a gale, or some violent, ungovernable, unintelligent destroyer of that sort."[1]

The coffin was subsequently put to use as a seachest, and then converted into the life-buoy which saved Ishmael's life in the final catastrophe.

159

A similarly unconcerned and unchristian approach to death is described by Lev Tolstoy in *Three Deaths*.[2] In this short story, unlike the rich lady who faces her inevitable death with bitter reluctance, a mortally sick peasant placidly gives away his boots to a young man, taking in return the man's promise to buy him a tombstone. Tolstoy does not revive his old peasant as Melville does Queequeg to complete "a little duty ashore", but has the cook sleeping near the dying man, dream that "uncle Fyodor got down from the stove and went out to chop wood". What exactly he meant in this story Tolstoy later explained in a letter to his cousin, Countess Alexandra Tolstoy:

> "The peasant dies calmly, being no Christian at all. His religion is something else, although he has kept up the Christian rites by force of habit; his religion is Nature having lived with her. He himself felled trees and sowed the grain and held the harvest; he killed lambs, and lambs had been born around him, and children were born and old men died—quite thoroughly and firmly does he know this law he never went beyond (as did the lady) in the simplicity of his perception."[3]

Melville's respect for this "simplicity of perception" regarding death, one devoid of fear, is also manifest in *Billy Budd*. In this novel, which Melville wrote not long before his own death, Billy Budd, the sailor hero, is innocently sentenced to death. Yet he "freely referred to his death as a thing close at hand" and "was wholly without irrational fear of it, a fear more prevalent in highly civilized communities than those so-called barbarous ones which in all respects stand nearer to unadulterate Nature." (Chapter 25).

Would Christianity make a better or a worse harpooner out of Queequeg? This is the question Bildad and Peleg, the two part-owners of the *Pequod* argue about, when considering his employment.

Devout Captain Bildad sternly admonishes Queequeg:

> "If thou still clingest to thy Pagan ways, which I sadly fear, I beseech thee, remain not for aye a Belial bondsman. Spurn the idol Bell, and the hideous dragon; turn from the wrath to come; mind thine eye, I say: oh! goodness gracious! steer clear of the fiery pit!"

But Bildad's more practical partner, Captain Peleg thinks differently:

> "Pious harpooneers never make good voyagers—it takes the shark out of 'em; ... There was young Nat Swaine, once the bravest boat-header out of all Nantucket ...; he joined the meeting, and never came to good. He got so frightened about his plaguy soul, that he shrinked and sheered away from whales, for fear of after-claps in case he got stove and went to Davy Jones."*

* Nautical slang: spirit of the sea; the sailors' devil.

At which, horrified Bildad remonstrates:

> "Peleg! Peleg! ... thou knowest, ... what it is to have the fear of death; how, then, can'st thou prate in this ungodly guise. ... Tell me, when this same Pequod here had her three masts overboard in that typhoon on Japan, that same voyage when thou went mate with Captain Ahab, did'st thou not think of Death and the Judgement then?"

Yet Peleg retorted angrily and with healthy secularism nurtured in the collective struggle for survival exclaims:

> "When every moment we thought the ship would sink! Death and the Judgement then? What? With all three masts making such an everlasting thundering against the side; and every sea breaking over us, fore and aft. Think of Death and the Judgement then? No! no time to think about Death then. Life was what Captain Ahab and I was thinking of; and how to save all hands—how to rig jury-masts—how to get into the nearest port; that was what I was thinking of."[4]

In a business, where fatal accidents were "matters of common occurence", Bildad's "dyspeptic" religious notions were clearly irrelevant and hypocritical. An Epicurean unconcern with life after death and concentration on survival against overwhelming odds would seem to be the only conduct befitting "this whaling world".[5]

2. Self-reliance

Thinking of death as part of life was one of the things whaling had taught Ishmael. Another, no less important, lesson was thinking of life in terms of human bondage.

In his obsession with "that inscrutable thing" behind the White Whale's "pasteboard mask" and "ready to sacrifice all mortal interests to that one passion" of capturing Moby Dick, Ahab chafed against this bond. He was "socially ... inaccessible" and in "the isolated subterraneousness" of his cabin there was "no companionship".[6]

Concurring in his ambition with Emerson's idea of the Self-Reliant Man, who, in Emerson's word, "godlike ... has cast off the common motives of humanity and has ventured to trust himself for a taskmaster", ("It is only as a man puts off all foreign support and stands alone that I see him to be strong and to prevail. He is weaker by every recruit to his banner"[7], Ahab was embittered even by his dependence on the carpenter for his ivory leg:

> "Oh, Life! Here I am, proud as a Greek god, and yet standing debtor to this blockhead for a bone to stand on! Cursed be that mortal inter-indebtedness which will not do away with ledgers. I would be free as air; and I'm down in the whole world's books."[8]

161

"Proud as a Greek god" as Ahab was, this duly affected his relationship with his subordinates. "Who's over him, he cries", Starbuck remarks to himself "aye, he would be a democrat to all above; look, how he lords it over all below".

"Ye are not other men, but my arms and my legs; and so obey me"[9] — Ahab blurted out in the heat of the last day's chase. But until then, he was more careful and calculating in conditioning his men into "flat obedience", whilst, at the same time, "distrustful of his crew's fidelity", going even to the cautious extreme of smuggling into the ship a private crew of five "subordinate phantoms"[10], Fedallah one of them, in case the ship's company should rise in mutiny, not a rare occurrence on open sea in those days. But the *Pequod*'s company remained loyal to Ahab, right to the bottom of the sea. Ahab had brought the art of leadership to its very perfection. "My one cogged circle fits into all their various wheels, and they revolve"—he pertinently averred to himself.

Ahab appealed to his crew's compassion: "Aye, . . . my hearties all round; it was Moby Dick that dismasted me; . . . that accursed white whale that razeed me; made a poor pegging lubber of me for ever and a day!" he told his men at the outset, "with a terrific, loud, animal sob, like that of a heart-stricken moose". He bribed them: "Whosoever of ye . . . raises me that white-headed whale, . . . he shall have this gold ounce, my boys!"

Besides, in a suffering world, vengeful hatred is easily stirred to fierce and relentless action. What better focus for the whalemen's exasperate pugnacity than the monstrous and redoubtable white whale? Ishmael spoke for the crew when he stated: "A wild, mystical, sympathetical feeling was in me; Ahab's quenchless feud seemed mine. With greedy ears I learned the history of that murderous monster against whom I and all the others had taken our oaths of violence and revenge."

An excellent manipulator of his subordinates' minds, Ahab made good use of his superior knowledge and "his subtile skill" "to revive the spirits of his crew". When in a violent storm lightning transpointed the compass needle, he replaced it with a sail-maker's needle which he skilfully magnetized, going "through some small strange motions with it—whether indispensable to the magnetizing of the steel, or merely intended to augment the awe of the crew, is uncertain". The whole chapter on "The Needle" is an exquisite presentation of skilfully engineered magic, calculated to inspire superstitious awe.

An efficient leader, Ahab also knew how to squelch panic and the thought of mutiny by a show of fortitude and firmness. During the typhoon, as Starbuck urged Ahab to stop his pursuit of Moby Dick against the eastward wind and rather let the wind drive them homeward, Ahab's harpoon was suddenly struck by lightning so that "from the keen steel barb there . . . came a levelled flame of pale, forked fire". As the superstitious, "panic-stricken crew . . . raised a half mutinous cry", Ahab snatched the burning harpoon, "waved it like a torch among them; swearing to transfix with it the first sailor that but cast loose a rope's end". Then "with one blast of his breath he extinguished the flame", exclaiming: "thus I blow out the last fear!"—and so he did, for henceforth "their fear of Ahab was greater than their fear of Fate". Even Starbuck, the first mate, was cowed into "flat obedience", though fully aware that "this crazed old man" ought rather to be "put aside" in his sleep, than "be tamely suffered to drag a whole ship's company down to doom with him".[11]

As a result, as they neared the haunts of the White Whale,

> "Ahab's purpose . . . fixedly gleamed down upon the constant midnight of the gloomy crew. It domineered above them so, that all their bodings, doubts, misgivings, fears, were fain to hide beneath their souls, and not sprout forth a single spear of leaf.
> In this foreshadowing interval too, all humor . . . vanished. . . . Alike, joy and sorrow, hope and fear, seemed ground to finest dust, and powdered, for the time, in the clamped mortar of Ahab's iron soul. Like machines, they dumbly moved about the deck, ever conscious that the old man's despot eye was on them."

Ahab was fully successful in regimenting his crew and eliminating all opposition to his fatal drive:

> "They were one man, not thirty. For as the one ship that held them all; though it was put together of all contrasting things—oak, and maple, and pine wood; iron, and pitch, and hemp—yet all these ran into each other in the one concrete hull, which shot on its way, both balanced and directed by the long central keel; even so, all the individualities of the crew, this man's valor, that man's fear; guilt and guiltlessness, all varieties were welded into oneness, and were all directed to that fatal goal which Ahab their one lord and keel did point to."[12]

Yet Ahab, too, had "his humanities" and he suffered from the loneliness of his self-reliance. Looking back on his life, he bemoans

> "the desolation of solitude it has been; the masoned, walled-town of a Captain's exclusiveness, . . . the . . . Guinea-coast slavery of solitary command"

and longs to "look into a human eye; it is better than to gaze into sea or sky; better than to gaze upon God". In an emotional moment on the second day of the final chase, he tells Starbuck:

> "Aye, aye, Starbuck, 'tis sweet to lean sometimes, be the leaner who he will; and would old Ahab had leaned oftener than he has."[13]

Just before his last onslaught on the Whale, from his boat casting a farewell glance at the *Pequod,* Ahab suddenly realized that the crew meant more to him than mere "arms and legs":

"When Ahab was sliding by the vessel, so near as plainly to distinguish Starbuck's face as he leaned over the rail, he hailed him to turn the vessel about, and follow him, not too swiftly, at a judicious interval. Glancing upwards, he saw Tashtego, Queequeg, and Daggoo, eagerly mounting to the three mast-heads; while the oarsmen were rocking in the two staved boats which had but just been hoisted to the side, and were busily at work in repairing them. One after the other, through the portholes, as he sped, he also caught flying glimpses of Stubb and Flask, busying themselves on deck among bundles of new irons and lances. As he was all this; as he heard the hammers in the broken boats; far other hammers seemed driving a nail into his heart. But he rallied."[14]

Ahab was also touched by deranged little Pip's attachment to him, but Pip's tragedy also reminded him of his quenchless feud:

"Oh, ye frozen heavens! look down here. Ye did beget this luckless child, and have abandoned him, ye creative libertines. ... Lo! ye believers in gods all goodness, and in man all ill, lo you! see the omniscient gods oblivious of suffering man; and man, though idiotic, and knowing not what he does, yet full of the sweet things of love and gratitude. Come! I feel prouder leading thee by thy black hand, than though I grasped an Emperor's!"[15]

Yet, in his defiance, all that this self-reliant Commander achieved was disaster and death.

3. The monkey-rope

In contrast to Ahab's "desolation of solitude" in his isolated and lonely cabin, Ishmael looks at the world from the forecastle, surrounded by "the godly, honest, unostentatious, hospitale, sociable, free-and-easy"[16] whalers. It should be noted here, that the *Pequod*'s crew is different from those of the *Julia* in *Omoo*, the *Highlander* in *Redburn*, the *Neversink* in *White-Jacket*, or even of "The Town Ho's Story" in *Moby-Dick*. In these narratives, Melville shows how the brutal oppression on board a man-of-war, a merchant vessel or a whaler depraves the men. In *Moby-Dick*, Melville warns his readers in an early chapter that he would present the whalemen "in the ideal", for

"men may have mean and meagre faces; but man, in the ideal, is so noble and so sparkling, such a grand and glowing creature, that over any ignominious blemish in him all his fellows should run to throw their costliest robes".

Addressing himself to his potential critics, he then declares his purpose:

"This august dignity I treat of, is not the dignity of kings and robes, but that abounding dignity which has no robed investiture. Thou shalt see it shining in the arm that wields a pick or drives a spike; that democratic dignity which, on all hands, radiates without end from God; Himself! The great God absolute! The centre and circumference of all democracy! His omnipresence, our divine equality!

If, then, to meanest mariners, and renegades and castaways, I shall hereafter ascribe high qualities, though dark; weave round them tragic graces; if even the most mournful, perchance the most abased, among them all, shall at times lift himself to the exalted mounts; if I shall touch that workman's arm with some ethereal light; if I shall spread a rainbow over his disastrous set of sun; then against all mortal critics bear me out in it, thou just Spirit of Equality, which hast spread one royal mantle of humanity over all my kind! Bear me out in it, thou great democratic God! ... Thou who, in all Thy mighty, earthly marchings, ever cullest Thy selectest champions from the kingly commons; bear me out in it, O God!"[17]

Ishmael establishes his first relationship with "the kingly commons" of the forecastle in the Spouter-Inn of New Bedford.

His first whaler friend is a cannibal from one of the South Sea Islands. Sharply differing from Ishmael's wonted company, Queequeg is aptly representative of the multi-racial whaling crews of the day, when, as Melville writes,

"not one in two of the many thousand men before the mast employed in the American whale fishery, are Americans born, though pretty nearly all the officers are."[18]

Melville sets great store by Ishmael's friendship with Queequeg. The relevant chapters (3, 4, 10, 11, 12, 13, 17, 18, 72, 78 and 90) testify to a rare sense of human identity. What creates their endearing humour is the way in which Melville, as he had already done in *Typee* and *Omoo,* deflates the myth of the moral superiority of Christian civilization over primitive society. He does so partly by exploding conventional prejudices regarding people living outside the Christian pale*, and partly by drawing parallels between heathen and Christian religious practices, thus at one stroke both identifying them and exposing their fallacies.

At first, Ishmael was horrified at seeing that his bedfellow in the Spouter-Inn was a "purple" and "abominable savage", a heathen and a cannibal. But after a while, he realized that "for all his tattooings he was on the whole a clean, comely looking cannibal" and thought to himself:

---

* Much in the spirit of Montaigne's essay "On Cannibals": "We may ... call them barbarians, with respect to the rules of reason, but not by comparison with ourselves, for we surpass them in all sorts of barbarism."[19]

"The man's a human being just as I am: he has just as much reason to fear me, as I have to be afraid of him. Better sleep with a sober cannibal than a drunken Christian."

Then American pragmatism takes over and altogether deflates the gothic horror, a device Mark Twain would often revert to:

"'Landlord,' said I, 'tell him to stash his tomahawk there, or pipe, or whatever you call it; tell him to stop smoking, in short, and I will turn in with him. But I don't fancy having a man smoking in bed with me. It's dangerous. Besides, I aint insured'."[20]

When Ishmael, "growing grim about the mouth" and requiring "a strong moral principle" to prevent him "from . . . methodically knocking people's hats off", set out to "sail about a little and see the watery part of the world", he left "nothing particular to interest"[21] him on shore, where "by how much the more pains" the "Sub-Subs" take "to please the world, by so much the more" shall they "for ever go thankless", and where men "strike but splintered hearts together".[22]

With friendship growing between Queequeg and himself, Ishmael "began to be sensible of strange feelings":

"I felt a melting in me. No more my splintered heart and maddened hand were turned against the wolfish world. This soothing savage had redeemed it. There he sat, his very indifference speaking a nature in which there lurked no civilized hypocrisies and bland deceits. Wild he was; . . . yet I began to feel myself mysteriously drawn towards him. . . . I'll try a pagan friend thought I, since Christian kindness has proved but hollow courtesy. . . . Soon I proposed a social smoke; and, producing his pouch and tomahawk, he quietly offered me a puff. And then we sat exchanging puffs from that wild pipe of his, and keeping it regularly passing between us.

If there yet lurked any ice of indifference towards me in the Pagan's breast, this pleasant genial smoke we had, soon thawed it out, and left us cronies . . . and when our smoke was over, he pressed his forehead against mine, clasped me round the waist, and said that henceforth we were married; meaning, in his country's phrase, that we were bosom friends; he would gladly die for me, if need should be. In a countryman, this sudden flame of friendship would have seemed far too premature, a thing to be much distrusted; but in this simple savage those old rules would not apply."

One day, Ishmael witnessed a demonstration of Queequeg's attitude to human relations.

On board the schooner which took them from New Bedford to Nantucket where they were to enlist on a whaling craft, the passengers were passing jeering glances, marvelling "that two fellow beings should be so companionable; as

166

though a white man were anything more dignified than a whitewashed negro". Queequeg caught one of the "boobies and bumpkins ... mimicking him behind his back". In no time he "sent him high up bodily into the air; then ... turning his back upon him, lighted his tomahawk pipe and passed it" to Ishmael "for a puff", reassuring the enraged captain that "Queequeg no kill-e so small fish-e; Queequeg kill-e big whale!"

Shortly afterwards, a blast swept "the poor fellow whom Queequeg had handled so roughly" overboard. In the general panic that ensued, Queequeg dived into the water and saved him. From that hour, Ishmael "clove to Queequeg like a barnacle".

Captain, crew and passengers celebrated Queequeg as a hero. But "he did not seem to think that he at all deserved a medal from the Humane and Magnanimous Societies. ... He ... put on dry clothes, lighted his pipe, and leaning against the bulwarks, and mildly eyeing those around him, seemed to be saying to himself— 'It's a mutual, joint-stock world, in all meridians. We cannibals must help these Christians'."[23]

It was on similar considerations that in a later chapter, with "great skill in obstetrics" Queequeg delivered Indian Tashtego from out a sperm-whale's head where he had accidentally fallen.

On board the *Pequod,* Ishmael came to a profound understanding of this "joint-stock world". And the *monkey-rope,* which for a while linked him to Queequeg, taught him an important lesson.

A whale had just been killed and fastened to the ship. It was then Queequeg's job as harpooneer "to descend upon the monster's back" and floundering about "half on the whale and half in the water",[24] insert a hook into the whale's back[25] to attend to the business of "flensing or stripping" the blubber off the carcass. For security reasons, one end of a rope was fastened to his belt, and the other to the belt of Ishmael standing on board:

> "So that for better or for worse, we two, for the time, were wedded; and should poor Queequeg sink to rise no more, then both usage and honor demanded, that in stead of cutting the cord, it should drag me down in his wake. So, then, an elongated Siamese ligature united us. Queequeg was my own inseparable twin brother; nor could I any way get rid of the dangerous liabilities which the hempen bond entailed.
>
> ... I seemed distinctly to perceive that my own individuality was now merged in a joint stock company of two: that my free will had received a mortal wound; and that another's mistake or misfortune might plunge innocent me into unmerited disaster and death. Therefore, I saw that here was a sort of interregnum in Providence; for its even-handed equity never could have sanctioned so gross an injustice. ... I saw that this situation of mine was the precise situation of every mortal that breathes; only, in most cases, he, one way or other, has this Siamese connexion with a plurality of other mortals. If your banker breaks, you snap; if your apothecary by

167

mistake sends you poison in your pills, you die. True, you may say that, by exceeding caution, you may possibly escape these and the multitudinous other evil chances of life. But handle Queequeg's monkey-rope heedfully as I would, sometimes he jerked it so, that I came very near sliding overboard. Nor could I possibly forget that, do what I would, I only had the management of one end of it."[26]

All true art is based on the realization of the existence of this monkey-rope. Poetically expressed by John Donne in Devotion XVII, it has often been quoted:

"No man is an island, entire of itself; every man is a piece of the continent, a part of the main; . . . any man's death diminishes me, because I am involved in mankind, and therefore never send to know for whom the bell tolls; it tolls for thee."

Melville might have been inspired by Donne when he wrote:

"They were nearly all Islanders in the Pequod, *Isolatoes* too, I call such, not acknowledging the common continent of men, but each *Isolato* living on a separate continent of his own. Yet now, federated along one keel, what a set these Isolatoes were! An Anacharsis Clootz deputation from all the isles of the sea, and all the ends of the earth, accompanying Old Ahab in the Pequod to lay the world's grievances before that bar from which not very many of them ever come back."[27]

4. Merger

In giving maximum emphasis to the friendship between Queequeg and Ishmael, Melville underscores the longing of the individual to transcend his particularity by merging with other fellow-beings.

In April, 1851, whilst still working on *Moby-Dick,* Melville told Hawthorne in a letter how much he was "struck" by the scene in *The House of the Seven Gables,* "where Clifford, for a moment, would fain throw himself forth from the window to join the procession".[28] Clifford had this sudden urge to join a demonstration after his release from jail where he had been innocently incarcerated for thirty years.

As Queequeg and Ishmael lie in their shared bed, Melville calls them "a cosy, loving pair". Ishmael indulges in the glories of transcending individual boundaries and sensing the oneness with a fellow-human:

"We had lain thus in bed, chatting and napping at short intervals, and Queequeg now and then affectionately throwing his brown tattooed legs over mine, and then drawing them back; so entirely sociable and free and easy were we; . . .

168

... our recumbent position began to grow wearisome, and by little and little we found ourselves sitting up; the clothes well tucked around us, leaning against the head-board with our four knees drawn up close together, and our two noses bending over them, as if our knee-pans were warming-pans."[29]

Several times in the course of the novel, Melville uses similar metaphors of corporeal unity to express the oneness of men in the same situation.

In Chapter 64, after having killed a whale, the crew of three boats are exerting themselves to tow the trophy to the ship:

"We eighteen men with our thirty-six arms, and one hundred and eighty thumbs and fingers, slowly toiled hour after hour upon that inert, sluggish corpse in the sea."

In Chapter 67, in the process of peeling the blubber off the whale's carcass

"the main body of the crew striking up a wild chorus, now commence heaving in one dense crowd at the windlass".

In Chapter 91, when a French whaleship is spotted, towing a "blasted" whale, that is, one which had been captured a corpse and was exhaling an intolerable stench of decomposition,

"the many noses on the Pequod's deck proved more vigilant discoverers than the three pairs of eyes aloft".

When, on the second day of the final chase, "Moby Dick bodily burst into view", Ahab

"struck the key-note to an orchestra, that made the air vibrate as with the combined discharges of rifles. The triumphant halloo of thirty buckskin lungs was heard".[30]

In the final chapters, Melville uses a metaphor in three escalating variants. When the unfortunate *Rachel* came into view, "all her spars" were "thickly clustering with men" on the look-out for two missing boats. When, after Ahab's refusal to assist, she sailed on, "weeping for her children, because they were not", "her masts and yards were thickly clustered with men, as three tall cherry trees, when the boys are cherrying among the boughs". And as the *Pequod* braced herself for the second day of the final chase,

"The rigging lived. The mast-heads, like the tops of tall palms, were outspreadingly tufted with arms and legs. ... all the spars in full bearing of mortals, ready and ripe for their fate".[31]

169

Whatever that fate would be, Ishmael in the meantime exults over merging his personality with his "co-laborers", when they are all set to squeeze the congealed lumps of the extracted spermaceti back into fluid, prior to its being tried out:

> "No wonder that in old times this sperm was such a favorite cosmetic. Such a clearer! such a sweetener! such a softener! such a delicious mollifier! After having my hands in it for only a few minutes, my fingers felt like eels, and began, as it were, to serpentine and spiralize.
>
> As I sat there ... cross-legged on the deck; ... as I bathed my hands among those soft, gentle globules of infiltrated tissues, ...; as I snuffed up that uncontaminated aroma, ... like the smell of spring violets; ... I felt divinely free from all ill-will, or petulence, or malice, of any sort whatsoever.
>
> Squeeze! squeeze! squeeze! all the morning long; I squeezed that sperm till a strange sort of insanity came over me; and I found myself unwittingly squeezing my co-laborers' hands in it, mistaking their hands for the gentle globules. Such an abounding, affectionate, friendly, loving feeling did this avocation beget; that at last I was continually squeezing their hands, and looking up into their eyes sentimentally; as much as to say,—Oh! my dear fellow beings, why should we longer cherish any social acerbities, or know the slightest ill-humor or envy! Come; let is squeeze hands all round; nay, let us all squeeze ourselves into each other; let us squeeze ourselves universally into the very milk and sperm of kindness."[32]

5. A wicked book

In November, 1851, Melville wrote to Hawthorne, overjoyed by his friend's favourable reception of *Moby-Dick:*

> "I have written a wicked book, and feel spotless as the lamb. Ineffable socialities are in me. I would sit down and dine with you and all the gods in old Rome's Pantheon."

It was a wicked book indeed that exploded the mid-nineteenth century American reading public's most vaunted ideas: private enterprise and ownership, self-reliance and faith in divine providence.

A woeful drama too, of "sound and fury", yet not lacking the vigour of secular conviviality, and pride in the heroic struggle of Americans grappling with nature's forces. Ahab stands forth as a hero, epitomizing in his fierce remonstrance the assurance of the American frontiersman, unsubmissive to god or man and undauntedly defying the overpowering forces of nature. His unexpected suffering and his outrage dramatically heightened assume universal proportions. But Ahab falls victim to fatal misguidance. Challenging an illusion, his single-minded heroism becomes futile. His fall is all the more tragic, as it is hardly noticed.

170

Paradoxically, the outcome of his expedition is just the opposite of its intention. Instead of redressing undeserved suffering, it increases it. Instead of vindicating the sovereignty of the individual, it reduces a whole ship's company into the helpless "arms and legs" of their all-powerful captain.

Before he wrote *Moby-Dick*, Melville had exultingly voiced in *White-Jacket* the hopeful plebeian expectations of equity and democracy beguiling American minds ever since the foundation of their Republic:

> "We Americans are the peculiar, chosen people—the Israel of our time; we bear the ark of the liberties of the world . . . We are the pioneers of the world; the advance-guard, sent on through the wilderness of untried things, to break a new path in the New World that is ours . . . The Past is, in many things, the foe of mankind: the Future is, in all things, our friend. The Past is the text-book of tyrants; the Future the Bible of the Free. Those who are solely governed by the Past stand like Lot's wife, crystallized in the act of looking backward, and forever incapable of looking before . . . More shall come after us than have gone before; the world is not yet middle-aged."

But the discrepancy between what was expected and what was happening engendered a frustration and resentment that assumed cosmic proportions in Melville's artistic vision, one that was embodied in Ahab's abortive defiance.

With no more faith left in the "manifest destiny" of the United States than in divine providence, Melville never lost confidence in "the kingly commons", "the meanest mariners, and renegades and castaways" from "all the ends of the earth", whose steadfastness he had learned to admire during his whaling years. In *Moby-Dick*, he raises an epic monument to their pluck and endurances and celebrates the forecastle companionship of "Isolatoes" as the only saving force in a "whaling world"[33] where "vultureism" is the universal law of nature, possession is often the whole of human law, and sorrow outweighs joy.

Notes

PART I

1. Hugh W. Hetherington, "A Tribute to the Late Hiram Melville", *Modern Language Quarterly*, 16 (December, 1955).
2. *Ibid.*
3. *The Press*, 29 September, 1891. Quoted from Jay Leyda: *The Melville Log*, Vol II, p. 836. All citations to the *Log* are from the Gordian Press edition (New York, 1969).
4. Quotations from Hugh W. Hetherington: *op. cit.*
5. *Ibid.*
6. Quoted from *Moby-Dick As Doubloon, Essays and Extracts (1851–1970)*, edited by Hershel Parker and Harrison Hayford. New York: W. W. Norton and Co., 1970
7. 1825–1903. Author, editor and critic.
8. Watson G. Branch, ed., *Melville: The Critical Heritage*. London and Boston: Routledge and Kegan Paul, 1974. pp. 423, 425.
9. *Log*, II, p. 826.
10. Merrell R. Davis and William H. Gilman, eds., *The Letters of Herman Melville*. New Haven, Conn.: Yale University Press, 1960. p. 130.
11. *Ibid.*, p. 76. Murray eventually refused *Mardi* on account of its fictitious character and the book was published by Richard Bentley, who thought it advisable to remind readers of *Typee* and *Omoo* on the title-page.
12. Eleanor Melville Metcalf, ed., *Journal of a Visit to London and the Continent by Herman Melville. 1849–50*. Cambridge: Harvard University Press, 1948. p. 18.
13. *Letters*, p. 199.
14. *Melville: The Critical Heritage*, pp. 422–3.
15. Hugh W. Hetherington, *op. cit.*, p. 330.
16. Evert A. and George L. Duyckinck, *Cyclopaedia of American Literature*. New York: Charles Scribner, 1855. Vol. II, pp. 672–5.
17. *Letters*, p. 241.
18. *Log*, II, pp. 605, 787.
19. Cf. *Moby-Dick*, p. 422: "The truest of all men was the Man of Sorrows, and the truest of all books is Solomon's, and Ecclesiastes is the fine hammered steel of woe." All page references to *Moby-Dick* are to the Hendricks House edition, edited by Luther S. Mansfield and Howard P. Vincent, New York, 1962.
20. *Letters*, pp. 128, 130.
21. *Letters*, p. 80.
22. Quoted from the Norton Critical Edition of *Moby-Dick*, Harrison Hayford and Hershel Parker eds., New York: W. W. Norton and Co., 1967. p. 542.
23. 1834–1882, author of *The City of Dreadful Night*. British atheist, poet and essay writer.
24. 1858–1932, lawyer and classical scholar, President of the Leicester Literary and Philosophical Society in 1893–4.
25. James Thomson, *Essays and Phantasies*. London: Reeves and Turner, 1881, pp. 116–7.
26. *Letters*, pp. 280–1.

27. *Pierre*, p. 264. All page references to *Pierre* are to the Northwestern-Newberry Edition, Harrison Hayford, Hershel Parker and G. Thomas Tanselle eds., Evanston and Chicago: Northwestern University Press and The Newberry Library, 1971.
28. *Letters*, p. 127.
29. Letter of E. A. Poe to Frederick W. Thomas, 4 July, 1841: ". . . I would be glad to get almost any appointment—even a $ 500 one—so that I have something independent of letters for a subsistence. To coin one's brain into silver, at the nod of a master, is to my thinking, the hardest task in the world . . . " Quoted from Arthur Hobson Quinn, *E. A. Poe. A Critical Biography*. New York: D. Appleton-Century Co., 1941. p. 323.
30. *Letters*, pp. 67, 128.
31. *Mardi*, p. 369. All page references to *Mardi* are to the Northwestern-Newberry Edition, Harrison Hayford, Hershel Parker and G. Thomas Tanselle eds., Evanston and Chicago: Northwestern University Press and The Newberry Library, 1970.
    In a letter to his father-in-law, dated 23 April, 1849, ten days after the American publication of *Mardi*, Melville wrote: "Time, which is the solver of all riddles, will solve 'Mardi.'" *Letters*, p. 85.
32. Frank Luther Mott, *Golden Multitudes. The Story of Best Sellers in the United States*. New York: Macmillan, 1947.
    Ironically, in the country that risked disruption over the issue of protective tariffs, no International Copyright Law was in force up to 1891. This put American authors at a great disadvantage, for publishers were reluctant to run risks *and* pay royalties to American Authors, when they could be sure of their profits by publishing pirated editions of famous British novels. Some authors, Melville among them, managed to arrange a previous or simultaneous British edition of their works, thus assuring at least the protection of a British copyright.
33. Since 1838 the voyage by steam had taken less than a fortnight. Hugh W. Hetherington, *op. cit.*
34. *Log*, I, 1. 265.
35. In a letter to the *Saturday Review of Literature* (24 November, 1928), Bernard de Voto pointed out that the Revised Edition was the culmination of a progressive bowdlerization which had already been exercised on the two reissues of the First Edition (he calls them "variant First Editions"), without consultation with Melville.
36. *Letters*, pp. 38–40.
37. Merrell R. Davis suggests it was "for reasons of publishing expenses". *Melville's Mardi. A Chartless Voyage*. New Haven: Yale University Press, 1952. p. 28.
38. Meade Minnigerode, ed., *Some Personal Letters of Herman Melville and a Bibliography*, New York: Edmund Byrne Hackett, 1922.
39. Hugh W. Hetherington, *Melville's Reviewers, British and American, 1846–1891*. Chapel Hill, North Carolina: North Carolina University Press, 1961.
40. *Mardi* (1849) had "Typee" and "Omoo" on its title page in the English edition only, issued by Bentley's, but not in Harper's edition in the United States.
    Redburn (1849) had "Typee", "Omoo", and "Mardi" after the author's name in both editions.
    White-Jacket (1850) carried all previous titles, but only in Harper's edition.
    Moby-Dick (1851) had all previous titles mentioned in editions on both sides of the Atlantic. Yet no title-page of his works issued during his lifetime referred to Melville as "author of 'Moby-Dick'" and the *Berkshire County Eagle* was quite exceptional when on 26 August, 1853, it referred to "Herman Melville, author of 'Pierre', 'Moby-Dick' and those witching tales of the Marquesas."
    Pierre (1852) mentioned no previous work on its title-page, but was advertised by Harper's in the *New York Evening Post* as "By Herman Melville, Author of 'Typee', 'Omoo', 'Redburn', etc."
    Israel Potter (1855) and *Piazza Tales* (1856) only mentioned "Typee" and "Omoo" with one and three "etc."s respectively added.
    The Confidence-Man (1857) referred to "Piazza Tales" as well as "Omoo" and "Typee", adding "etc., etc.".
    Battle Pieces (1866) mentioned no previous work, nor did *Clarel*, (1876), both published at the expense of Melville's uncle, or *John Marr* (1888) and *Timoleon* (1891), both privately published. (Cf. Meade Minnigerode, *op. cit.*) *Billy Budd* does not figure in this list, as it was published posthumously, in 1924.

41. Thomas Philbrick, *J. F. Cooper and the Development of American Sea Fiction*. Cambridge: Harvard University Press, 1961, p. 3.
42. *Ibid.*, p. 325.
43. See letter to Hawthorne, June, 1851. *Letters*, p. 128.
44. See letter to Lemuel Shaw, 6 October, 1849. *Letters*, p. 91.
45. Meade Minnigerode, *op. cit.*
46. Quotations from Hugh W. Hetherington, *op. cit.*
47. Quoted from *Moby-Dick As Doubloon*, Hershel Parker and Harrison Hayford eds. p. 55.
48. Hugh W. Hetherington *op. cit.*
49. Quoted from the Norton Critical Edition of *Moby-Dick*, Harrison Hayford and Hershel Parker eds. pp. 618, 616.
50. Quoted from the London *Morning Post* of 14 November, 1851, in *Moby-Dick As Doubloon*, pp. 28, 30.
51. Quotations from *Moby-Dick As Doubloon*, pp. 22, 24, 10, 13, 8, 72, 80, 7–10, 8, 28, 66.
52. Quoted from the Norton Critical Edition of *Moby-Dick*, p. 615.
53. Quotations from *Moby-Dick As Doubloon*, pp. 40, 53, 84, 94–6.
54. Meade Minnigerode, *op. cit.*
55. Hugh W. Hetherington, *op. cit.*
56. *Melville: The Critical Heritage:* pp. 294–6, 310.
57. Quoted from the Charleston *Southern Quarterly* Review in Hugh W. Hetherington, *op. cit.* p. 235.
58. *Melville: The Critical Heritage.*
59. Leon Howard and Hershel Parker, Historical Note to the Northwestern-Newberry Edition of *Pierre*, p. 379.
60. Hugh W. Hetherington, *op. cit.*
61. Meade Minnigerode, *op. cit.*
62. London: The Authors' Syndicate, 1903. New York: A. S. Barnes and Co., pp. 136, 143.
63. In the light of Melville's correspondence these statements seem gross exaggerations.
64. Cf. Meade Minnigerode, *op. cit.* p. 3. "... the same country that ignored him living—the same native city that forgot that he had not yet died, until it discovered that he had—will now tardily honor him with widespread curiosity."
65. *Letters*, pp. 82–3.
66. *Doubloon*, p. 121.
67. Jay B. Hubbell, *Who Are the Major American Writers? A Study of the Changing Literary Canon.* Durham, North Carolina: Duke University Press, 1972.
68. R.   . Stevenson, *Letters to Charles Baxter*. Eds. De Lancey Ferguson and Marshall Waingrow. New Haven: Yale University Press; Oxford University Press, 1956. p. 236.
69. Unsigned but identifiable review of the new issues in 1892 of *Typee, Omoo, Moby-Dick* and *White-Jacket* by Putnam's Sons, London.
70. See reference to H. S. Salt on p. 35.
71. *Log*, II, p. 819.
72. *Letters*, pp. 294–5.
73. See reference to William Clark Russell on p. 27.
74. 1862–1933.
75. Cf. p. 14.
76. Cf. p. 31.
77. Meade Minnigerode, *op. cit.*
78. Quoted from Raymond M. Weaver, *Herman Melville: Mariner and Mystic* (New York: George H. Doran Co., 1921) by V. L. O. Chittick in "The Way Back to Melville. Sea-Chart of a Literary Revival", *Southwest Review*, 40 (Summer, 1955), p. 242.
79. *Letters*, p. 291. Most likely referring to *Billy Budd*.
80. Cf. the definition of Secularism in Joseph McCabe, *A Biographical Dictionary of Ancient, Medieval and Modern Freethinkers*. Kansas: *Haldeman–Julius* Publications, 1945, p. 533: A word coined by G. J. Holyoake 'to express the extension of Freethought to Ethics', as he made in 1840. In

1851 he began to use the terms 'Secularism' and 'Secularist' . . . in his paper *The Reasoner*, . . . after consultation with J. S. Mill, and after that date he began to found Secular Societies. The name 'Agnostic' was not coined by Huxley until 1869, and the word 'Rationalist' was at that time still associated with R. Owen's Rational Religion or Socialism. Holyoake felt that 'Secularist' had a positive meaning, indicating that the rejection of religion was accompanied by humanitarian feeling and endeavour, and so was preferable to the words in current use: 'Atheist', 'Freethinker', 'Sceptic', 'Infidel', etc. A conference at the Secular Institute at Manchester in 1852, was attended by representatives of twenty-two Secular Societies. Many of them built Halls of Science, and some of them schools. . . . In 1866 . . . the National Secular Society was founded. The Independent Leicester Secular Society which has a handsome institute of its own, retains Holyoake's broader ideal and interests, but in other societies the name stands for the rejection and criticism of religion."
81. See reference to H. S. Salt on p. 35.
82. See note 23.
83. Joseph McCabe, *A Biographical Dictionary of Modern Rationalists*. London: Watts and Co., 1920, p. 218.
84. Henry S. Salt, *Seventy Years Among Savages*. London: George Allen and Unwin, 1921.
85. Bertram Dobell: *The Laureate of Pessimism*. London, 1910. pp. 48–9. See also: Joseph McCabe, *Life and Letters of George Jacob Holyoake*. London: Watts and Co., 1908, Vol. II, pp. 79–80: "The Leicester Secularists . . . had built a fine Institute in 1873 and were led by . . . Josiah Gimson (an old Owenite, head of the engineering firm of that name) and Michael Wright."
86. *Op. cit.* p. 279.
87. John W. Barrs, who had become "Jack" to Thomson.
88. *Letters*, pp. 275–6.
89. *Letters*, p. 289.
90. *The Life of James Thomson (B. V.)*. London: Bertram Dobell, 1889. Salt had been requested by Dobell to write this biography.
91. *Letters*, p. 292–3.
92. *The City of Dreadful Night. Poems and Some Letters of James Thomson*. Edited and introduced by Anne Ridler. London: Centaur Press, 1963.
93. Herman Charles Merivale, barrister and author. Born in London, 1839. Died in 1906. George John Whyte Melville, novelist, writing in the 1870s 80s, and 90s. Salt's complaint was certainly not unfounded. Recollecting his relationship with Henry S. Salt, G. B. Shaw in his Preface to Stephen Winsten's *Salt and His Circle* (London: Hutchinson & Co., 1951) wrote: "The bond between us was that we were Shelleyans and Humanitarians . . . We agreed about Herman Merivale's Moby-Dick, another of his pets."
94. Some twenty years later, at the age of 70, in 1938, Frank Jewett Mather once more reminisced in the *Princeton Alumni Weekly* (25 March, 1938, pp. 555–6, reprinted in *Doubloon* pp. 180–3) about how he became a "Melvilleite" (a "Mellvillian" in the 1938 article) as early as 1891. Subsequently, in 1902, he was introduced by Edmund Clarence Stedman, banker and poet, to Melville's daughter, Elizabeth, who granted him several interviews and offered him access to various Melville archives, including diaries and the unpublished MS of *Billy Budd*. With this assistance, "a book on Melville by myself seemed obvious to me. Unluckily it didn't seem obvious at all to my publisher, who felt there was no interest in Melville that justified risking of the few hundred dollars that such a book would then have cost. . . . Then came the centenary of Melville's birth in 1919, and, as good luck would have it, I was again in weekly journalism on the shortlived *Review*. That meant I had an editor who almost had to print me, and I'm afraid I sorely taxed my friend Dr. Fabian Franklin's indulgence when I imposed on him two long essays on Herman Melville in successive August numbers. I may have thus hastened the demise of his excellent journal. In view of what has since been done on Melville, these do not now come to much, but at least they were the first serious attempt to appraise Melville on the basis of all his work. Previous criticism had pretty well confined itself to *Typee* and *Moby-Dick*. The Melville Centenary woke up literary America. Mr. Raymond Weaver . . . with more energy and better luck than mine found a publisher for the first, and in my feeling still the best, biography, *Herman Melville, Mariner and Mystic* (1921). This set the ball rolling. There has been an increasing flood of Melville literature ever since. . . .

As look back over forty-five years of reading and collecting Melville, there is a pale satisfaction in recalling that I was right about Melville in 1902. But I was right at the wrong time."

95. "Herman Melville (1819–1891): A Centenary Tribute," London *Bookman*, 56 (August, 1819) pp. 164–7.
96. Quotations referring to period 1921–1923 from *Moby-Dick As Doubloon*.
97. *Mardi*, p. 369.
98. *Letters*, p. 82.
99. From Raymond Weaver, "The Centennial of Herman Melville", New York *Nation*, 109 (2 August, 1919). Reprinted in and quoted from the Norton Critical Edition of *Moby-Dick*, p. 627.
100. William S. Ament, "Bowdler and the Whale; Some Notes on the First English and American Editions of *Moby-Dick*", *American Literature* 4 (1932), pp. 39–46. For a list of "Substantive Variants Between *Moby-Dick* and *The Whale*" see the Norton Critical Edition of *Moby-Dick*, pp. 477–486.
101. *Herman Melville: A Reference Bibliography, 1900–1972*. Compiled by Beatrica Ricks and Joseph D. Adams. Boston: G. K. Hall and Co., 1973.
102. George R. Stewart, "The Two Moby-Dicks" *American Literature*, 25 (January, 1954), pp. 417–448.
103. Robert Zoellner, *The Salt-Sea Mastodon. A Reading of Moby-Dick*. Berkeley, Los Angeles, London: University of California Press, 1973.
104. "Melville as Symbolist", *University of Kansas City Review*, 15 (Autumn, 1949), pp. 38–49. Reprinted in and quoted from Paul Gerhard Buchloh and Hartmut Krüger eds., *Herman Melville*, Darmstadt: Wissenschaftliche Buchgesellschaft, 1974.
105. *Moby-Dick*, p. 396.

PART II

CHAPTER 1

1. This might refer to a contemporary experiment in Stockbridge, near Pittsfield, of planting some Egyptian wheat seed taken from the inside of a mummy case. See *Letters*, p. 130, footnote.
2. *Letters*, p. 130.
3. Allan Melvill's letter to his father, *Log*, p. 3.
4. Allan Melvill's letter to his father, 12 June, 1820. *Log*, p. 6.
5. L. M. Hacker, *The Course of American Economic Growth and Development*. New York: John Wiley and Sons, 1970, pp. 70–77.
6. Quoted from William H. Gilman, *Melville's Early Life and Redburn*. New York University Press, 1951, pp. 12–13.
7. "Before we conclude this title, we think proper to observe, that it appears that the Melvills of Boston in New England, also John Melvill, Esq; a member of his majesty's council at Granada, are descended of the same branch of the Melvill family with this." *Douglas's Baronage of Scotland*, Edinburgh, 1798. Under "Melvill of Strathkinnes and Craightoun", pp. 527–9.
8. "The Earl of Leven & Melville is chief of the ancient family of Melville, who, it is said, derive their descent from a person of Anglo–Norman lineage, called Male. This person settled under King David I on some lands in the county of Edinburgh, which he called Maleville; and from this local appellation his posterity were distinguished by the surname of Maleville. Others assign a Hungarian origin to this family, the first of whom, they say, attended Margaret, Queen of Malcolm Canmore, into Scotland, and gave his name of Melville to the lands he acquired in Mid-Lothian; and it is asserted that there are some of the name of Melville still in Hungary, who carry arms similar to those borne by the Earls of Melville." Sir Robert Douglas, *The Peerage of Scotland*. 2nd Edition. Revised & corrected by John Philip Wood. Edinburgh, 1813. Vol. 2. p. 110.
9. Queen Margaret of Scotland—1045-93—was probably born in Hungary as daughter of the exiled

176

Saxon royal prince: Edward the Aetheling and of Agatha, believed to be kinswoman to Gisela, Queen of Stephen I of Hungary and sister of the German emperor Henry II. She was brought up in the Hungarian court and returned to England at the age of 12, together with her brother Edgar the Aetheling. They submitted to William the Conqueror in 1066, but fled to Scotland in 1068 where Margaret married King Malcolm III in 1070.

10. The myth of the Hungarian origin of the Melville family was exploded by Sir William Fraser in his three-volume work on *The Melvilles and the Leslies* (Edinburgh, 1890): "According to tradition, the original ancestor of the family of Melville was one of those Hungarian noblemen who are said to have accompanied from their exile in Hungary the Saxon Prince Edgar Aetheling and his sisters the Princesses Margaret and Cristina, to Scotland in the year 1068. To this it is added that this nobleman afterwards received from King Malcolm Canmore, who married the Princess Margaret, a grant of various lands in Midlothian, on which he built Castle Melville, and became the progenitor of all the Melvilles in Scotland. This account of the origin of the Melvilles in Scotland ... resembles the mythical tale of Prince Maurice, the fabled ancestor of the Drummonds ... " The Drummonds traced their lineage to a Hungarian nobleman called Maurice, whom some believed to have been "son of George, a younger son of Andrew, King of Hungary". (William Fraser: *The Red Book of Menteith*. Edinburgh, 1880. Vol 1. pp. LII–LV. Sir William Fraser establishes the Norman origin: "On the other hand, there is good reason to believe that the Melvilles are of Norman descent. Among those who accompanied William, Duke of Normandy, on his expedition against England in 1066 appears the name of Guillaume de Malleville, who probably, like other adherents of the Conqueror, obtained lands and settled in England, whence his descendants, like so many other Anglo–Normans, came to Scotland." (pp. 1–2.) The 1909 edition of Douglas's *Peerage of Scotland* drops the theory of the Hungarian origin altogether and only refers to the Norman extraction.

11. See Elizabeth Melville's letter to her niece, Catherine Lansing, 28 May, 1891. *Log*, II. p. 835.

12. Robert Greenhalf Albion, *The Rise of New York Port (1815–1860)*. New York, London: Charles Scribner's Sons, 1939, pp. 285–6. Cf. "But as it is said of the merchants that ninety-seven in a hundred fail, so the life of men generally, tried by this standard, is a failure, and bankruptcy may be surely prophesied." Henry Thoreau: *Life Without Principle* (1863), in *The Portable Thoreau*, ed. Carl Bode (New York: The Viking Press, 1947), p. 637.

13. Letter of Peter Gansevoort to his brother-in-law, Thomas Melvill, Jr., 10 January, 1832. *Log*, I. p. 51.

14. W. H. Gilman, *op. cit.* p. 309.

15. *Ibid.*

16. *Log*, I, p. 85.

17. Robert Greenhalf Albion, *op. cit.* pp. 266, 243.

18. Letter of Peter Gansevoort to Lemuel Shaw, 4 October, 1839. *Log*, I. p. 96.

19. *Journals*, Cambridge Riverside Press, 1913. Vol. IX. p. 9. Quoted from W. H. Gilman, *op. cit.* p. 341.

20. *Log*, I, p. 110.

21. *Log*, I, p. 111.

22. Cf. p. 55.

CHAPTER 2

1. *Moby-Dick*, p. 110.

2. *John Marr and Other Sailors. Selected Poems of Herman Melville.* Ed. Hennig Cohen. Carbondale: Southern Illinois University Press, 1964, pp. 101–2.

3. "Pardon me, if I have unintentionally translated your patronymick into the Sanscrit or some other tongue—'What's in a name?' says Juliet a)—a strange combination of vowels and consonants, at least in Mr. Duyckinck's, Miss, is my reply." Postscript to letter to Evert A. Duyckinck, 3. July, 1846. *Letters*, p. 36. a) *Romeo and Juliet*, Act II, Scene 1.

4. W. H. Gilman, *Melville's Early Life and Redburn*, p. 165.

5. Merton M. Sealts, Jr., *Melville's Reading: A Check-List of Books Owned and Borrowed.* Madison: Wisconsin University Press, 1966.

6. *Pierre,* p. 283.

7. See, for instance, Henry F. Pommer, *Milton and Melville.* Pittsburgh: Pittsburgh University Press, 1950.

8. Letters to John Murray, October 29, 1847 and January 1, 1848, *Letters,* pp. 66, 68.

9. Letter to E. A. Duyckinck, 5 April, 1849. *Letters,* p. 83.

10. Letter to John Murray, 19 June, 1848. *Letters,* p. 72.

11. Letter to John Murray, 28 January, 1849. *Letters,* p. 76.

12. Letter to E. A. Duyckinck, 5 April, 1849. *Letters,* p. 83.

13. In fact, John Murray, having purchased the English copyright of *Typee* and *Omoo* for the duration of Melville's lifetime, reissued these novels seven and six times respectively, between 1847 and 1866.

14. Later Lord Shaftesbury.

15. Abode of John Murray's publishing house.

16. The Home and Colonial Library, started by John III. Murray in 1843, was meant "to consist of a series of useful and entertaining volumes, ... which would contain nothing offensive to morals and good taste, and would appeal, it was hoped, to heads of families, clergymen, school teachers and employers of labour." George Paston (Pseud. of Emily Morse Symonds), *At John Murray's. Records of a Literary Circle. 1843–1892.* London: John Murray, 1932. p. 39.

17. *Ibid.,* p. 53.

18. *Log,* I, p. 302.

19. *The Athenaeum,* 24 March, 1849. Quoted from *Log,* p. 293.

20. Letter to Richard Bentley, 5 June, 1849, *Letters,* p. 85.

21. Richard Bentley's letter to Melville, 20 June, 1849. *Log,* II, p. 920.

22. Richard Bentley to Melville, 5 May, 1852. *Log,* II. p. 931.

23. Melville's letters to Richard Bentley, June 5 and July 20, 1849. *Letters,* pp. 86, 87.

24. Cf. "Away with your logic and conic sections." *Mardi,* p. 606.

25. Melville's letter to Richard Bentley, 4 June, 1849. *Letters,* p. 86.

26. Melville's letter to Lemuel Shaw, 6 October, 1849. *Letters,* p. 91.

27. 14 December, 1849. *Letters,* pp. 95–6.

28. Cf. Iago's repetition of the phrase, "Put the money in thy purse", *Othello,* I, iii.

PART III

CHAPTER 1

1. *Moby-Dick,* p. 131.

2. Author of *Two Years Before the Mast,* 1840.

3. *Letters,* p. 108.

4. *Redburn,* Northwestern-Newberry edition, Harrison Hayford, Hershel Parker, and G. Thomas Tanselle, eds. Evanston and Chicago: Northwestern University Press and The Newberry Library, 1969, pp. 84, 176, 178.

5. *Moby-Dick,* pp. 239, 106–7.

6. J. Ross Browne, *Etchings of a Whaling Cruise.* First published by Harper and Brothers, New York, 1846. New edition in facsimile, John Seelye ed., Cambridge, Mass.: The Belknap Press of Harvard University Press, 1968, p. IV.

7. See similar satirical references to the same poem in *Moby-Dick,* p. 156 and *Redburn,* p. 116.

8. *The Literary World,* 6 March, 1849. Reprinted in and quoted from the Norton Critical Edition of *Moby-Dick,* pp. 529–533.

9. *Typee,* Ch. 29; *Redburn,* Ch. 30; *White-Jacket,* Ch. 23 and 90; *Billy Budd,* Ch. 3.

10. From "Bill Bobstay". *Songs of Charles Dibdin*. Collected and arranged by T. Dibdin. 3rd Edition. London: Harrison and Son, 1850, p. 57.
11. From "The True English Sailor", *Songs of Charles Dibdin*, pp. 56–7.
12. *Billy Budd*, Signet Classics edition, New York, 1961, p. 19.
13. *White-Jacket*, Northwestern-Newberry edition, p. 383.
14. *Moby-Dick*, p. 360.
15. Francis Rabelais, *The Histories of Gargantua and Pantagruel*. Transl. by J. M. Cohen. London: Penguin, 1970, p. 521.
16. Saint Augustine, *Confessions*. Translated by R. S. Pine-Coffin. London: Penguin, 1970, p. 108.
17. *Moby-Dick*, p. XXXIX.
18. *Ibid.*, 452–3.
19. *Ibid.*, XXXIX.
20. *Redburn*, p. 116.
21. *Moby-Dick*, p. 156.
22. Pierre Bayle, *Dictionnaire historique et critique*, 1695–7. The English edition Melville used has not been identified. All citations to Bayle's Dictionary in this book are from *The Dictionary Historical and Critical of Mr. Peter Bayle*. Second Edition. London: D. Midwinter, 1737. Five vols.
23. Pierre Bayle, *op. cit.* Vol. I. p. 124.
24. *Redburn*, p. 60.
25. *Pierre*, p. 89.
26. *The Confidence-Man*, Signet Classics edition, New York, 1964, p. 146.
27. *Genesis*, XXVIII, 18.
28. Pierre Bayle, *op. cit.* Vol. I. pp. 124–5.
29. *The Confidence-Man*, pp. 107, 112–3, 115–7.
30. *Moby-Dick*, p. 6.
31. *Ibid.*,p. 118.
32. *Ibid.*, p. 567.
33. *Genesis*, XVI, 12; "And he will be a wild man; his hand *will* be against every man, and every man's hand against him; . . . "
34. George R. Stewart, "The Two *Moby-Dicks*", *American Literature* 25 (January, 1954).
35. Cf. p. 67.
36. *Moby-Dick*, pp. 180, 372.
37. *Ibid.*, pp. 276, 176, 180, 181, 566.
38. Melville named his fictitious whaler after a North-American Indian tribe, ruthlessly exterminated in 1637 by the colonists.
39. *Moby-Dick*, pp. 201, 200, 203.
40. *Ibid.*, pp. 202–4.
41. Cf. Explanatory Notes, *Moby-Dick*, pp. 720–1.
42. *Ibid.*, p. 546.
43. Elizabeth Melville's Memoir, in the spring of 1853. *Log*, T. p. 469.
44. Maria Melville's letter to Peter Ganseevoort, 20 April, 1853. *Log*, T. p. 469.
45. *Moby-Dick*, pp. 452–3.
46. *Ibid.*, p. 228.
47. *Ibid.*, p. 36. On p. 178 Melville refers to chances of being "torn into a quick eternity".
48. *Ibid.*, pp. 35, 203.
49. *Ibid.*, pp. 133, 204, 373, 208, 176, 180, 438–9.
50. "Song of the Broad-Axe," Walt Whitman, *Complete Poetry and Selected Prose and Letters*. London: The Nonesuch Press, 1938, p. 181.
51. "Song of the Open Road," Walt Whitman, *op. cit.* p. 138.
52. *Moby-Dick*, pp. 491, 310, 131.
53. Melville's letter to Evert A. Duyckinck, 3 March, 1849. *Letters*, p. 79.
54. *Moby-Dick*, pp. 105. 273–4.
55. *Ibid.*, pp. 566, 274, 422–3.
56. *Ibid.*, pp. 122, 167, 487, 564–4, 460–1, 501, 428, 425–6.

57. *The Encantadas.* Signet Classics edition, pp. 293–40.
58. Albert Camus, *The Myth of Sisyphus.* Translated from the French by Justin O'Brien. London: Hamish Hamilton, 1969, pp. 96–8. Originally published as *Le Mythe de Sisyphe,* Gallimard, 1942. Camus, in his essay on Melville, published in *Les Écrivains Célebres,* Edition Mazenod, Vol III, 1952, and reprinted in Albert Camus, *Lyrical and Critical,* London: Hamish Hamilton, 1967, pp. 205–9, extols Melville as one of "the greatest geniuses of the West". Estimating Melville's art much above that of Kafka, Camus emphasizes, that "like the greatest artist, Melville constructed his symbols out of concrete things, not from the material of dreams . . . In Kafka, the reality which he describes is created by the symbol, the fact stems from the image, whereas in Melville the symbol emerges from reality, the image is born of what we see with our own eyes. This is why Melville never cut himself off from flesh or nature, which are barely perceptible in Kafka's work."
59. *Moby-Dick,* pp. 411–565.
60. *Ibid.,* pp. 277–80, 288–9.
61. *Ibid.,* pp. 436, 550–1,
62. *Ibid.,* pp. 226.
63. *Ibid.,* p. 244.
64. *Ibid.,* p. 470.
65. *Ibid.,* pp. 286–7, 281.
66. *Ibid.,* pp. 225–7.
67. *Ibid.,* pp. 7, 8.
68. On p. 142 Melville uses the same metaphor: "small erections may be finished by their first architects; grand ones, true ones, ever leave the copestone to posterity."
69. *Ibid.,* p. 9.
70. *Ibid.,* p. 181.
71. *Ibid.,* p. 307.
72. *Ibid.,* p. 274.
73. *Ibid.,* p. 562.
74. *Ibid.,* p. 301.
75. "Canst thou draw out leviathan with an hook? or his tongue with a cord which thou lettest down? Canst thou put an hook into his nose? or bore his jaw through with a thorn?
    . . . .
    Canst thou fill his skin with barbed irons? or his head with fish spears?
    . . . .
    None is so fierce that dare stir him up: who then is able to stand before me?"
    118 years after the publication of *Moby-Dick,* the *New Catholic Commentary on Holy Scripture* (London: Nelson, 1969. p. 438.) seems to be embarrassed by these verses:
    "The hyperbole is such that the artistic value of the latter part of the Lord's speech has been called in question. The Lord God, it has been said, brings out a zoological garden—to refute Job or crush him with wonderment at God's achievements. Moreover the display of beasts and birds is enhanced with that of two half-mythological creatures, Behemoth and Leviathan."
    The authors of the *Commentary* wish that Chapter XLI and verses 15–24 of Chapter XL had never been written:
    "The epilogue would, in the eyes of some, come better after XL, 1–14, where Yahweh has brought the discussion to a close by showing that man cannot set himself up as judge of God's purposes."
76. *Moby-Dick,* pp. 291–2.
77. *Ibid.,* p. 299.
78. *Ibid.,* p. 297.
79. creatures.
80. *Moby-Dick,* p. 294.
81. *Mardi,* pp. 40, 42.
82. Thomas Carlyle, *Sartor Resartus.* London: Everyman, 1967, p. 198.
83. Reference to *Exodus,* XXXIII, 23, where the Lord says to Moses: "And I will take away mine hand, and thou shalt see my back parts: but my face shall not be seen". Pierre Bayle in his *Dictionary* (Vol. V. p. 823) presents an indirect quotation of Calvin's interpretation of this verse:

"The Mysteries of God belong unto God, but the things which are revealed, to us and to our children. Moses heard the voice of God, but did not see his face, because we walk by faith and not by sight, and of that God the glory of whose majesty we are not able to bear, we behold, with Moses, the works, only as it were in their back parts."

This argument, in its turn, was taken up and used by Melville in "The Tail" chapter of *Moby-Dick* in regard to the whale. As usual, here too, the Biblical reference serves the satirical purpose of reversing apology into scepticism:

"Thou shalt see my back parts, my tail, he seems to say, but my face shall not be seen. But I cannot completely make out his back parts; and hint what he will about his face, I say again he has no face." (p. 377.)

84. Cf. *Romans*, I, 20: "For the invisible things of him from the creation of the world are clearly seen, being understood by the things that are made, even his eternal power and Godhead; ..." *The Essential Montaigne*. Translated by Serge Hughes. New York: New American Library, 1970, pp. 120–1. Montaigne had translated from Spanish into French Raymond Sebond's *Natural Theology*, a book purporting, in Montaigne's words: "to defend the Christian faith against atheists, with arguments based on natural reason." (p. 114.) in his essay "in defence" of the book, Montaigne follows in Pierre Bayle's footsteps, and under the pretence of defending the book against its critics, with exquisite satire refutes all its apological arguments. "Montaigne sur Sebond joue le même personnage que Bayle sur les Manichéens"—C. A. Sainte-Beuve writes in an essay on Pascal (*Port Royal*. Paris: La Connaissance, 1925, p. 46).

85. *Moby-Dick*, p. 174.
86. *Ibid.*, pp. 274, 320.
87. *Ibid.*, pp. 232, 257.
88. *Ibid.*, p. 412. Note the three alliterations.
89. *Ibid.*, p. 413.
90. *Ibid.*, pp. 516, 540, 549.
91. *Ibid.*, pp. 558, 555, 232.
92. *Ibid.*, p. 310.
93. R. W. Emerson, *Selected Prose and Poetry*. New York: Holt, Rinehart and Winston, 1965. p. 15.
94. *Moby-Dick*, p. 422.
95. *Ibid.*, pp. 274, 307.
96. *Ibid.*, pp. 10–4.
97. *Ibid.*, pp. 68–9.
98. *Ibid.*, pp. 61–2.
99. *Ibid.*, p. 66.
100. *Ibid.*, p. 35.
101. *Ibid.*, pp. 32–3.
102. *Moby-Dick*, Explanatory Notes, p. 635.
103. *Ibid.*, pp. 73–7.
104. *Ibid.*, pp. 274, 412, 395.
105. *Ibid.*, p. 393. "Fast" here means bound to end, close to.
106. *Ibid.*, pp. 395–6.

CHAPTER 2

1. *Moby-Dick*, pp. 348, 145
2. Thomas Carlyle, *Sartor Resartus*, p. 145.
3. *Moby-Dick*, p. 166.
4. *Ibid.*, p. 161.
5. *Ibid.*, p. 470.
6. *Ibid.*, p. 181

7. *Ibid.*, pp. 534, 535.
8. *Ibid.*, pp. 162, 176, 180, 181.
9. *Ibid.*, pp. 79, 469.
10. *Ibid.*, pp. 104, 161, 181–4.
11. *Ibid.*, p. 161.
12. *Ibid.*, pp. 470–1.
13. *Ibid.*, p. 507.
14. *Ibid.* p. 166.
15. J. Ross Browne, *op. cit.* p. 76.
16. *Moby-Dick*, pp. 237–9.
17. *Ibid.*, pp. 79. 150.
18. *Ibid.*, pp. 236, 235.
19. *Ibid.*, p. 238.
20. *Ibid.*, pp. 349, 488.
21. *Ibid.*, pp. 401, 406.
22. *Ibid.*, pp. 488–9.
23. *Ibid.*, pp. 166, 177, 241.
24. *Ibid.*, pp. 312–6.
25. *Ibid.*, p. 524. Quotation from *Jeremiah*, XXXI, 15.
26. *Ibid.*, p. 521.
27. *Ibid.* p. 181.
28. *Ibid.*, pp. 523–4.
29. *Ibid.*, p. 316.
30. *Ibid.*, p. 181.
31. *Ibid.*, p. 122.
32. *Ibid.*, p. 165.
33. *Ibid.*, pp. 524, 545.
34. *Ibid.*, pp. 531–2.
35. *Ibid.*, p. 439.
36. *Ibid.*, p. 470.
37. *Pierre*, pp. 214, 206.
38. As stated by Harrison Hayford and Merton M. Sealts, Jr. in their edition of *Billy Budd, Sailor (An Inside Narrative): Regarding Text and Genetic Text* (Chicago: Chicago University Press, 1962), an intermediate stage of the manuscript of *Billy Budd,* the order of the last two chapters was reversed, the story ending with the press report that called Claggart "respectable" and "patriotic", and Billy Budd an "assassin", not even an Englishman, but "one of those aliens adopting English cognomens". To this Melville added this pencil-draft coda, reprinted in the *Reading Text and Genetic Text:*

> "Here ends a story not unwarranted by what sometimes happens in this incomputable world of ours—innocence and infamy, spiritual depravity and fair repute."

In the final stage of the manuscript this coda was omitted. Harrison Hayford and Merton M. Sealts, Jr. present it in Melville's handwriting and remark that "the coda, it seems apparent, was meant to bring out the main point of the story as it then stood." (p. 8.) Later (p. 201), they observe that the word preceding "world" has been given as "incongruous" by Raymond Weaver and as "incomprehensible" by John Freeman, but they do not accept either reading as satisfactory. I suggest that the enigmatic word is "incomputable". Melville often uses this word in his writings, his handwriting can be unequivocally identified as far as "incomput", and the "able" seems to be abbreviated in Melville's usual way.
39. *Moby-Dick*, pp. 165, 543.
40. Cf. *Moby-Dick*, p. 126. Ahab's pipe "no longer soothes" him and he tosses it into the sea.
41. *Moby-Dick*, p. 145.
42. *Ibid.*, p. 144.
43. *Ibid.*, p. 126.
44. *Ibid.*, p. 79.

45. *Ibid.*, pp. 167, 210.
46. *Ibid.*, pp. 565, 534–5.
47. *Ibid.*, pp. 180–2.
48. *Ibid.*, pp. 161–2.
49. Thomas Carlyle, *op. cit.* p. 54.
50. *Moby-Dick*, pp. 166, 500, 536.
51. *Ibid.*, p. 500.
52. Pierre Bayle, *op. cit.* Vol. V, pp. 635–6.
53. *Ibid.*, p. 515.
54. *Moby-Dick*, pp. 500–1.
55. Letter to Hawthorne, June, 1851, *Letters*, p. 129.
56. Letter to Hawthorne, 16, April, 1851. *Letters*, pp. 124–5.
57. *Moby-Dick*, p. 536.
58. *Ibid.*, pp. 118–9.
59. *Letters*, p. 83.
60. Pierre Bayle, *op. cit.*, Vol. V, p. 822.
61. From entry on the Paulicians, Vol. IV, p. 515.
62. From entry on the Manichees, Vol. IV, pp. 95–6.
63. From entry on the Paulicians, Vol. IV, p. 513.
64. From entry on the Manichees, Vol. IV, p. 96.
65. *Mardi*, pp. 426–8.
66. Pierre Bayle, *op. cit.*, Vol. IV, p. 516.
67. *Ibid.*, Vol. V, pp. 822–3.
68. *Moby-Dick*, pp. 500, 413.
69. *Ecclesiastes*, I, 13, 14, 17, 18.
70 *Moby-Dick*, pp. 422–3, 166, 482, 182.
71. *King Lear*, Act IV, Scene VI, 175–6.
72. *Moby-Dick*, p. 161, 181.
73. *Ibid.*, p. 533.
74. *Ibid.*, pp. 1–3.
75. *Ibid.*, pp. 156–7.
76. *Ibid.*, pp. 421–2.
77. *Ibid.*, pp. 340, 343.
78. *Ibid.*, pp. 161–2, 536.
79. *Ibid.*, p. 408.
80. Reference to *Genesis* I, 29, 30.
81. *The Confessions of St. Augustine*, Translated by Rex Warner. New York: New American Library, 1963, pp. 341, 343.
82. *Images or Shadows of Divine Things by Jonathan Edwards*. Perry Miller ed. New Haven: Yale University Press, 1948, pp. 82–3.
83. *Moby-Dick*, p. 235.
84. *Ibid.*, p. 501.
85. *Ibid.*, p. 310, 428, 466–7.
86. *Ibid.*, p. 157.
87. R. W. Emerson, *op. cit.* pp. 15, 20, 21.
88. *Moby-Dick*, pp. 161, 126, 199–200, 561, 565.
89. *Ibid.*, p. 200.
90. *Ibid.*, p. 492.
91. *Ibid.*, p. 546.
92. *Ibid.*, p. 492.
93. *Macbeth*, Act IV, Scene I, 80–1, 92–4, 98–100.
94. *Moby-Dick*, p. 565.
95. *Macbeth*, Act V, Scenes V, 43–4, VII, 48–51, 59–62.
96. *Moby-Dick*, p. 565.
97. *I Kings*, XXII, 30, 34–5, 38; XII, 23, XXII, 6.

12*

98. Pierre Bayle, *op. cit.*, Vol. V, p. 822.
99. *Moby-Dick*, pp. 5–6, 67.
100. *Ibid.*, p. 168.
101. *Ibid.*, pp. 247, 244, 257, 348, 548–9, 409, 541, 512, 257, 564–5.
102. *Ibid.*, pp. 412–3, 514.
103. *Ibid.*, pp. 536, 181, 471, 553–4.
104. *Ibid.*, p. 484.
105. *Mardi*, pp. 428, 430.
106. *Moby-Dick*, p. 213.
107. *Ibid.*, pp. 566, 413.
108. *Ibid.*, pp. 463–4, 519.
109. *Ibid.*, pp. 539, 335, 344–5, 328, 247, 258, 550, 345.
110. *Ibid.*, pp. 193, 185–6, 189, 192–3.
111. *Log*, II, p. 529.
112. *Mardi*, p. 577.
113. *Moby-Dick*, p. 48, 193, 412–3.
114. *Ibid.*, pp. 193–4.
115. *Ibid.*, pp. 345, 369, 500.
116. *Pierre*, pp. 134–5, 204.
117. *Moby-Dick*, pp. 387, 305, 345, 376–7.
118. Sir Thomas Browne, *Religio Medici*. Cambridge University Press, 1963, p. 15.
119. Pierre Bayle, *op. cit.* Vol. V, p. 823. See "Pierre Bayle and Moby-Dick," by Millicent Bell. *PMLA*, 66 (September, 1951), pp. 626–648. I should here like to underscore my gratitude to Professor Millicent Bell, whose article first showed me the effect Pierre Bayle had on Melville.
120. *Moby-Dick*, pp. 305, 345, 452.
121. *Ibid.*, pp. 12, 68, 180, 435, 203, 159, 195, 470, 482, 483, 181, 541, 542, 543.
122. *Ibid.*, pp. 539, 483, 452–4.
123. *Ibid.*, pp. 181, 535, 557, 274.
124. *Ibid.*, p. 453–4.
125. *Ibid.*, p. 413.
126. See "Melville and Geology", by Elizabeth S. Foster. *American Literature*, 17 (March, 1945), pp. 50–65.
127. *Omoo*, Harrison Hayford, Hershel Perker, and G. Thomas Tanselle eds., Northwestern-Newberry Edition, Evanston and Chicago: Northwestern University Press and The Newberry Library, 1968, pp. 62–3.
128. *Moby-Dick*, p. 194.
129. *Ibid.*, pp. 486–7, 567.
130. *Ibid.*, pp. 265–6.
131. *Ibid.*, pp. 370–1.
132. *Ibid.*, p. 261.
133. William Scoresby, Jr., whose *Journal of a Voyage to the Northern Whale Fishery* was one of Melville's chief reference books on whaling.
134. *Moby-Dick*, p. 268.
135. *Ibid.*, p. 267. Louis Garneray was himself a veteran of South Sea travel, and painted marine scenes. See Explanatory Notes, *Moby-Dick*, p. 749.
136. *Ibid.*, p. 451.
137. *Mardi*, pp. 428, 430.
138. The Muggletonians were followers of Lodowicke Muggleton (1609–1698) and John Reeve, who called themselves the two witnesses of Revelation ("And I will give power unto my two witnesses, and they shall prophesy a thousand two hundred and threescore days, clothed in sackcloth." *The Revelation of St. John.*, XI, 3.). They declared their ideas to be divine in origin. In the passage quoted Melville's definition of "Muggletonian Scots and Yankees" refers to the followers of Carlyle and Emerson. See Henry Murray's explanatory note in the Hendricks House edition of *Pierre*, New York, 1949, p. 439.

139. *Pierre*, p. 208.
140. *Moby-Dick*, pp. 500, 345, 431.
141. *Mardi*, p. 428.
142. *Moby-Dick*, pp. 359, 361.
143. Pierre Bayle, *op. cit.* Vol. III, p. 578.
144. *Moby-Dick*, pp. 363–4.
145. Pierre Bayle, *op. cit.* p. 579.
146. *Moby-Dick*, 364.
147. Cf. p. 17.
148. See Explanatory Notes, *Moby-Dick*, p. 782.
149. *Moby-Dick*, pp. 446–7.
150. *Complete Stories of Herman Melville.* Jay Leyda ed., London: Eyre and Spottiswoode. (1951), p. 202.
151. *Moby-Dick*, p. 514.
152. *Ibid.*, p. 36.
153. *Genesis*, II, 17.
154. *Moby-Dick*, p. 413.
155. *Ibid.*, pp. 447–8.
156. *Ibid.*, pp. 51–2, 48, 28, 83–4, 67–8.
157. See Explanatory Notes, *ibid.*, p. 630.
158. *Ibid.*, p. 81, 85.
159. Thomas Carlyle, *Sartor Resartus.* London: Dent, 1967, p. 1.
160. Merton M. Sealts, Jr., *Melville's Reading*, p. 48.
161. *Moby-Dick*, p. 86–7, 54–6, 566.

CHAPTER 3

1. *Moby-Dick*, pp. 472–7.
2. Lev Tolstoy, *Tales.* Translated by Constance Garnett. London: The Folio Society, 1947.
3. Letter dated 1 May, 1858. *The Letters of Tolstoy and His Cousin, Countess Alexandra Tolstoy, 1857–1903.* Translated by Leo Islavin. London: Methuen and Co., 1929, pp. 13–4. For both references and quotations see Lukács György, *Az esztétikum sajátossága,* Budapest, Akadémiai Kiadó, 1965. Vol. II, pp. 740–1.
4. *Moby-Dick*, p. 89–90.
5. *Ibid.*, p. 320.
6. *Ibid.*, p. 150.
7. R. W. Emerson, "Self-Reliance", from *Selected Prose and Poetry.* New York: Holt Rinehart and Winston, 1965, pp. 183, 191.
8. *Moby-Dick*, p. 468.
9. *Ibid.*, pp. 167, 561.
10. *Ibid.*, pp. 507, 529, 229.
11. *Ibid.*, 160–1, 159, 177, 164, 484, 166, 175, 511, 501–2, 510, 507.
12. *Ibid.*, pp. 527, 548.
13. *Ibid.*, pp. 80, 534–5, 552.
14. *Ibid.*, p. 561.
15. *Ibid.*, pp. 514–5.
16. *Ibid.*, pp. 534, 538.
17. *Ibid.*, p. 114.
18. *Ibid.*, p. 118.
19. *The Essential Montaigne,* Sel. and translated by Serge Hughes, New American Library, Mentor Books, 1970. p. 271.

20. *Moby-Dick.*, pp. 21–2, 24.
21. *Ibid.*, p. 1.
22. *Ibid.*, p. XXXIX.
23. *Ibid.*, pp. 50–1, 59–61.
24. *Ibid.*, pp. 342, 317.
25. Cf. God's taunting question to Job: "Canst thou draw out leviathan with an hook?" LI, 1.
26. *Moby-Dick*, pp. 317–9.
27. *Ibid.*, pp. 118–9.
28. *Letters*, p. 124.
29. *Moby-Dick*, pp. 52–3.
30. *Ibid.*, pp. 289, 302, 400, 549.
31. *Ibid.*, pp. 521, 524, 548–9.
32. *Ibid.*, pp. 414–5.
33. *Ibid.*, p. 320.

Selected bibliography

Primary sources

The Evanston and Chicago: Northwestern University Press and The Newberry Library Editions, 1968, 1969, and 1971, Harrison Hayford, Hershel Parker, and G. Thomas Tanselle editors, of: *Typee: A Peep at Polynesian Life; Omoo: A Narrative of Adventures in the South Seas; Mardi, Redburn, His First Voyage; White-Jacket, or the World in a Man-of-War; Pierre.*

Moby-Dick. Luther S. Mansfield and Howard P. Vincent, eds. New York: Hendricks House, 1962.

Moby-Dick. An authoritative text. Reviews and letters by Melville. Analogues and sources. Criticism. Pictorial materials prepared by John B. Putnam. Harrison Hayford and Hershel Parker eds. New York: W. W. Norton & Co, 1967.

The Confidence-Man: His Masquerade. An Authoritative Text. Hershel Parker, ed. New York: W. W. Norton & Co., 1971.

Billy Budd and Other Tales (Including *Bartleby* and *The Encantadas*). Signet Classics edition. New York: The New American Library, 1961.

Billy Budd, Sailor (An Inside Narrative): Reading Text and Genetic Text. Edited from the Manuscript with Introduction and Notes by Harrison Hayford and Merton M. Sealts, Jr. Chicago: Chicago University Press, 1962.

Billy Budd and Other Prose Pieces (including *The Tartarus of Maids*). Raymond W. Weaver, ed. New York: Russell and Russell, 1963.

Selected Poems. Hennig Cohen, ed. With Introduction and Notes. Carbondale: Southern Ill. University Press, 1964.

The Letters of Herman Melville. Merrell R. Davis and William H. Gilman, eds. New Haven, Conn.: Yale University Press, 1960.

Journal of a Visit to London and the Continent by Herman Melville, 1849–50. Eleanor Melville Metcalf, ed. Cambridge, Mass.: Harvard University Press, 1948.

Journal of a Visit to Europe and the Levant, October 11, 1856—May 6, 1857, by Herman Melville. Howard C. Horsford, ed. Princeton, N. J.: Princeton University Press, 1955.

Secondary sources

Aaron, Daniel, "Melville and the Missionaries." *New England Quarterly*, 8 (June, 1935).

Albion, Robert Greenhalf, *The Rise of New York Port (1815–1860)*. New York, London: Charles Scribner's Sons, 1939.

Ament, William S., "Bowdler and the Whale." *American Literature*, 4 (1932).

Anderson, Charles Roberts, *Melville in the South Seas*. New York: Columbia University Press, 1939.

Anderson, David D., "Melville Criticism: Past and Present." *Midwest Quarterly*, 2 (1961).

Appleton's Cyclopaedia of American Biography, James Grant Wilson and John Fiske eds. New York: Appleton and Co., 1888.

187

Arvin, Newton, "Melville and the Gothic Novel." *New England Quarterly,* 22 (March, 1949). *Herman Melville.* New York: Sloane, 1950.

Ashley, Clifford W., *The Yankee Whaler.* London: Martin Hopkinson and Co., 1926.

Aspiz, Harold, "Phrenologizing the Whale." *Nineteenth Century Fiction,* 23 (June, 1968.)

St. Augustine, *Confessions.* Translated by Rex Warner. New York: New American Library, 1963.

Barr, James, *Old and New in Interpretation. A Study of the Two Testaments.* London: SCM Press, 1964.

Bayle, Pierre, *The Dictionary Historical and Critical.* London: D. Midwinter, 1737.

Beaver, Harold, Introduction to *Moby-Dick,* London: Penguin, 1972.

Becke, Louis, Introduction to *Moby-Dick.* London: G. P. Putnam's Sons, 1901.

Belgion, Montgomery, "Heterodoxy on *Moby Dick?*" *Sewanee Review,* 55 (1947).

Bell, Millicent, "Pierre Bayle and *Moby Dick*". *Publications of the Modern Language Association of America,* 66 (September, 1951).

Bernstein, John, *Pacifism and Rebellion in the Writings of Herman Melville.* The Hague: Mouton and Co., 1964.

Berthoff, Warner, *The Example of Melville.* Princeton: Princeton University Press, 1962.

Bewley, Marius, *The Eccentric Design.* New York: Columbia University Press, 1959.

Bezanson, Walter E., Introduction and notes to *Clarel: A Poem and Pilgrimage in the Holy Land.* New York: Hendricks House, 1954.

Birrell, Augustine, "The Great White Whale: A Rhapsody." *Athenaeum,* 4735 (January 28, 1921).

Blackmur, R. P., "The Craft of Herman Melville: A Putative Statement." *The Lion and the Honeycomb.* London: Methuen and Co., 1956.

Boas, George, ed., *Romanticism in America.* Papers contributed to a Symposium held at the Baltimore Museum of Art, May, 1940. New York: Russell and Russel, 1961.

Boas, Ralph Philip and Katherine Burton, *Social Backgrounds of American Literature.* Boston: Little, Brown and Co., 1933.

Bonney, T. G., *Geology and Genesis.* London: Society for Promoting Christian Knowledge, 1920.

Booth, Thornton Y., *"Moby Dick:* Standing Up to God." *Nineteenth Century Fiction,* 17 (June, 1962).

Borton, John, *Herman Melville: The Philosophical Implications of Literary Technique in Moby Dick.* Amherst, Mass.: Amherst College Press, 1961.

Bowen, Merlin, *The Long Encounter: Self and Experience in the Writings of Herman Melville.* Chicago: Chicago University Press, 1960.

Branch, E. Douglas, *The Sentimental Years. 1836–1860.* D. Appleton-Century Co., 1934.

Branch, Watson G., ed., *Melville. The Critical Heritage.* London and Boston: Routledge and Kegan Paul, 1974.

Braswell, William, "The Satirical Temper of Melville's *Pierre.*" *American Literature,* 7 (January, 1936). "Melville as a Critic of Emerson." *American Literature,* 9 (November, 1937). "Melville's Use of Seneca." *American Literature,* 12 (1940). "Melville's *Billy Budd* as 'An Inside Narrative'." *American Literature,* 29 (May, 1957). *Melville's Religious Thought: An Essay in Interpretation.* New York: Pageant Book Co., 1959.

Brauer, Jerald C., ed., *Reinterpretation in American Church History.* Chicago and London: Chicago University Press, 1968.

Brée, Germaine, *Camus.* New Brunswick, N. J.: Rutgers University Press, 1959.

Brockway, Philip Judd, "Sylvester Judd: Novelist of Transcendentalism." *New England Quarterly,* 13 (December, 1940).

Brodtkorb, Paul, Jr., *Ishmael's White World: A Phenomenological Reading of Moby Dick.* New Haven: Yale University Press, 1965.

Brooks, Van Wyck, *The Times of Melville and Whitman.* London: Dent, 1948. *The Writer in America.* New York: Dutton and Co., 1953.

Browder, Earl, *Marx and America.* London: Victor Gollancz, 1959.

Brown, Stuart Gerry, "Emerson's Platonism." *New England Quarterly,* 18 (September, 1945).

Browne, J. Ross, *Etchings of a Whaling Cruise.* New York: Harper & Brother, 1846. New edition in facsimile, Cambridge, Mass.: The Belknap Press of Harvard University Press, 1968.

Browne, Ray B., *"Billy Budd:* Gospel of Democracy." *Nineteenth Century Fiction,* 18 (March, 1963).

188

Browne, Sir Thomas, *Religio Medici*. (1643) London: Cambridge University Press, 1963.

Brush, Craig B., *Montaigne and Bayle. Variations on the Theme of Scepticism*. The Hague: Martinus Nijhoff, 1966.

Buchloh, Paul Gerhard, and Hartmut Krüger, eds., *Herman Melville*. Darmstadt: Wissenschaftliche Buchgesellschaft, 1974.

Byron, Kenneth Hugh, *The Pessimism of James Thomson* (B. V.) *in Relation to His Times*. The Hague: Mouton and Co., 1965.

Campbell, Harry Modean, "The Hanging Scene in Melville's *Billy Budd Foretopman*." *Modern Language Notes*, 66 (June, 1951).

Camus, Albert, *The Myth of Sisyphus*. Translated by Justin O'Brien. London: Hamish Hamilton, 1969 (1955). "Herman Melville", *Lyrical and Critical*. Selected and translated by Philip Thody. London: Hamish Hamilton, 1967.

Canby, Henry Seidel, "Conrad and Melville." *Definitions: Essays in Contemporary Criticism*. First Series. New York: Harcourt Brace, 1922. *Classic Americans*. New York: Harcourt Brace and Co., 1931.

Carlyle, Thomas, *Sartor Resartus*. (1836) London: Dent, 1967.

Chandler, Alic, "Captain Vere and the 'Tragedies of the Palace'." *Modern Fiction Studies*, 13 (Summer, 1967).

Channing, W. E., *The Moral Argument Against Calvinism*. Tracts published by the Edinburgh Unitarian Library and Tract Society, 1845.

Chase, Owen, *Narrative of the Most Extraordinary and Distressing Shipwreck of the Whaleship Essex of Nantucket*. (1821) Edited and introduced by B. R. McElderry, Jr. New York: Corinth Books, 1963.

Chase, Richard, "An Approach to Melville." *Partisan Review*, 14 (May-June, 1947). "Dissent on *Billy Budd*." *Partisan Review*, 15 (November, 1948). *Herman Melville: A Critical Study*. New York: Macmillan, 1949. *The American Novel and Its Tradition*. New York: Doubleday and Co., 1957.

Chase, Richard, ed., *Twentieth Century Views. Melville. A Collection of Critical Essays*. Englewood Cliffs, N. J.: Prentice-Hall, 1962.

Chittick, V. L. O., "The Way Back to Melville: Sea-Chart of a Literary Revival." *Southwest Review*, 40 (Summer, 1955).

Coan, Titus Munson, "Herman Melville." *Literary World*, 22 (December, 1891).

Cook, Charles H., Jr. "Ahab's 'Intolerable Allegory'." *Boston University Studies in English*, 1 (Spring-Summer, 1955).

Dana, Richard Henry, Jr. *Two Years Before the Mast*. (1840) New York: Signet Classics edition of The New American Library, 1964.

Davis, Merrell R., "Melville's Midwestern Lecture Tour, 1859." *Philological Quarterly*, 20 (January, 1941). *Melville's Mardi: A Chartless Voyage*. New Haven, Conn.: Yale University Press, 1952.

Dibdin, Charles, *Songs*. 3rd edition. London: Harrison and Son, 1850.

Dobell, Bertram, *The Laureate of Pessimism*. London: Bertram Dobell, 1910.

Douglas, Sir Robert, *The Peerage of Scotland*. Edinburgh: Fleming, 1964. Second revised edition, Edinburgh: John Philip Wood, 1813. Revised edition, Edinburgh: David Douglas, 1909. *The Baronage of Scotland*. Edinburgh, 1798.

Dow, George Francis, *Whale Ships and Whaling*. Salem, Mass.: Marine Research Society, 1925.

Driver, Samuel Rolles, *The Book of Genesis. A Critical and Exegetical Commentary*. Edinburgh: T. & T. Clark, 1921.

Drummond, Andrew Landale, *Story of American Protestantism*. London: Oliver and Boyd, 1949.

Duyckinck, Evert A. and George L., *Cyclopaedia of American Literature*. New York: Charles Scribner, 1855.

Eldridge, Herbert G., "'Careful Disorder': The Structure of *Moby Dick*." *American Literature*, 39 (May, 1967).

Elliott-Binns, L. E. D.D., *Religion in the Victorian Era*. London: Lutterworth Press, 1964.

Emerson, Ralph Waldo, *Selected Prose and Poetry*. New York: Holt, Rinehart & Winston, 1965.

189

Fagin, Bryllion, "Hermann Melville and the Interior Monologue." *American Literature*, 6 (January, 1935).

Faulkner, Harold Underwood, *American Economic History*. 8th edition. New York: Harper & Row, 1960.

Finkelstein, Sidney Walter, "Cooper, Melville, James, Dreiser." *Mainstream*, December, 1960

Fogle, Richard Harter, "Billy Budd—Acceptance or Irony." *Tulane Studies in English*, 8 (1958); "Melville and the Civil War". *Tulane Studies in English*, 9 (1959); "Melville's Clarel: Doubt and Belief." *Tulane Studies in English*, 10 (1960); "*Billy Budd:* The Order of The Fall." *Nineteenth Century Fiction*, 15 (December, 1960).

Forrey, Robert, "Herman Melville and the Negro Question." *Mainstream*, 15 (February, 1962).

Foster, Charles H., "Something in Embles: A Reinterpretation of *Moby-Dick*." *New England Quarterly*, 34 (March, 1961).

Foster, Elizabeth S., "Melville and Geology." *American Literature*, 17 (March, 1945).

Foster, Elizabeth S., ed. *The Confidence Man*. With Introduction and Explanatory Notes. New York: Hendricks House, 1954.

Franklin, H. Bruce, *The Wake of the Gods: Melville's Mythology*. Stanford: Stanford University Press, 1963.

Fraser, Sir William, *The Melvilles and the Leslies*. Edinburgh: 1890.

Freeman, John, *Herman Melville*. London: Macmillan & Co., 1926.

Friedman, Maurice, *Problematic Rebel: An Image of Modern Man*. (Melville, Dostoievsky, Kafka, Camus.) New York: Random House, 1963.

Friedrich, Gerhard, "A Note on Quakerism and Moby Dick." *Quaker History*, 54 (Autumn, 1965).

Fuller, R. G., L. Johnston, Conleth Kearns, *A New Catholic Commentary on Holy Scripture*. London: Nelson, 1969.

Gabriel, Ralph Henry, *The Course of American Democratic Thought: An Intellectual History Since 1815*. New York: The Ronald Press Co., 1940.

Geiger, Don, "Melville's Black God: Contrary Evidence in 'The Town-Ho's Story'." *American Literature*, 25 (January, 1954).

Geist, Stanley, *Herman Melville: The Tragic Vision and the Heroic Ideal*. Cambridge, Mass.: Harvard University Press, 1939.

Gilenson, Boris, "Melville in Russia: For the 150th Anniversary of His Birth." *Soviet Literature*, (1969).

Gilman, William H., *Melville's Early Life and Redburn*. New York: New York University Press, 1951.

Gilmore, Michael T., ed., *Twentieth Century Interpretations of Moby-Dick. A Collection of Critical Essays*. Englewood Cliffs, N. J.: Prentice-Hall, 1977.

Gleim, William S., "A Theory of *Moby-Dick*." *New England Quarterly*, 2 (July, 1929). *The Meaning of Moby Dick*. (1938) New York: Russel & Russel, 1962.

Glick, Wendell, "Expediency and Absolute Morality in *Billy Budd*." *Publications of the Modern Language Association of America*, 68 (March, 1953).

Gordis, Robert, *The Wisdom of Kohelet*. A New Translation with a Commentary and an Introductory Essay. London: The Horovitz Publishing Co., 1950.

Graham, Gerald S., "The Migration of the Nantucket Whale Fishery: An Episode in British Colonial Policy." *New England Quarterly*, 8 (June, 1935).

Green, Jesse D., "Diabolism, Pessimism, and Democracy: Notes on Melville and Conrad." *Modern Fiction Studies*, 8 (Autumn, 1962). Herman Melville Special Number.

Gross, John J., "Melville, Dostoevsky, and the People." *Pacific Spectator*, 10 (Spring, 1956).

Guetti, James, *The Limits of Metaphor: A Study of Melville, Conrad, and Faulkner*. Ithaca: Cornell University Press, 1967.

Hacker, L. M., *The Triumph of American Capitalism*. New York: Columbia University Press, 1946. *The Course of American Economic Growth and Development*. New York: John Wiley and Sons, 1970.

Halverson, John, "The Shadow in *Moby Dick*." *American Quarterly*, 15 (Fall, 1963).

Hanson, R. P. C. D.D., *Allegory and Event*. London: SCM Press, 1959.

190

Harding, Walter, *"A Note on the Title of 'Moby-Dick'." American Literature*, 22 (January, 1951).

Hawthorne, Nathaniel, *The American Notebooks*. Randall Stewart ed. New Haven: Yale University Press, 1932.

Hayford, Harrison, "Poe in *The Confidence-Man." Nineteenth Century Fiction*, 14 (December, 1959).

Hayman, Allen, "The Real and the Original: Herman Melville's Theory of Prose Fiction." *Modern Fiction Studies*, 8 (Autumn, 1962).

Heimert, Alan, *"Moby Dick* and American Political Symbolism." *American Quarterly*, 15 (Winter, 1963).

Hetherington, Hugh W., "A Tribute to the Late Hiram Melville." *Modern Language Quarterly*, 16 (December, 1955). *Melville's Reviewers, British and American, 1846–1891*. Chapel Hill, North Carolina: North Carolina University Press, 1961.

Hicks, Granville, "A Re-Reading of *Moby Dick." Twelve Original Essays on Great American Novels*. Charles Shapiro, ed. Detroit: Wayne State University Press, 1958.

Hill, Christopher, *Society and Puritanism in Pre-Revolutionary England*. London: Panther, 1968. *Puritanism and Revolution*. London: Panther, 1969

Hillway, Tyrus, "Melville's Use of Two Pseudo-Sciences." *Modern Language Notes*, 64 (March, 1949). "Pierre, the Fool of Virtue." *American Literature*, 21 (May, 1949). *Herman Melville*. New York: Twayne, 1963.

Hillway, Tyrus and Luther S. Mansfield, eds., *Moby-Dick Centennial Essays*. Edited for the Melville Society. Dallas: Southern Methodist University Press, 1953.

Hohman, Elmo Paul, *The American Whaleman. A Study of Life and Labor in the Whaling Industry*. New York, London: Longmans, Green and Co., 1928.

Holman, C. Hugh, "The Reconciliation of Ishmael: *Moby-Dick* and the *Book of Job." South Atlantic Quarterly*, 57 (Autumn, 1958).

Horsford, Howard C., "The Design of the Argument in *Moby-Dick." Modern Fiction Studies*. 8 (Autumn, 1962), Herman Melville Special No.

Howard, Leon, "Melville's Struggle with the Angel." *Modern Language Quarterly*, 1 (June, 1940). *Herman Melville: A Biography*. Berkeley, California: California University Press, 1951.

Hubbell, Jay B., *Who Are the Major American Writers? A Study of Changes in Literary Canon*. Durham, North Carolina: Duke University Press, 1972.

Hudson, Winthrop S., *Religion in America*. New York: Charles Scribner's Sons, 1965.

Hull, William, *"Moby Dick:* An Interpretation." *Etc. A Review of General Semantics*, 5 (Autumn, 1947).

Humphreys, A. R., *Melville*. London: Oliver and Boyd, 1962.

Hutchinson, William R., "Liberal Protestantism and the 'End of Innocence'." *American Quarterly*, Summer, 1963.

Inge, William Ralph, C. V. O., D.D., *The Platonic Tradition in English Religious Thought*. London: Longmans, 1926.

Ionesco, Eugene, *Notes and Counter-Notes*. London: John Calder, 1964.

Isani, Mukhtar Ali, "Zoroastrianism and the Fire Symbol in *Moby-Dick." American Literature*, 44 (November, 1972).

Jaffé, David, "Some Origins of *Moby-Dick." American Literature*, 29 (November, 1957).

James, Cyril Lionel Robert, *Mariners, Renegades, and Castaways*. New York: C. L. R. James, 1953.

Jerrold, Douglas, *Black-Ey'd Susan*. A Drama in Three Acts. London: Thomas Richardson, 1829.

Jones, Rufus M., *Quakers in the American Colonies*. London: Macmillan, 1923.

Kaiser, Walter, *Praisers of Folly: Erasmus, Rabelais, Shakespeare*. London: Victor Gollancz, 1964.

Kaplan, Harold, *Democratic Humanism and American Literature*. Chicago and London: University of Chicago Press, 1972.

Kaplan, Sidney, "Explications on *Billy Budd." Melville Society Newsletter*, Summer, 1951.

Kaul, A. N., *The American Vision: Actual and Ideal Society in Nineteenth-Century Fiction*. New Haven: Yale University Press, 1963.

Kovalev, Yu., *Herman Melville i Amerikansky Romantism*. Leningrad: Hudozhestvennaia Literatura, 1972.

Keach, Benjamin, *Tropologia: A Key to Open Scripture Metaphors. Together with Types of the Old Testament*. London: 1779.

Kitchener, William, *A Brief Memoir of Charles Dibdin*. London: M. Walbrook, 1823.

Kittredge, George Lyman, *Witchcraft in Old and New England*. Cambridge, Mass.: Harvard University Press, 1929.

Krieger, Murray, *The Tragic Vision*. New York: Holt, Rinehart & Winston, 1960.

Kroeber, Rudi, *Der Prediger*. Berlin: Akademie-Verlag, 1963.

Lanzinger, Klaus, *Primitivismus und Naturalismus im Prosaschaffen Herman Melvilles*. Innsbruck: Universitätsverlag Wagner, 1959.

Lawrence, D. H., *Studies in Classic American Literature*. New York: Doubleday and Co., 1953. Copyright 1923 by Thomas Seltzer.

Leach, Edmund, "The Legitimacy of Solomon. Some Structural Aspects of Old Testament History." *Structuralism. A Reader*. Michael Lane, ed. London: Jonathan Cape, 1970.

Lebowitz, Alan, *Progress into Silence: A Study of Melville's Heroes*. Bloomington: Indiana University Press, 1970.

Levin, Harry, "Don Quixote and Moby-Dick", *Contexts of Criticism*. Cambridge: Harvard University Press, 1957. *The Power of Blackness*. New York: Alfred A. Knopf, 1958.

Lewis, R. W. B., *The American Adam: Innocence, Tragedy, and Tradition in the Nineteenth Century*. Chicago: Chicago University Press, 1955. *Trials of the Word*. New Haven: Yale University Press, 1965.

Leyda, Jay, *The Melville Log*. New York: Gordian Press, 1969. Originally published by Harcourt, Brace, and Co., 1951.

Loewenberg, Bert James "The Controversy over Evolution in New England, 1859–73." *New England Quarterly*, 8 (June, 1935).

Lott, F. B., *A Centenary Book of the Leicester Literary and Philosophical Society*. Leicester: W. Thornley and Son, 1935.

Lovejoy, Arthur O., "Milton and the Paradox of the Fortunate Fall." *Essays in the History of Ideas*. New York: 1955.

Lukács, György, *Az esztétikum sajátossága*. Budapest, Akadémiai Kiadó, 1965.

MacCabe, Joseph, *A Biographical Dictionary of Modern Rationalists*. London: Watts and Co., 1920. *A Biographical Dictionary of Ancient, Medieval, and Modern Freethinkers*. Haldeman Julius Publications, 1945.

MacCabe, Joseph, *A Rationalist Encyclopaedia*. London: Watts and Co., 1948.

MacKay, Charles, ed., *The Book of English Songs*. London: Houlston & Wright, 1857.

MacMechan, Archibald, "The Best Sea Story Ever Written." *Queen's Quarterly*, 7 (October, 1899).

Markus, R. A. and A. H. Armstrong, *Christian Faith and Greek Philosophy*. London: Darton, Longman & Todd, 1964.

Marx, Karl and Friedrich Engels, *Letters to Americans, 1848–95*. Translated by Leonard E. Mins. Alexander Trachtenberg, ed. New York: International Publishers, 1953.

Marx, Leo, *The Machine in the Garden: Technology and the Pastoral Ideal in America*. New York: Oxford Univ. Press, 1964.

Mason, Ronald, *The Spirit Above the Dust: A Study of Herman Melville*. London: John Lehmann, 1951.

Mather, Frank Jewett, Jr., "Herman Melville." *The Review*, 1 (August 9 and 16, 1919).

Matthiessen, F. O., *American Renaissance*. New York: Oxford University Press, 1941.

Maugham, W. Somerset, *"Moby Dick." Atlantic Monthly*, 181 (June, 1948).

May, Henry F., *The End of American Innocence*. London: Jonathan Cape, 1960.

Mayoux, Jean-Jacques, *Melville*. Translated by John Ashbery. London: Evergreen Books; New York: Grove Press, 1960.

Meynell, Viola, "Herman Melville." *Dublin Review,* 166 (January–March, 1920). Introduction to *Moby Dick.* London: Oxford University Press, 1920.

Miller, Perry and Thomas H. Johnson, eds., *The Puritans.* New York: Harper and Row, 1963. (First published in 1938.)

Miller, Perry, *The New England Mind. The Seventeenth Century.* (1939) Boston: Beacon Press, 1970. (First published in 1939). "Melville and Transcendentalism." *Virginia Quarterly Review,* 29 (Autumn, 1953); *The Raven and the Whale.* New York: Harcourt, Brace, and Co., 1956; *Errand into the Wilderness.* Cambridge, Mass.: The Belknap Press of Harvard University Press, 1956; *The Life of the Mind in America. From the Revolution to the Civil War.* London: Gollancz, 1966.

Miller, Perry, ed., *Images or Shadows of Divine Things by Jonathan Edwards.* With Introduction and Notes. New Haven: Yale University Press, 1948.

Minnigerode, Meade, ed., *Some Personal Letters of Herman Melville and a Bibliography.* New York: Edmund Byrne Hackett, 1922.

Montaigne, Michel de, *The Essential Montaigne.* Selected, translated, and edited, with an Introduction by Serge Hughes. New York: New American Library, 1970.

Moorman, Charles, "Melville's *Pierre* and the Fortunate Fall." *American Literature,* 25 (March, 1953).

Morgan, Edmund S., "New England Puritanism: Another Approch." *William and Mary Quarterly,* 18 (April, 1961).

Mott, Frank Luther, *Golden Multitudes. The Story of Best Sellers in the United States.* New York: Macmillan, 1947.

Mumford, Lewis, *Herman Melville: A Study of His Life and Vision.* (1929) Revised edition, New York: Harcourt, Brace, & World, 1962.

Murray, Henry A., "In Nomine Diaboli." *New England Quarterly,* 24 (December, 1951).

Murry, John Middleton, "Herman Melville's Silence." *Times Literary Supplement,* July 10, 1924.

Myers, Henry Alonzo, "Captain Ahab's Discovery: The Tragic Meaning of *Moby Dick.*" *New England Quarterly,* 15 (March, 1942).

Oliver, Egbert S., "Melville's Picture of Emerson and Thoreau in *The Confidence Man.*" *College English,* 8 (October, 1946).

Olson, Charles, *Call Me Ishmael.* New York: Grove Press, 1947.

Owlett, F. C., "Herman Melville (1819–1891): A Centenary Tribute." London *Bookman,* 56 (August, 1919).

Paley, William, *Natural Theology.* London: R. Faulder, 1802.

Parke, John, "Seven *Moby-Dicks.*" *New England Quarterly,* 28 (1955).

Parker, Hershel, "A Reexamination of *Melville's Reviewers.*" *American Literature* 42 (May, 1970).

Parker, Hershel, ed., *The Recognition of Herman Melville. Selected Criticism Since 1846.* Ann Arbor: Michigan University Press, 1967.

Parker, Hershel, and Harrison Hayford, eds., *Moby-Dick As Doubloon: Essays and Extracts (1851–1970).* New York: W. W. Norton & Co., 1970.

Paston, George (pseud. of Emily Morse Symonds). *At John Murray's. Records of a Literary Circle, 1843–1891.* London: John Murray, 1932.

Pauck, Wilhelm, *The Heritage of the Reformation.* (1950) London: Oxford University Press, 1968.

Percival, M. O., *A Reading of Moby Dick.* Chicago: Chicago University Press, 1950.

Philbrick, Thomas L., *James Fenimore Cooper and the Development of American Sea Fiction.* Cambridge, Mass.: Harvard University Press, 1961.

Pochmann, Henry A., *German Culture in America: Philosophical and Literary Influences, 1600–1900.* Madison: University of Wisconsin Press, 1957.

Pommer, Henry F., *Milton and Melville.* Pittsburgh: Pittsburgh University Press, 1950.

Popkin, Richard Henry, *The History of Scepticism. From Erasmus to Descartes.* (1964) New York: Harper & Row, 1968.

Ricks, Beatrice and Joseph D. Adams, comps., *Herman Melville: A Reference Bibliography, 1900–1972.* Boston: G. K. Hall & Co., 1973.

Riegel, O. W., "The Anatomy of Melville's Fame." *American Literature,* 3 (1931).

Robinson, Howard, *Bayle the Sceptic.* New York: Columbia University Press, 1931.

Rosenberry, Edward H., *Melville and the Comic Spirit.* Cambridge, Mass.: Harvard University Press, 1955.

Roudiez, Leon A., "Strangers in Melville and Camus." *French Review,* 31 (January, 1958); "Camus and *Moby Dick.*" *Symposium,* 15 (Spring, 1961).

Salt, Henry S., *Seventy Years Among Savages.* London: George Allen and Unwin, 1921; *Company I have Kept.* London: George Allen and Unwin, 1930.

Schaefer, William David, *The Speedy Extinction of Evil and Misery.* Selected Prose of James Thomson. (B. V.) Berkeley, California: California University Press, 1967.

Schiffman, Joseph, "Melville's Final Stage, Irony: A Re-examination of *Billy Budd* Criticism." *American Literature,* 22 (1950).

Schless, Howard H., "*Moby Dick* and Dante." *Bulletin of the New York Public Library.* 65 (May, 1961).

Schroeter, James, "*Redburn* and the Failure of Mythic Criticism." *American Literature,* 39 (November, 1967).

Scott, Sumner W. D., "Some Implications of the Typhoon Scenes in *Moby Dick.*" *American Literature,* 12 (1940).

Sealts, Merton M., Jr., "Melville's 'Neoplatonical Originals'," *Modern Language Notes,* 67 (February, 1952); *Melville as Lecturer.* Cambridge, Mass.: Harvard University Press, 1957; *Melville's Reading: A Check-List of Books Owned and Borrowed.* Madison: Wisconsin University Press, 1966.

Sedgwick, William Ellery, *Herman Melville: The Tragedy of Mind.* (1944) New York: Russel & Russel, 1962.

Seelye, John D., "The Golden Navel: The Cabalism of Ahab's Doubloon." *Nineteenth Century Fiction,* 14 (March, 1960).

Seelye, John D., *Melville: The Ironic Diagram.* Evanston, Illinois: Northwestern University Press, 1970.

Seltzer, Leon F., "Camus's Absurd and the World of Melville's *Confidence-Man.*" *Publications of the Modern Language Association of America,* 82 (March, 1967).

Shulman, Robert, "The Serious Functions of Melville's Phallic Jokes." *American Literature,* 33 (May, 1961).

Simons, A. M., *Social Forces in American History.* New York: MacMillan, 1911.

Skinner, John, *A Critical and Exegetical Commentary on Genesis.* T. & T. Clark, 1910.

Slochower, Harry, "*Moby Dick:* The Myth of Democratic Expectancy." *American Quarterly,* 2 (1950).

Smart, James D., *The Old Testament in Dialogue with Modern Man.* London: The Epworth Press, 1965.

Smith, Paul, "*The Confidence-Man* and the Literary World of New York." *Nineteenth Century Fiction,* 16 (March, 1962).

Spector, Robert D., "Melville's Bartleby and the Absurd." *Nineteenth Century Fiction,* 16 (September, 1961).

Stafford, John, *The Literary Criticism of "Young America": A Study in the Relationship of Politics and Literature, 1837–1850.* Berkeley and Los Angeles: California University Press, English Studies, No. 3, 1952.

Stafford, William T., ed., *Melville's Billy Budd and the Critics.* San Francisco: Wadsworth Publishing Co., 1961.

Stafford, William T., "The New *Billy Budd* and the Novelistic Fallacy." *Modern Fiction Studies,* 8 (Autumn, 1962), Herman Melville Special Number.

Stern, Milton R., *The Fine Hammered Steel of Herman Melville.* Urbana, Illinois: Illinois University Press, 1957.

Stern, Milton R., ed., *Discussion of Moby Dick.* With Introduction. Boston: D. C, Heath and Co., 1960.

Stern, Milton R., *Introduction to Typee and Billy Budd.* London: Dent, 1958.

Stewart, George, "The Two Moby-Dicks." *American Literature,* 25 (January, 1954).

Stoddard, Richard Henry, *Recollections Personal and Literary.* New York: A. S. Barnes & Co., 1903.

Stoll, Elmer E., "Symbolism in Coleridge." *Publications of the Modern Language Association of America,* 63 (March, 1948); "Symbolism in *Moby-Dick.*" *Journal of the History of Ideas,* 12 (June, 1951).

194

Storr, Vernon F., *The Development of English Theology in the Nineteenth Century, 1800–1860*. London: Longmans, Green & Co., 1913.

Stovall, Floyd, ed., *Eight American Authors: A Review of Research and Criticism*. New York: Modern Language Association of America, 1956.

Taylor, Dick, Jr., "Milton and the Paradox of the Fortunate Fall." *Tulane Studies in English*, 9 (1959).

Temple, Frederick, D. D., *The Present Relations of Science to Religion*. A Sermon preached on Act Sunday, July 1, 1860, before the University of Oxford. Oxford and London: J. H. and Jas. Parker, 1860.

Thompson, Lawrence, *Melville's Quarrel with God*. Princeton: Princeton University Press, 1952.

Thomson, James, *Essays and Phantasies*. London: Reaves and Turner, 1881; *Satires and Profanities*. London: Progressive Publishing Co., 1884; *Walt Whitman. The Man and the Poet*. London: Bertram Dobell, 1910; *Poems and Some Letters*. Anne Ridler, ed., with Introduction and Notes. London: Centaur Press, 1963.

Thorn, Henry G., *Charles Dibdin, One of Southampton's Sons*. London: Geo. Vickers, 1888.

Thorp, Willard, ed., *Herman Melville: Representative Selections*. With Introduction. New York: American Book Company, 1938.

Townsend, Harvey G., *The Philosophy of Jonathan Edwards*. University of Oregon, 1955.

Vargish, Thomas, "Gnostic Mythos in *Moby Dick*." *Publications of the Modern Language Association of America*, 81 (June, 1966).

Vincent, Howard P., *The Trying-Out of Moby-Dick*. Boston: Houghton Mifflin Co., 1949

Walcutt, Charles Child, "The Fire Symbolism in Moby Dick." *Modern Language Notes*, 59 (May, 1944).

Ward, Joseph A., "The Function of the Cetological Chapters in *Moby-Dick*." *American Literature*, 28 (May, 1956); *"Moby Dick." London Mercury*, 3 (December, 1920).

Watson, E. L. Grant, "Melville's Testament of Acceptance." *New England Quarterly*, (June, 1933).

Watters, Reginald E., "Melville's Metaphysics of Evil." *University of Toronto Quarterly*, 9 (January, 1940); "Melville's Isolatoes." *Publications of the Modern Language Association of America*, 60 (December, 1945); "Melville's Sociality. *American Literature*, 17 (March, 1945).

Way, Brian, *Herman Melville: Moby Dick*. London: Edward Arnold, 1978.

Weaver, Raymond M., *Herman Melville: Mariner and Mystic*. New York: George H. Doran Co., 1921.

Weisinger, Herbert, *Tragedy and the Paradox of the Fortunate Fall*. London: Routledge & Kegan Paul 1953.

Wellek, René, "The Minor Transcendentalists and German Philosophy." *New England Quarterly*, 15 (December, 1942).

Wells, Whitney Hastings, "Moby Dick and Rabelais." *Modern Language Notes*, 38 (February, 1923).

Wheeler, Otis, "Humor in *Moby-Dick:* Two Problems." *American Literature*, 29 (May, 1957).

Widmer, Kingsley, "The Negative Affirmation: Melville's 'Bartleby'." *Modern Fiction Studies*, 8 (Autumn, 1962), Herman Melville Special Number.

Williams, Mentor L., "Two Hawaiian Americans Visit Herman Melville." *New England Quarterly*, 23 (March, 1950).

Wilson, R. McL., *The Gnostic Problem*. London: A. R. Mowbray, 1958.

Winsten, Stephen, *Salt and His Circle*. Preface by G. B. Shaw. London: Hutchinson & Co., 1951.

Winters, Yvor, *In Defense of Reason*. Denver: Denver University Press, 1943.

Wright, Nathalia, *Melville's Use of the Bible*. Durham, North Carolina: Duke University Press, 1949; "The Head and the Heart in Melville's *Mardi*." *Publications of the Modern Language Association of America*, 66 (June, 1951).

Young, James Dean, "The Nine Gams of the *Pequod*." *American Literature*, 25 (January, 1954).

Young, Philip, *Introduction to Typee*. London: Cassel, 1967.

Zoellner, Robert, *The Salt-Sea Mastodon. A Reading of Moby-Dick*. Berkeley and Los Angeles, California: California University Press, 1973.

Akadémiai Nyomda, Budapest